Language

Michael Kelly
Editor

Languages after Brexit

How the UK Speaks to the World

Editor
Michael Kelly
Department of Modern Languages and Linguistics
University of Southampton
Southampton, UK

ISBN 978-3-319-65168-2   ISBN 978-3-319-65169-9   (eBook)
https://doi.org/10.1007/978-3-319-65169-9

Library of Congress Control Number: 2017956098

Cover illustration: Cover design by Fatima Jamadar

This Palgrave Macmillan imprint is published by Springer Nature
The registered company is Springer International Publishing AG
The registered company address is: Gewerbestrasse 11, 6330 Cham, Switzerland

For Jo

Preface

The UK has always needed people who speak other languages and understand other countries. Now that negotiations to leave the EU have begun, we have more need than ever of such people. Without them, our country will struggle to renegotiate its cultural and commercial relationships with the rest of Europe, and will struggle to build new relationships with other international partners.

Initially, the result of the referendum vote encouraged a spate of public hostility towards languages other than English. If sustained, this would make it more difficult to develop our country's capacity to engage with the wider world, just when we have greatest need. More recently, evidence has emerged that the prospect of Brexit has prompted larger numbers of people to start learning other languages, whether through formal classes or through informal routes. If this continues, it could help to close the gap between our language needs and our capability.

The essays that follow aim to spell out what language capability the UK is likely to need in in the new climate, how well prepared we are and what we can do to be better prepared. There is no area of social life where languages have no impact, and we look at a selection of areas where language needs are a prominent issue. Language capability can take many forms and we focus on the main ways in which language support is provided across the UK. The discussion is designed to respond to the particular circumstances of the UK in the period of uncertainty opened by the referendum. This does not mean that all of the language issues are unique to the UK. On the contrary, we share many of them with other English-speaking countries, with other European countries and with other countries around the world. That could be the basis of another book.

Brexit is a loosely defined and contested concept, but the title 'Languages after Brexit' recognises that the result of the referendum marked a significant change in our country's position in Europe and in the wider world. Consequently, it has brought our relationship with other languages into sharper perspective. Contributors have emphasised the impact of Brexit in its most general sense rather than focus on the situation at a given moment, but our texts undoubtedly reflect the state of affairs at the time of writing or revising. The chapters of this book were all completed by the middle of June 2017 and do not reflect political changes since then. There have been many twists and turns over the past year. No doubt there will be many more to come.

The idea for this book came from a short piece I wrote for the *French Studies Bulletin* in autumn 2016, asking 'What Does the Brexit Vote Mean for Us?' Judith Allan at Palgrave Macmillan suggested that it would be timely to publish a book on the impact of Brexit on languages while the negotiation process was under way. I jumped at the suggestion and proposed an edited book that would bring together specialists in different areas of language and language policy. I was sure they would rapidly be able to distil their knowledge in a form that would be clear and succinct, presenting the current state of play, and looking forward while learning the lessons of the past. They responded with enthusiasm to the challenge.

Part I provides views on the UK's situation in a multilingual world. It looks at why many people are resistant to other languages, and why the international role of English brings definite benefits but also the drawbacks of being dependent on the goodwill of others. Part II asks what the UK needs in languages. It explores the needs of the economy, business, science and social services, such as the legal system or support for refugees. And it looks at the potential benefits of working in several languages, both for social development and individual mental development.

Part III assesses where the UK currently stands in language capacity. It pays particular attention to language education in the four home nations, with a particular focus on schools. It looks at what is provided in higher education, in community-based learning and in informal learning. It also examines the UK's capacity in translators, interpreters and language teachers. Part IV draws together recommendations for steps that need to be taken to improve our capability in languages and help our country to thrive in the new international environment. It suggests public initiatives, potential actions by government and a long-term strategy for the UK. The recommendations are outlined in summary form in the Appendix.

I am grateful for the enthusiasm of so many friends and colleagues who encouraged me to work on this book, for the support of the editorial team at Palgrave Macmillan and for the helpful comments of the anonymous reviewers. I am grateful to the 25 contributors, who have worked to tight deadlines, bringing together a huge amount of knowledge and fresh insights about this complex area. I am particularly grateful to my wife, Jo Doyle, whose love and support has been a *sine qua non* throughout.

Southampton, UK   Michael Kelly

Contents

Notes on Contributors

Wendy Ayres-Bennett is Professor of French Philology and Linguistics, University of Cambridge. She specialises in the history of French and the history of linguistic thought, on which she has published widely. Her research interests include standardisation and codification, linguistic ideology and policy, variation and change. She is Principal Investigator on the multidisciplinary, multi-institution research project, Multilingualism: Empowering Individuals, Transforming Societies, funded by the AHRC under its Open World Research Initiative (2016–20). The project is working closely with policymakers and practitioners to promote the value of languages for key issues of our time, and the benefits of language learning for individuals and societies.

Kate Borthwick is Senior Enterprise Fellow in Modern Languages and Linguistics at the University of Southampton. She is a founding trustee of the Community Languages Trust and served as chair from 2015 to 2016. She leads innovative enterprise projects in the area of technology enhanced learning (TEL); teaches on postgraduate courses in blended/online learning; trains staff; and develops online courses and materials. Her recent work has been in the area of open educational resources in language teaching including leading teams to create Massive Open Online Courses (MOOCs) within the Faculty of Humanities. She directed an annual e-learning symposium for languages professionals (2010–16) and is chair of the 2017 EuroCALL conference (European Association of Computer Assisted Language Learning).

Helen J.L. Campbell was a staff member of the European Commission Interpreting Directorate-General from 1973 until 2011. During this time, she was active in IAMLADP, the UN-run forum of Heads of Language and Conference Services, where she set up the Universities Contact Group in 2006. As a conference interpreter and trainer she has sat on many test and competition juries as speaker and assessor, and she frequently speaks at university careers events. She is chief examiner and external trainer for the Master of Conference Interpreting at Glendon, York University, Toronto. Her publications include five volumes on legal translation and one on recruitment of conference interpreters. She is a Director of the Educational Trust Board and member of the Council of the Chartered Institute of Linguists as well as a member of the Irish Translators and Interpreters' Association.

Ann Carlisle is Chief Executive of the Chartered Institute of Linguists and the IoL Educational Trust. She is a specialist in French and language management and strategy. She was previously Director of Language Training at the Foreign and Commonwealth Office (2004–7) and a senior consultant to the Metropolitan Police Service on language strategy and assessment (2007–13), in both capacities sitting on the Cross-Whitehall Languages Group. She has a particular interest in language use professionally in the workplace—by specialist linguists and non-specialist language professionals—and in promoting the recognition and status of languages as a chartered profession.

Janice Carruthers is AHRC Priority Area Leadership Fellow in Modern Languages and former Head of the School of Modern Languages at Queen's University, Belfast. Her research is in the field of French linguistics, particularly in sociolinguistics, orality, temporality (tense, aspect, connectors, frames), corpus linguistics and language policy. The research project attached to her Leadership Fellowship is on language policy in the three devolved administrations of Scotland, Wales and Northern Ireland. She is a Co-Investigator on the AHRC MEITS project, leading the Queen's strand, which focuses on questions of language and identity in France and Ireland.

Svetlana Carsten is an Honorary Fellow in Translation Studies at the University of Leeds, where she was the Director of Postgraduate Programmes in Interpreting from 2001 to 2010. From 2007 to 2012, she led the National Network for Interpreting, which was a part of the UK government-funded Routes into Languages programme. From 2010 she has led the EU-funded ORCIT project (Online Resources for Conference Interpreter Training) in partnership with eight EU universities. She has published in the field of interpreting and interpreting studies and holds a visiting teaching position at the University of Manchester.

Tim Connell is Professor Emeritus at City, University of London, having been head of languages there for nearly 20 years. He is deputy chair of the international course board of ESCP Europe, the French *grande école*. He is a graduate of Oxford, Liverpool, City and London universities, and has also studied in Spain and Mexico. He is a Fellow and Vice-President of the Chartered Institute of Linguists. Tim sits on the Academic Board of Gresham College where he is a Life Fellow, and is also Chair of the Gresham Society. He maintains close links in the Square Mile as a Liveryman of the Stationers' and Newspaper Makers' Company, where he sits on the Court of Assistants.

Baroness Jean Coussins Following a career spanning the public, private and NGO sectors, Jean Coussins was made a life peer in 2007 and sits as an independent cross-bench peer in the House of Lords. She also works as an adviser on corporate responsibility. A modern languages graduate from Newnham College Cambridge, she now co-chairs the All-Party Parliamentary Group on Modern Languages, and is a Vice-President of the Chartered Institute of Linguists and President of the Speak to the Future Campaign. Jean takes a special interest in linguists as well as languages, and campaigns to promote the interests of interpreters working in conflict zones and those working in public service in the UK.

David Crystal is Honorary Professor of Linguistics at the University of Bangor, and works from his home in Holyhead as a writer, editor, lecturer and broadcaster. He studied English at University College London, then lectured in linguistics, mainly at Reading University, where he eventually became professor. Among his publications related to the theme of his chapter are *Language Death* and *The Cambridge Encyclopedia of Language*. He is an Honorary Vice-President of the Association for Language Learning and the Chartered Institute of Linguists. He received an OBE for services to the English language in 1995 and became a Fellow of the British Academy in 2000.

Hannah Doughty works as Professional Development Officer for SCILT, Scotland's National Centre for Languages. She is editor of the organisation's electronic open access journal, *The Scottish Languages Review*, and leads on a number of cross-sector and interdisciplinary initiatives. She initially worked in industry, both in the UK and abroad, before moving into education, teaching French and German across all education sectors. Before moving to her present post at SCILT she was in charge of language and tourism provision at a further education college and her doctoral thesis explored the reasons behind the decline of modern languages in Scottish further education.

Charles Forsdick is James Barrow Professor of French at the University of Liverpool. He is currently the Arts and Humanities Research Council's theme leadership fellow for 'Translating Cultures'. He has published on travel writing, colonial history, postcolonial and world literature and the memorialisation of slavery. Recent publications include *The Black Jacobins Reader* (Duke University Press, 2016) and *Toussaint Louverture: Black Jacobin in an Age of Revolution* (Pluto, 2017). Co-Director of the Centre for the Study of International Slavery 2010–13, he is currently Chair of the Editorial Advisory Board at Liverpool University Press and a member of the Academy of Europe.

Claire Gorrara is Professor of French at Cardiff University and a specialist on literary and visual cultures of the Second World War. She has been Academic Director of Routes into Languages Cymru since 2014 and is the Academic Lead for the Modern Languages Student Mentoring Project currently funded by the Welsh government as part of its Global Futures programme. She is active as an advocate for modern languages in higher education, within Wales and beyond, and works with partners such as the British Council and the European Commission. She is co-editor of two book series with University of Wales Press, on French and francophone cultures and European crime fictions.

Philip Harding-Esch studied French and Linguistics at St John's College, Oxford and is also a qualified translator. From 2000 to 2011, he worked for CILT, the National Centre for Languages, supporting the national primary and secondary programmes. Since then he has worked freelance on language and education projects including script and language consultancy for television and online media work, school outreach for education initiatives in the UK, and abroad for national and international institutions, and contributing to research projects looking at issues of multilingualism including urban languages, story-telling in language learning and online hate speech. He has been a supporter of Speak to the Future, the national campaign for languages, and provides the Secretariat for the All-Party Parliamentary Group on Modern Languages on behalf of the British Council.

Gabrielle Hogan-Brun is the author of *Linguanomics: What is the Market Potential of Multilingualism?* (Bloomsbury Academic, 2017). She is Senior Research Fellow at the University of Bristol and has worked with various European organisations on language policy in multilingual settings. She is Series Editor of Palgrave Studies in Minority Languages and Communities.

Bernardette Holmes MBE is Director of *Speak to the future*, the national campaign for languages, and Past President of the Association for Language Learning. She is Director of CLERA (Cambridge Language Education and Research Advisers) and Trustee/Director of CIOL/IoLET. Bernardette actively advises government on language policy and curriculum reform for modern languages and is drafter of the new AS and A-level Subject Content Criteria for French, German and Spanish and writer of the GCSE criteria for both modern and ancient languages. Her current research focus is on languages and employment.

Jennifer Jenkins is Professor of Global Englishes at the University of Southampton, where she is the founding director of the Centre for Global Englishes. She has been researching English as a lingua franca (ELF) for nearly 30 years, most recently in relation to higher education, and has published three monographs on the subject as well as numerous articles and chapters, and a university course book, *Global Englishes*, now in its third edition. She is the founding editor of the De Gruyter Mouton book series, *Developments in English as a Lingua Franca*, and co-editor of the forthcoming (2017) *Routledge Handbook of ELF*.

Michael Kelly is Emeritus Professor of French at the University of Southampton and a specialist in modern French culture and society. He directed the UK Subject Centre for languages, linguistics and area studies (2000–12) and the government-funded Routes into Languages programme (2006–16) to promote the learning of languages. He is particularly active in developing public policy on languages and cultural diversity, in the UK and internationally. He is editor of the *European Journal of Language Policy*. His recent books have focused on languages in war and conflict, and he co-edits a book series on this topic for Palgrave Macmillan. He is a trustee of the *Speak to the future* campaign to promote languages in the UK.

René Koglbauer is Senior Lecturer and Executive Director of the North Leadership Centre at Newcastle University. René is a former President of the Association for Language Learning and is currently its chair of Board of Trustees. René is also Director of Network for Languages North East and is the UK representative to the International German Teacher Association (IDV).

Mícheál B. Ó Mainnín is Professor of Irish and Celtic Studies at Queen's University, Belfast and a specialist in Irish and Scottish Gaelic language and literature. He is Director of the Northern Ireland Place-Name Project (www.placenamesni.org) and co-investigator on Strand 3 of the AHRC OWRI project

'Multilingualism: Empowering Individuals, Transforming Societies' (www. meits.org). His research on place names as a reflection of linguistic diversity and the role of multilingualism in conflict resolution in divided societies links these two projects. He has also published on aspects of dialectology and historical linguistics, and on medieval and early modern literary texts.

Dina Mehmedbegovic currently works as a lecturer at UCL. She co-leads the MA TESOL pre-service programme and leads the PGCE EAL Pathway. Her research focuses on attitudes to bilingualism/multilingualism, minority languages and the positioning of languages in relation to dominance, political power and language disappearance. Her previous roles include that of Deputy Director of the London Education Research Unit (2009–11) and editor of the IOE publication the *London Digest*, with the brief of generating and sharing knowledge on key educational issues in London and global cities generally.

Maria K. Norton is Regional Business Development Manager at the British Council in Italy and a specialist in teacher development, blended learning, bilingualism and CLIL. She has worked with government on three continents over 15 years with the British Council, on postings in Belgium, Portugal, South Korea and Tunisia. With a PGCE (Secondary) in Teaching Modern Foreign Languages and an MA in Applied Linguistics (University of Southampton, 2000) she has trained thousands of teachers around the world. She is particularly active on the language education conference circuit.

Alison Phipps holds the UNESCO Chair in Refugee Integration through Languages and the Arts. She is Co-Convener of Glasgow Refugee, Asylum and Migration Network (GRAMNET); and Principal Investigator for a £2 million AHRC Large Grant, and for a number of other funded projects. In 2012 she received an OBE for Services to Education and Intercultural and Interreligious Relations in the Queen's Birthday Honours. She is an elected Fellow of the Royal Society of Edinburgh and of the Academy of Social Sciences, and appears regularly in the media as well as being a published poet. Her publications and practice-based creative arts research attend to themes of language pedagogy, migratory aesthetics and forms of displacement, and the everyday practices of integration and hospitality.

Myriam Salama-Carr is Senior Research Fellow at the Centre for Translation and Intercultural Studies, University of Manchester. Her research focuses on the history of translation, with particular focus on the translation of science and the transmission of knowledge. She is the author of *La Traduction à l'époque abasside* (Didier Erudition 1990) and the editor of *Translating and Interpreting*

Conflict (Rodopi 2007) and of a special issue of *Social Semiotics* on Translation and Conflict (2007). She has co-edited a special issue of *Forum* (2009) on Ideology and Cross-Cultural Encounters, and of *The Translator* (2011) on Science in Translation. She is investigator in a QNRF-funded project on the construction of an anthology of the Arabic Discourse on Translation (2015–18) and co-editor of a handbook on Languages at War (for the Palgrave series Languages at War) to be published in 2018. She was the Director of the National Network for Translation (www.nationalnetworkfortranslation.ac.uk) from 2007 to 2017, and Chair of the Training Committee on IATIS (www.iatis.org) from 2011 to 2016.

Marion Spöring is Senior Lecturer at the University of Dundee and the Chair of the University Council for Modern Languages in Scotland (UCMLS). She trained as a teacher of German and Russian in Hamburg and worked in schools, colleges and universities across Germany and the UK for over 35 years.

Teresa Tinsley is a linguist, researcher and author with more than 30 years' experience in national organisations devoted to languages education. As Director of Communications at CILT, the National Centre for Languages (2003–11), she led the organisation's information, research and publications activities and established the Language Trends series of annual research reports charting the health of languages in schools. In 2011, she founded Alcantara Communications, a specialist consultancy for policy-focused research on languages, whose output has included the *State of the Nation* report on demand and supply for language skills, for the British Academy, and publications on Arabic, Chinese and 'Which Languages the UK Needs Most and Why' for the British Council.

Jocelyn Wyburd is Director of the Language Centre at the University of Cambridge, and is responsible for promoting multilingualism for academic, professional and personal purposes. She was Chair of the University Council of Modern Languages (UCML) (2014–17), serving previously in other roles, over a period of nine years. She was Chair of the National Advisory Board for the government-funded Routes into Languages programme (2013–16), and from 2017 she will serve on the Advisory Boards of the AHRC-funded Creative Multilingualism project and the British Academy Flagship Skills project. She is a Trustee of the Institute of Linguists Education Trust.

List of Figures and Tables

1

Introduction

Baroness Jean Coussins and Philip Harding-Esch

The trouble with languages is that too many Brits seem to think English will do. Since the referendum on EU membership, there have even been media reports of school students sighing with relief that they don't need to bother with their French lessons any more because they won't need it in future. What a contradictory world these young people live in: on the one hand retreating into a post-Brexit 'little island' mindset, and on the other, being in instant contact every second of the day via their smart digital devices with anyone and everyone in the world.

Someone needs to tell them that there are more blogs in Japanese than English; that Arabic is the fastest-growing language across all social media platforms; that the proportion of web content in English is diminishing, while the share of Mandarin is rapidly expanding; that French and German top the list of UK employers' language skill-set wish list; and that only 6% of the world's population are native English speakers, with 75% speaking no English at all.

J. Coussins
House of Lords, London, UK

P. Harding-Esch (✉)
Secretariat, All-Party Parliamentary Group on Modern Languages, London, UK

© The Author(s) 2018
M. Kelly (ed.), *Languages after Brexit*,
https://doi.org/10.1007/978-3-319-65169-9_1

There is no doubt that speaking English is vital for success in the twenty-first century, whether in business, diplomacy, cultural understanding or research. But speaking *only* English is a huge disadvantage. This doesn't just apply to an internationally mobile elite: a survey in 2011 showed that in the UK, 27% of clerical and admin vacancies went unfilled because of a lack of language skills (UK Commission for Employment and Skills' (UKCES) Employer Skills Survey 2011. Available at: https://www.gov.uk/government/publications/ukces-employer-skills-survey-2011). Post-Brexit, the UK needs to up its game in language skills more than ever, if we are to fulfil the government's ambition of becoming a leader in global free trade and a key player on the international stage.

Politically, though, the trouble with languages is that they belong everywhere a bit, but nowhere holistically or strategically. The Department for Education deals with schools, Further Education and Higher Education; the Foreign and Commonwealth Office (FCO) handles diplomacy and our role in international institutions such as the United Nations; the Treasury is concerned with export growth; the Ministry of Justice and the Department of Health supply public service interpreters; and the Ministry of Defence teaches the armed forces the languages they'll need to be effective on the ground when deployed. The list goes on: the Home Office, and the Departments for Business, Energy and Industrial Strategy, International Trade, International Development and others all have a key interest in languages, whether they realise it or not—and that's before we even get to the new Department for Exiting the European Union. What we see is an approach to language skills and needs that is piecemeal, short-term and self-defeating. Taking what appears to be the easy way out by employing native speakers or turning to instant online translation services simply masks the problem, possibly compounds it, but certainly doesn't solve it.

Brexit presents a new opportunity to get languages right in the UK. By doing so, the Brexit process itself will be easier and post-Brexit Britain will be more successful. If the government can grasp the significance of the language issues highlighted in this book, the UK could take some vital steps towards setting itself up for a confident long-term future well beyond Brexit as a diplomatic and commercial player in the world, and especially in the interests of the future life chances and employability of the next generation. There are four essential language-specific objectives for the government to take on board as part of our Brexit negotiations. These were published in October 2016 by the All-Party Parliamentary Group on Modern Languages. They are introduced below and will be discussed in more detail in later chapters.

First, the government should guarantee the residency status of non-UK EU nationals already living in the UK *and* agree favourable terms for the future recruitment of EU citizens who are needed in jobs for which British nationals can't compete because they don't have the language skills. The second part of this objective should in theory be needed only for the medium term until we have achieved other goals to improve our own supply pipeline of language skills through longer-term educational measures (see below).

In answer to parliamentary questions asked in November 2016, the government said that it did want to protect the status of EU nationals already living and working in the UK, but only if British citizens' rights in other EU member states were protected in return.[1] As far as future migration arrangements were concerned, the government's only answer was that 'various options' were being considered.

This is a good example of how language-related issues are all interconnected and why the government must take a holistic and strategic approach, rather than deal with Brexit department by department. The reason residency status and the future access to employment of EU nationals is so important for languages is that without these people, the teaching of modern foreign languages (MFL) in our schools will collapse. An estimated 35% of MFL teachers and 85% of modern language assistants in our schools are non-UK EU nationals. The UK does not currently produce anything like enough modern language graduates to fill the teacher shortage already predicted, never mind if we make it hard for EU nationals to stay or be recruited. So the Home Office needs to be talking to the Department for Education about this aspect of Brexit.

The interconnectedness goes beyond education. Around one-third of the public service interpreters working in our courts, police stations and the NHS are also non-UK EU nationals. Without them, large numbers of people would have justice or healthcare delayed or denied in what is already a stretched system. So the Home Office also needs to be talking to the Ministry of Justice and the Department of Health.

The second language-specific objective for the Brexit negotiators should be to ensure that the UK retains access to and participation in the EU's Erasmus+ programme, which funds study and work experience abroad. In principle, this one should be a no-brainer. There is precedent for non-EU participation, as both Norway and Switzerland are in Erasmus+. It is also clearly an issue of self-interest. We know that employers favour graduates (in all subjects, not just linguists) who have spent a year abroad and acquired language and intercultural skills. A 2014 study showed that Erasmus+ students had an unemployment rate 23% lower than that of non-mobile students. Without Erasmus+, UK graduates would therefore be disadvantaged in a global labour market. Erasmus+ also plays a crucial role in the supply chain of language recruits to teaching and research in schools and universities. If the government stands any chance of achieving its English Baccalaureate (EBacc) target of 90% of school leavers achieving A–C grade in a modern foreign language by 2020, then we need as many MFL teachers coming through the system as possible.

The viability of modern language degrees at UK universities is already very fragile: over 50 universities have scrapped some or all of their modern language degree courses since 2000, because of a sustained drop in applications. Prospective students, even if they have done one or more languages at A level, don't necessarily relish the increased debt they will accumulate if they undertake a four-year course. Before the referendum, there were already concerns that the present funding arrangements, which limit the cost to students of their Erasmus+ year abroad to 15% of the usual tuition fee, could come to an end. Now, the prospect of the UK coming out of Erasmus+ is already having an impact on undergraduate recruitment. Anecdotal evidence is emerging of university departments having to work hard to convince the worried parents of prospective students that the year abroad will still be an affordable proposition by the time students matriculating in 2017 reach their third year. The year abroad is the jewel in the crown of a good modern languages degree and the government should do all it can to help students and universities continue to fund it and preserve it as an essential part of the value and quality of the course.

The third objective is very specific. The government should give a firm commitment to legislate to replicate the rights enshrined in the 2010 European Directive on the Right to Interpretation and Translation in Criminal Proceedings. Natural justice and the human rights of defendants and witnesses will suffer if good-quality interpreting services are not guaranteed as of right. The UK's record of compliance with this Directive is not flawless, so it would be risky to leave the provision of court and police interpreters to the policy of individual courts and constabularies, rather than at least having common standards and objectives as set out in legislation, especially regarding the need for quality.

The final language-specific objective is the most challenging, complex and long-term. It is the need for a comprehensive strategic plan, consisting of specific actions to ensure that the UK produces sufficient linguists to meet its future requirements post-Brexit as a leader in global free trade and on the international stage. This plan was already needed before, and irrespective of, the EU referendum, of course. But now we know that in some shape or form the UK has a future outside the EU, the need for a languages strategy is all the more acute. Trade negotiations and other key functions currently carried out by the EU will require UK officials with language skills in the future. Research shows that our language skills deficit is already currently estimated to cost 3.5% of GDP and that the UK is already overdependent on Anglophone export markets. Brexit should be seized on as the catalyst to turn this around (The Costs to the UK of Language Deficiencies as a Barrier to UK Engagement in Exporting: A Report to UK Trade & Investment by James Foreman-Peck and Yi Wang, UKTI, 2014. Available at: https://www.gov.uk/government/publications/the-costs-to-the-uk-of-language-deficiencies-as-a-barrier-to-ukengagement-in-exporting).

Any languages strategy must be fully comprehensive, covering not only all ages and stages of education, from primary school to postgraduate research and including apprenticeships, but also business and the civil service. Who knows what linguistic resources we may already have at our disposal, if only we thought it important enough to find out: oddly, the government remains persistently averse to conducting any sort of languages audit across the civil service. Businesses, particularly small and medium-sized enterprises (SMEs), at least seem to appreciate what they're missing. Eighty-three per cent of SMEs operate only in English, yet over half of them say that language skills would help expand business opportunities and build export growth. Unfortunately, the government's support for exporters in terms of language and culture still does not seem adequate. It appears that the new contracts between the regions and the

Department for International Trade (formerly UKTI) have done away with the previously available one-to-one advice on language and culture.

In answer to a parliamentary question asked in November 2016, the government said it recognised the importance of language skills to the export success of our country, and pointed to its new GREAT website, and the country guides available on it, written for exporters.[2] However, the page on 'Face to face communication' fails to mention language at all, and the advice on researching the market mentions 'language barriers' without any guidance on what these might be and how to overcome them. Even the 'more detailed guides' for China, France, Germany, India and the USA make scant reference to language skills, simply advising exporters to get a local agent if they are not fluent themselves. The British Academy's *Lost for Words* report underlines the need for a cross-government strategy, concluding that the UK will be unable to meet its security, defence and diplomacy requirements without one.[3] Cambridge University's *Value of Languages* report further develops this in some detail, with several compelling case studies from a range of sectors.[4]

If an audit of the civil service would be useful in finding out what language resources we may already have, then how much more helpful for the future would it also be to take advantage of the fact that over 1 million school pupils in the UK are bilingual? Too often, these children are seen as an educational problem rather than an educational asset. We know that to realise the potential for the UK to be more successful in world trade we will need a wider range of languages than just the traditional Western European ones taught in our schools, yet we've had to fight hard to keep GCSE and A levels in a number of lesser-taught languages. Children who speak languages like Arabic, Korean, Turkish, Farsi and others at home should have their linguistic skills recognised, nurtured and accredited, and be shown how much more employable they will be as a result, whether in business, diplomacy or education.

We should nevertheless cite existing, homegrown examples of good practice. Scotland's 1+2 (or Mother Tongue Plus Two) policy and Wales's 2+1 (or Bilingual + 1) policy are ambitious, and well thought-out, systems to ensure children have a real opportunity to learn not one but two languages other than English, and include serious plans for the provision of Gaelic and Welsh teaching. It is particularly pleasing to see Wales's new 'Global Futures' MFL strategy for schools being so innovative and ambitious, after years of underperforming (even by UK standards!). The Department for Education's £10m Mandarin Excellence Programme, which is being delivered by the Institute of Education Confucius Institute for Schools in partnership with the British Council, is more proof that we are capable of implementing new MFL strategies in secondary education when we put our minds to it.

University College London (UCL) shows us that it is perfectly possible to have a modern languages entry requirement for university matriculation. Its policy has been a huge success: those students who have to study a modern language after matriculation in order to meet the requirement have been feeding back that they find these skills to be applicable, and the courses to be enjoyable; and the number of students taking a modern language as part of their degree has increased fourfold since 2000. And even within the civil service, solutions are already there if you look for them.

It was encouraging to see assurances recently from Lord Howe, the Minister of State for Defence, that the FCO is now 'actively working to improve the teaching of Arabic dialects and the scope for including immersion training as part of our in-country training for Arabic students', and to see that the FCO's annual budget for essential language training has been increased by nearly 12% in the last two years. It is also good to see the government recognising that 'the importance of effective local language capability … whether it be a humanitarian crisis or a military operation, the ability to communicate with local partners is vital to any response'.

The Ministry of Defence boasts extensive collaboration with allied partners and its programme of exchanges with those partners is to be applauded, with participants, once qualified, being seen as a 'defence resource' for that language, to be reused in future. It also ensures its language training conforms to NATO Standardisation Agreement 6001 for language proficiency. Liaison with local partners includes work with the UN, the Red Cross and the Red Crescent Societies. The FCO Language Centre is now able to provide training in fully 86 different languages, and the Defence Centre for Language and Culture has the capacity for 40 languages. Most significantly, the armed forces now require language skills for promotion and are conducting personnel audits of 'latent language skills'. Could this approach not be implemented more widely across the civil service?

The challenge of Brexit has provided the opportunity to demonstrate the *urgency* of rebuilding (building?) the UK's capacity in languages. It is also urgent that the government realise that this cannot wait until after the UK leaves the EU, but is an important aspect of the exit process itself, as well as a keystone of future success. Neither is it an issue solely important in its own right; on the contrary, language skills and a serious commitment to improve them will affect the degree to which we can succeed and influence others across the board. In other words, languages are central and instrumental, not an optional extra or afterthought. This must be reflected in the way government organises and presents itself, right now, during the Brexit process, and beyond. The interconnectedness of language issues points to the need for a designated minister with responsibility for cross-government languages strategy, with the authority, research back-up and vision to connect the dots between the various departments and between departments and external bodies and agencies. The Treasury should realise that it is as much in its interests to see increased take-up of MFL at GCSE and A level as it is for the Department for Education.

The trouble with languages is it's easy to agree how important they are, but even easier to do nothing about it. Take, for example, the contradictory policies at play in the education system. Modern foreign languages are now part of the EBacc GCSE performance measure (achieving grade A–C in five core subjects including an MFL), but are not part of the National Curriculum after the age of 14 (which a majority of schools can opt out of anyway); nor are they necessary for schools to achieve full marks under the Progress 8 assessment regime (which measures progress over time in eight subjects, not necessarily including MFL). Evidence from last year's GCSE results suggested that schools are using Progress 8 to opt out of the MFL EBacc requirement. Meanwhile, official guidelines for checks on host families appear to be putting an end to school exchanges, and budgetary pressures are driving the fall in the number of modern language assistants. Universities, bar UCL as mentioned above, won't insist on a modern language GCSE for matriculation because they are too worried about compromising their 'widening access' efforts. Employers say better language skills in the workforce would be good for business, but very few invest in language training for their staff. (Note to Chancellor of the Exchequer: perhaps more would if there were a tax break for doing so.) Meanwhile, we are seeing the aforementioned new contracts between the Department for International Trade and the regions lead to a decimation of language and culture advice for exporting businesses. It is not enough to rely on the excellent support for language skills in exports provided by the Institute of Export, amongst others: language skills should not be so hard to come by in the UK workforce. And all of these issues were already present before the referendum took place.

The government could and should break this stalemate with some decisive leadership. The beauty of languages is that there's a win-win waiting to be claimed. Post-Brexit success, for the country and for individuals, requires cultural intelligence and agility, whether in business, diplomacy or research. Not everyone needs to be a specialist professional linguist. But the soft power advantage in the twenty-first century belongs to the multilingual citizen and nation, not the blinkered Brit of the past.

Notes

1. See Baroness Coussins's written questions, 15–16 November 2016:
   http://www.parliament.uk/business/publications/written-questions-answers-statements/written-question/Lords/2016-11-15/HL3194;
   http://www.parliament.uk/business/publications/written-questions-answers-statements/written-question/Lords/2016-11-15/HL3195/;
   http://www.parliament.uk/business/publications/written-questions-answers-statements/written-question/Lords/2016-11-15/HL3196/;
   http://www.parliament.uk/business/publications/written-questions-answers-statements/written-question/Lords/2016-11-16/HL3279/.
2. See Baroness Coussins' written question, 15 November 2016:
   http://www.parliament.uk/business/publications/written-questions-answers-statements/written-question/Lords/2016-11-15/HL3199/.
3. See *Lost for Words: The Need for Languages in UK Diplomacy and Security*, on the British Academy website:
   http://www.britac.ac.uk/publications/lost-words-need-languages-uk-diplomacy-and-security.
4. See *Report: The Value of Languages* on the Cambridge Language Sciences website:
   http://www.languagesciences.cam.ac.uk/national-languages-policy/report-the-value-of-languages/view.

Part I

Living in a World of Languages

2

Why Are Many People Resistant to Other Languages?

Michael Kelly

Struggling with Languages

Why is it that many people in the UK just don't seem to get on with other languages, don't like to hear or see them and are not keen to learn them? In this chapter I will look at some of the main factors that affect people's attitudes and suggest that there are reasons for people being resistant to other languages. We are not the only country that has this problem, so it is not just a matter of British cussedness. Languages are risky and challenging because they are inseparable from how we communicate, how we live and who we are. I will look in turn at these challenges and suggest why it makes sense to face up to them and learn to love languages.

It may not be very reassuring, but the UK is far from being alone in struggling with languages. A number of other European countries are also struggling, and so are many other countries around the world, not just in the English-speaking world. The detailed Eurobarometer surveys give a good guide to how we stand (Eurobarometer 386 2012). Its 2012

M. Kelly (✉)
University of Southampton, Southampton, UK

© The Author(s) 2018
M. Kelly (ed.), *Languages after Brexit*,
https://doi.org/10.1007/978-3-319-65169-9_2

13

survey showed that 39% of British people thought they could hold a conversation in at least one other language: a slight improvement since the same survey was conducted eight years previously. Fourteen per cent of Britons could use two other languages to this level, with 5% having this proficiency in three or more languages. Clearly we are not all tongue-tied.

Our performance did fall below the European average (54%), but was still a higher number than in Portugal, Italy or Hungary in the same survey. Looking at the English-speaking world, Ireland had a very similar score to the UK, with 40% proficient in one other language. This compares quite favourably with the 20–26% of Australians or Americans who said they could speak another language, in surveys taken at around the same time. Further afield, Japanese commentators routinely lament that the Japanese are poor communicators in foreign languages, (Hashimoto 2004: 1) and recently their government has introduced crisis measures to improve the country's capability in English. In most countries around the world, the first foreign language is English, seen as the international lingua franca. But many countries report a low level of capability in English. A recent ranking of 72 countries found that only 20 had high or very high proficiency: all but four of them are European (the others are Singapore, Malaysia, Philippines and Argentina).[1] Thirty-nine countries reported poor or very poor proficiency, including major economies such as Brazil, China, Japan, Russia, Saudi Arabia and Turkey.

While it may be some consolation that the UK is not alone in having difficulties with languages, it may also be chastening that very significant international trade partners do not have the level of capability in English that we may imagine. Naturally, their concern is not particularly with UK English, nor even with US English, despite the efforts of the British and American language-education industries. Their need is to speak to each other rather than to us, and therefore to be capable in English as a lingua franca (see Chap. 3). We should take note if we want to join the conversation.

In fact, the problem goes deeper. At least these potential partners are all agreed that their priority foreign language is English. In the UK, on the other hand, we don't have a priority foreign language. Historically, French was always the first foreign language and is still the most widely learned foreign language in Britain. But in the last two decades the pattern has shifted, with Spanish gaining greatly in popularity, while French and German have declined and a growing variety of other languages are learned in schools and spoken in the streets and at home. This has happened mainly because there is no overwhelming economic or social reason why everyone in the UK should opt for one particular foreign language, and governments do not wish to impose a single choice in the education system. It does leave something of a conundrum: which languages should people learn in the UK?

Various attempts have been made to promote the merits of particular languages, many of which have active advocates inside and outside of education. Most foreign embassies in the UK have cultural services or institutes that promote their particular language, and often provide tangible assistance to people who choose to learn or use it, in school or elsewhere. A concerted effort was recently made by the British Council to identify the most important languages for the needs of the UK (British Council 2014). It used a list of criteria to choose the ten languages that would best serve 'the UK's prosperity, security and influence in the world in the years ahead'.[2] The languages identified, in rank order of importance, were: Spanish, Arabic, French, Mandarin Chinese, German, Portuguese, Italian, Russian, Turkish and Japanese. This was a reasonable list in 2014, and priorities could well change, but particular languages and their rank order are less significant than the point that 'the UK needs to develop its citizens' competence in a wider range of languages, and in far greater numbers, in order to reap the economic and cultural benefits' (p. 3).

Most people in Britain learn some elements of a foreign language in school and pick up other elements outside school, but there is a great deal of variety in which languages they know and what level of proficiency they have. From that perspective, 39% of people being able to hold a conversation in another language is not so bad. We do need to improve on that capability, but the good news is that it doesn't really matter which specific language a person chooses to learn, because they are all likely to be useful.

The fact that many countries find it difficult to tackle their language deficits means that this is not just a UK problem. The normal solution for overcoming language deficits, in any country, is to look at how the education system might be improved to promote more or better language learning. This is a sensible reaction because education is the most obvious lever to increase the knowledge and skills of the population. Several later chapters in this book examine how different areas of education in the UK are attempting to address this. Other countries have their own circumstances, which affect their capability in languages, and there would be room for another book to draw lessons from what other countries have done. However, if the issues are so widely shared, we need to look for the common factors that shape how human beings feel about speaking other languages. There is something about languages, and if we can pinpoint what that is, perhaps we can do better.

Languages Are Risky, Like Life

There is a long list of reasons why we need to do better with languages. A study some years ago identified more than 700 reasons to learn languages,[3] and the main ones are discussed in the different chapters of this book. The UK has some great assets in a long history of living with many languages, and learning other languages. But the uncomfortable fact is that a lot of people are resistant to languages. Before encouraging them to be more positive, it is worth pausing to look at some of the good reasons they may have to be resistant.

The American writer Oliver Wendell Holmes famously said that language is the blood of the soul into which our thoughts run and out of which they grow.[4] Language is entwined with every aspect of our life. It is one of the main means by which we make sense of the world, express ourselves and interact with other people. From an early stage in our individual development, we acquire the language knowledge and skills we need to become fully functioning human beings. We take them from the people around us, we internalise them and the way we use language becomes part of who we are. We may have a large repertoire if we meet several languages in our daily life, or we may have a narrower range if our circles are less varied.

The result is that the experience of language and the way we use it is a risky business. It is tangled up with all the joys and struggles of our life, with money, power, love and death; with our sharpest emotions and our deepest beliefs. Every time we speak or listen, read or write, we open ourselves to new experiences that can change our lives, both for good and for ill. Small wonder then that some people are risk-averse with languages and prefer to look before they leap (and maybe not leap), while others are language risk-takers (nothing ventured nothing gained).

Since languages are so bound up with all aspects of life, speaking is never simple. There are three dimensions in particular that are always present and often in conflict. They can be summed up as communication, culture and identity. Communication is about conveying and understanding messages. Culture is about understanding and navigating your human environment. Identity is about revealing who you are and discovering who you are talking to. These distinctions lie at the heart of language. They have been recognised by linguists for centuries, but they have been understood implicitly since humans began to use language. In the discussion that follows, I will often talk about 'speaking' in the broad sense, as shorthand for all the ways we use language, though speaking, in a narrow sense, is only one dimension of our life in language.

Language and Communication

It is a curiosity of surveys into attitudes that people typically put a high positive value on communication, but a much lower value on languages.[5] A good communicator is a prized asset, but there tends to be an assumption that they will only need to work their magic in one shared language. This may have been a viable assumption in the past when people didn't get about so much, but looks rather shaky in the global environment.

There may be an underlying recognition that communication is difficult enough in one language without the complicating factor of other languages. There is some truth in this. Speaking any language requires a large range of knowledge, skills, and ways of being and behaving. Few people can be completely confident of mastering the whole range. The dimensions of language include the traditional 'four skills' of production (speaking, in the narrow sense, and writing) and reception (listening and reading). They also include the more recently emphasised skills of interaction (e.g. conversation, discussion, negotiation), mediation (translation and interpreting) and non-verbal communication (e.g. pointing, body language, visuals).[6]

Good communicators achieve a high level of mastery in at least some of these skills, and there may be an advantage in specialising in single-language communication. Attempting communication in a second or third language is often disappointing because you are unlikely to achieve the same level of mastery across the range of skills, without a great deal of commitment. However, there are new benefits in learning a second language. Most obviously, you can communicate at some level with a lot more people. But you can also learn to communicate more effectively, by learning more about how communication works, and by getting a more explicit understanding of the skills and knowledge you need. The benefits you get from your second language experience then feed back into your first language.

It is this benefit of communication that has driven the dominant approach to language learning of the past 40 years. The 'communicative approach' takes communication as the main reason for learning a language and focuses on how best to communicate effectively in a range of situations, from the simplest greetings to the most complex interactions. But, of course, language is more than just a tool or instrument for communicating messages; it is also a means of negotiating your presence in the world and interacting with other people.

Language and Culture

Culture is a sweeping concept encompassing the many ways in which people create the meanings and purposes for which we live. It ranges from the broadest sense of how we do things in our particular environment (e.g. eat, sleep, work, make families) through the artefacts we design to assist us (e.g. pottery, buildings, weapons, writing systems) to those we create to entertain and edify us (e.g. popular or high culture, art, music, stories, beliefs). Culture happens in language, whether it is accompanied and explained by speech or writing, or whether it is constructed in whole or in part from language, like a declaration of love, a talking cure or a work of literature.

The relationship of different cultures to different languages is a complex and often contested one. Many aspects of culture have always sprawled carelessly across national borders and language barriers. Even at the level of high culture, it is debatable whether there is such a thing as a unified culture, such as British or French or Chinese culture. Much of the effort of nation-state building over the past two centuries has been directed at selecting cultural landmarks around which a national identity can be built, for example on the works of Shakespeare, Molière or Confucius. But on inspection, most of these works have deep links with other countries and cultures: for example, Shakespeare set some of his best-known plays in Italy, Denmark, Cyprus and other places, and borrowed heavily from foreign sources. Moreover, the claim to fame of Shakespeare's works, and most other great works, rests on their ability to embody wider or even universal human values, rather than those of just one nation.

Great works also have a life outside their home country, through performances and exhibitions abroad, through inbound cultural tourism, and through translations and adaptations into different languages, forms and formats. They are the stock-in-trade of cultural diplomacy, as shown by the national cultural institutes named after Confucius, Cervantes or Goethe. Nonetheless, these landmarks do reveal a great deal about the countries in which they originated, and there is great value in careful study of them, whether as accomplished works of art or as reflections of the cultural context in which they were formed. Mastery of a language is extremely valuable for this purpose, since a work's full meaning and resonance only come into focus when it is experienced in its original language.

This is the arena of scholars and specialists. The traditional strength of studies in modern languages in the UK is to enable British students and teachers to grasp the complexities of foreign cultures, both for the deeper satisfaction that this brings to the individual, and for the ability to pass on their insights to a wider British public. As time has passed, the scope of specialist modern languages has broadened from the study of literary masterpieces to include a wide range of cultural artefacts and the social and political contexts in which they function. These studies continue to help us understand how people in other countries live and feel, and what makes them tick.

Understanding other cultures can be a daunting enterprise, especially if it means stepping through the mists of language barriers to achieve it. Not everyone has the time or inclination, in any event. However, there are strategies and workarounds that can ease the difficulty. A good deal of insight can be gained by using translations. Great strides have been made in recent years to increase the quality and availability of translated material. The growing internationalisation of culture has brought pressure to make material accessible to non-native-speaking audiences. These include audio guides in several languages in museums, galleries or theatres, and subtitles and surtitles in performance venues.

Encountering other cultures, whether through works of art or through conversations with people you meet calls on a further set of skills, now usually called intercultural skills, which are not dependent on specific knowledge of a language. You begin by suspending your assumptions about other cultures, and by recognising that people do things differently in different places. Your own way of living or working is not the only one and you should not rush to judge others by your own norms. There are many handbooks and guides that can introduce you to the ways people differ (Hofstede 2001; Jackson 2011). They outline, for example, different attitudes to time (punctilious or laid-back); personal space (touchy-feely or keep your distance); politeness (in your face or not presuming); giving information (spell everything out or a nod and a wink); and your place in life (independent individual or part of a community).

Other manuals offer broad generalisations about how people from different countries operate, sometimes verging on stereotypes, but helping you to avoid misinterpreting their behaviour. Taken together, these approaches can help you to see a 'Third Space', in which you can suspend your cultural assumptions about the people you meet, and build a shared relationship through dialogue and mutual respect.

Language remains an important element in intercultural encounters, because you can't communicate much without it. This is where you need to draw on your own linguistic repertoire and the language resources of the people you meet. You may have a shared language at a reasonable level: yours, theirs or a third language. You may find that you can understand some of each other's language even if you can't speak it, especially if there are enough common words for you to pick out the gist. You may be able to offer smatterings of different languages, use a phrase book or an app on your smartphone or make some headway with gestures and grimaces. You can have a meaningful conversation using some or any of these strategies, but the greater your language repertoire, the better the experience will be.

Language and Identity

In everyday life, the language you speak, or even the dialect or the accent you use, marks you out as distinctive. And you judge other people by their distinctive way of speaking. At the extreme end, the difference can be dangerous and even fatal. Warfare throws up the sharpest examples. For example, the Bible narrates that in a conflict between two tribes, the Gileadites defeated the Ephraimites beside the River Jordan. Fleeing Ephraimites who tried to talk their way through the Gileadite lines were asked to say the word 'shibboleth'. If they pronounced it as 'sibboleth' they revealed themselves as Ephraimites and were slaughtered on the spot (Judges 12:5–6). A more recent example from the conflict in Bosnia-Herzegovina recounts how a British soldier playfully used the Serbian word for bread when buying in a Bosnian Croat bakery. The baker pulled out a machine gun and the soldier was fortunate to escape with his life (Kelly and Baker 2013: 38).

Conversely, speaking the same language, whether literally or metaphorically, is well known to create a sense of belonging and solidarity with others. It is a strong feature of identity in many countries. States, regions and ethnic groups have used a wide variety of strategies to attach their political profile to a particular language. Some have rejuvenated older languages, some have sought to suppress minority languages and some have tried to purify their dominant language, for example. While some states successfully manage a multilingual population, many struggle to maintain unity across language divides. The result is that many people end up with the feeling that speaking a particular language is an endorsement of the country, region or group with whom the language is associated.

In the context of Brexit, the issues of language and identity have been a strong undercurrent. The most nationalistic voices in the UK have been shouting at people on the streets for speaking a language other than English. Signs and notices in foreign languages have been defaced. And many foreign residents have become fearful of speaking their own language in public. In parallel, the resistance to speaking English elsewhere in Europe has noticeably increased. The President of the EU Commission, speaking to diplomats in Florence, was applauded when he suggested that: 'Slowly but surely English is losing importance in Europe.'[7]

If the fate of the English language were solely tied to the political allegiances of the British government, M. Juncker would no doubt have a good point. However, the link between languages and individual countries is far more complex. In the case of English, as Jennifer Jenkins points out (see Chap. 3), native speakers are a shrinking minority of users of English, and the prevalent forms of English (as a lingua franca) are increasingly diverging from standard British usage.

Other languages are similarly complex. The major world languages have footprints that cross many national boundaries, including native speakers and second-language speakers. Almost all countries have resident populations who speak several different first languages and often several 'second' languages. This does not stop language from being a focus for struggles over identity. On the contrary, it is because languages refuse to fit neatly into convenient boxes that they get tangled up in whatever conflicts may arise in a society.

As an individual, whatever language you speak in a given context, you will convey a good deal about yourself. The French have an elegant way of distinguishing between the instrumental function of 'savoir-faire' and the existential function of 'savoir-être'. With *savoir-faire* you can get things done and get your message across. With *savoir-être* you can take people along with you and make your presence felt. This is both a risk and an opportunity. You certainly risk exposing yourself to the eyes and ears of other people who may or may not respond well. But you also have the opportunity to present yourself positively, and put your best foot forward.

Presenting yourself positively means being self-aware, recognising what other people are likely to see and thinking about how you want to appear. This can include being aware of your own attitudes, particularly how open you are to new experiences and how interested you are in other people. It will also include your motivations (what you are hoping to achieve), your values and beliefs, your way of thinking and your general personality. Fortunately, a little forethought will go a long way to enabling you to put your best foot forward, and will also have the side effect of making you a more effective communicator with people who also share your own language.

Conclusion

The UK is not alone in struggling with a deficit in its language capabilities. Other countries have a similar experience, even if most of them have the advantage of knowing which foreign language they need to prioritise: generally English, though perhaps not as we know it. I have argued that the experience of language and the way we use it is a risky business. People have very diverse attitudes to risk: some shy away where others feel that is part of the fun. And so it is with languages.

Not everyone is lucky enough to enjoy learning or speaking other languages, and there are real challenges to doing it, based in the nature of language itself. But the challenges are more than matched by the benefits of persevering. It may not be easy to get your message across in another language, but the effort of trying can make you a better all-round communicator. It may be difficult to get your head around a different culture, but if you are patient with it you may end up with surprising insights into your own culture. You may feel personally exposed, embarrassed or in a hostile environment, but if you step into the world of other languages and cultures you will expand your own repertoire and grow as a person.

Notes

1. See Education First, 'The World's Largest Ranking of Countries by English Skills', 6th edition, 2015: http://www.ef.co.uk/epi/.

2. The criteria used were: (1) current UK export trade; (2) the language needs of UK business; (3) UK government trade priorities; (4) emerging high growth markets; (5) diplomatic and security priorities; (6) the public's language interests; (7) outward visitor destinations; (8) UK government's International Education Strategy priorities; (9) levels of English proficiency in other countries; (10) the prevalence of different languages on the internet.

3. See Angela Gallagher-Brett, *Seven Hundred Reasons for Studying Languages*, *Southamptom: LLAS, 2004*, https://www.llas.ac.uk/sites/default/files/nodes/6063/700_reasons.pdf.

4. Oliver Wendell Holmes, Sr, *The Professor at the Breakfast Table* (1859), Kindle edition, p.28, accessed 24 August 2017.

5. See for example 'The Right Combination: CBI/Pearson Education and Skills Survey 2016': http://www.cbi.org.uk/cbi-prod/assets/File/pdf/cbi-education-and-skills-survey2016.pdf.

6. The skills are outlined in detail in the Common European Framework of Reference for Languages: https://www.coe.int/t/dg4/linguistic/Source/Framework_EN.pdf.

7. Jennifer Rankin, 'Brexit: English is losing its importance in Europe, says Juncker'. *The Guardian*, 5 May 2017: https://www.theguardian.com/politics/2017/may/05/brexit-english-is-losing-its-importance-in-europe-says-juncker.

References

British Council. (2014). Languages for the Future. Which Languages the UK Needs Most and Why. https://www.britishcouncil.org/sites/default/files/languages-for-the-future-report-v3.pdf.

Eurobarometer 386. (2012). *Europeans and Their Languages*. Brussels: European Commission.

Hashimoto, S. (2004). Foreign Language Education in Japan: A Japanese Perspective. In *Policy Forum: Global Approaches to Plurilingual Education*. Strasbourg: Council of Europe.

Hofstede, G. (2001). *Culture's Consequences. International Differences in Work-Related Values* (2nd ed.). London: Sage.

Jackson, J. (Ed.). (2011). *The Routledge Handbook of Language and Intercultural Communication*. London: Routledge.

Kelly, M., & Baker, C. (2013). *Interpreting the Peace. Peace Operations, Conflict and Language in Bosnia-Herzegovina*. London: Palgrave Macmillan.

3

Trouble with English?

Jennifer Jenkins

It has long been recognised in research into English as a lingua franca (henceforth ELF) that English mother tongue speakers, particularly those who are monolingual, are often at a linguistic disadvantage in settings where English is used as a lingua franca, despite English being their native language. Not only do those who are monolingual lack the ability to switch into the other languages of their non-native English speaker interlocutors, but even if multilingual, they tend to be more attached to native English and less able than their non-native speaking counterparts to adjust their English in order to ensure smooth, successful transcultural communication. In this chapter, I will discuss this further, go on to consider the implications of the latest thinking about ELF communication and finally explore how the situation is likely to be altered as a result of Brexit, both for the nature of English beyond its mother tongue countries and for the position of native English speakers in lingua franca communication.

ELF communication is, by its nature, very diverse, or more accurately, 'superdiverse', to use a term that has suffered badly from overuse since

J. Jenkins (✉)
University of Southampton, Southampton, UK

© The Author(s) 2018
M. Kelly (ed.), *Languages after Brexit*,
https://doi.org/10.1007/978-3-319-65169-9_3

25

Vertovec (e.g. 2007) first coined and published it. Increasing numbers of people from a growing range of first language groups around the world, including massive numbers in China, have been adopting English as their primary language for international communication. Their use of English is influenced on the one hand by their mother tongue and other languages they speak, and on the other hand by the kinds of English used by their interlocutors in ELF interactions, a combination which Mauranen (2012) describes as their 'similects' (see below). As a result, the various ways in which English is used in both speech and (albeit less so) in writing are expanding commensurably. Thus, it is often impossible to know what to expect at the start of a communication in which English is the lingua franca in terms of the other ELF user's English.

Transcultural communication skills are therefore paramount, and the more successful ELF communicators will be able to adjust (or accommodate) their own use of English or other languages (so as to make it more appropriate for their interlocutors), and their own receptive expectations (so as to more easily understand what is being said to them). Familiarity with a range of other ways of using English obviously plays an important role in being able to understand. Meanwhile, the process of having learnt another language or languages is helpful in being understood, by alerting speakers to what kinds of linguistic features non-native speakers may find difficult to understand in English.

However, many native English speakers lack both these skill sets. In particular, regardless of whether they are multilingual or monolingual, they seem to have difficulty in appreciating that people who did not grow up in an English mother tongue country do not necessarily understand native English idiomatic language. Because English has long been the primary global lingua franca, those native speakers who lack transcultural awareness perhaps assume that all non-natives who speak English speak, or should speak, native-like English, complete with all its local idioms. This situation, of course, is not helped by the English language teaching industry's mistaken assumption that people learn English to communicate in the main with native speakers rather than with other non-native speakers. They therefore include native idioms in language teaching materials and test the ability to use them in examinations for English as a Foreign Language. But as Sweeney and Zhu (2010) demonstrate, even when native speakers are transculturally aware, they are not necessarily able to translate their transcultural awareness into successful use of accommodation skills so as to make spontaneous conversational adjustments to their English.

A case in point, and one of numerous examples I could provide, was a monolingual BBC Radio 3 host interviewing the Italian opera singer, Roberto Alagna, who was in London to sing at the Royal Opera House. After initial pleasantries, the interviewer, wanting to know how Alagna was finding his London experience, asked 'Is it going swimmingly?' It was clear that Alagna did not have any idea of what this opaque idiom meant, and the interviewer, after an uncomfortable pause, realised this and asked instead 'Is it going well?' A second example involved a bilingual Channel 4 News presenter who was interviewing Emmanuel Macron, then a candidate in the 2017 French election. He and Macron had discussed the current move towards the right in France, and the presenter then went on to ask 'So how would you buck that trend?' Macron looked confused, and the presenter, realising his mistake, tried again, asking 'How would you go against it?' While in both cases, the interviewer, especially the second one, was able to paraphrase fairly speedily (which is by no means always the case), these two anecdotes demonstrate that native speakers who have experience of speaking English with non-natives, and even those who have other languages, may find it problematic to adjust spontaneously away from their local use of English. This seems to be true even when they are making an effort to be comprehensible in lingua franca settings. Having said that, native speakers with more experience of communicating with non-natives, and especially those who are themselves multilingual, seem likely to be better than others at making adjustments once they have noticed the problem.

Finally, an example from the EU itself. As Van Parijs (2011) recounts:

At many EU meetings, interpretation is provided for at least some combinations of languages, but more and more speakers choose to speak in English rather than in their own language … When they speak, no-one or hardly anyone in the audience listens to the interpreters. But when a British or Irish participant takes the floor, you can often notice that some participants suddenly grab their earphones and start fiddling with the channel selector. Ironically, the people whose language has been learned by every-one are becoming those who most need the expensive and stiffening inter-mediation of interpreters in order to be understood. (p. 219)

The point that Van Parijs is making, and one that has been made by several others with experience of EU meetings, is that the native speaker delegates speak as if they are addressing an audience of other native speak-ers, not an international audience made up of a majority of people who come from a large range of first languages other than English. As a result, they make few if any concessions in terms of the speed of their speech, use local British or Irish idioms and tend not to adjust their use of English for the benefit of their multilingual audience. Later in the chapter, I will return to the native speaker accommodation issue and discuss both how Brexit may exacerbate it and how steps might be taken to improve matters.

But it is not only accommodation skills *within* English (i.e. ELF) com-munication that present problems for native speakers. I have already mentioned that multilingual native speakers are shown in research to often communicate better than monolingual native speakers in ELF set-tings. This is because ELF is, by definition, a multilingual phenomenon, and the latest conceptualisation of ELF—English as a multilingua franca—makes this clear. In the early stages of ELF research until the early years of the first decade of the twenty-first century, ELF was under-stood as consisting of a range of varieties of English, much like mother tongue varieties such as British English, American English, Australian English and postcolonial varieties such as Indian English, Singapore English and the like. As increasing amounts of ELF corpus data were col-lected, it became clear that a 'variety' approach to ELF was inappropriate, because ELF communication was far too fluid, flexible and hybrid to be captured by the notion of bounded varieties. Variability thus began to be seen as one of, and possibly *the*, defining feature of ELF, and the idea of ELF 'varieties' was replaced with Mauranen's (2012) 'similects' to which I referred briefly above.

According to the notion of similects, most, if not all, ELF users have at least a trace of first language influence in their English. But they do not develop their English beyond the English language classroom in communication with their first language peer group, among whom they generally use their first language. The development of their English therefore depends on who they subsequently interact with: in other words, speakers of first languages other than their own, most of whom are also multilingual. This means that ELF is 'a site of unusually complex contact' (p. 29), which Mauranen terms 'second-order language contact: a contact between hybrids'. She goes on to observe that 'second-order contact means that instead of a typical contact situation where speakers of two different languages use one of them in communication ("first-order contact"), a large number of languages are in contact with English, and it is these contact varieties ("similects") that are, in turn, in contact with each other'. ELF is thus what she calls 'a hybrid of similects', and the way it develops among its users will vary widely from one to another, even if they share the same first language, as they will not share the same multilingual interlocutors.

But the variability of ELF goes even beyond this. Most recently, it has been increasingly recognised that multilingualism has been to an extent overlooked in ELF research. Whereas it has often been treated conceptually as if it were merely one of a number of characteristics of ELF communication, its significance goes far beyond this: multilingualism is the entire *raison d'être* for the existence of the phenomenon of ELF. In other words, ELF itself exists within a framework of multilingualism rather than vice versa. This means, in turn, that whereas the primary focus was hitherto on the 'E' of ELF, it has switched to the 'LF', that is, to the other languages of all but ELF's monolingual English users. I have therefore proposed a change in the definition of ELF to encompass this conceptual development. Up until recently, ELF has been defined in a number of similar ways, for example, as 'any use of English among speakers of different first languages for whom English is the communicative medium of choice' (Seidlhofer 2011: 7). I have argued that it should be redefined as 'multilingual communication in which English is available as a contact language of choice, but is not necessarily chosen' (Jenkins 2015: 73).

This reconceptualisation, which has gained widespread acceptance in the ELF research community, shifts the emphasis to the multilingualism of (most) ELF users. It recognises that they may choose to move strategically in and out of the various languages within their entire multilingual repertoire (a phenomenon known as 'translanguaging'; see García and Wei 2014), rather than speaking exclusively in English, despite English being known to everyone engaged in the interaction. For English as a multilingua franca, then, the crucial distinction is no longer between native and non-native English speakers, with its attendant implication that native speakers are the 'owners' of English. Instead, the crucial distinction becomes that between multi- and monolingual ELF users: between those who can and those who cannot slip in and out of other languages as and when appropriate. This presents further problems, going well beyond those of accommodation *within English*, for monolingual English speakers, who are by definition restricted to 'English only'.

Having explored the problems with ELF—and its essential multilingualism—for native English speakers, we turn now to consider the implications of Brexit for the English language, and hence for both its native and non-native speakers.

At the time of writing, the process of the UK leaving the EU is only just beginning, and it is too early to predict with any certainty whether English will remain the primary working language of the EU after the majority of its native speakers (that is, all but the Irish members and some Maltese) have departed. My guess, nevertheless, is that it will do so, regardless of arguments being put forward in favour of one of the other two working languages taking over this role. Assuming it remains with English, however, the issue then becomes: what kind of English will it be? Despite the native-normative attitude towards languages that the EU has favoured to date, in practice, the English in EU use has always been English as a lingua franca rather than native English, except when the speakers are, themselves, native speakers. Thus, both local non-native features, and features that have been found to occur frequently across speakers from different first languages in ELF corpora such as VOICE (Vienna-Oxford International Corpus of English; see Seidlhofer 2011) and ELFA (English as a Lingua Franca in Academic Settings; see Mauranen 2012), are likely also to have figured frequently in EU interactions. Examples include the countable use of nouns that are uncountable in native English (e.g. feedbacks, advices, informations), the non-marking of third-person singular in the present tense (e.g. 'she think'), and the conflation of 'who' and 'which' (e.g. 'the paper who', 'the delegate which'), among many other features that would not be used by native speakers of standard English.

The question is what will happen once the majority of native-speaking EU members are no longer present as examples of native English. And given all that is known from sociolinguistic research about language contact and its effect on language change, the likelihood is that with such a major reduction in contact with native speakers, EU English (i.e. ELF) will increasingly move away from native English, while the absence of monolingual native speakers in EU settings will lead to an increase in translanguaging, and hence in multilingualism per se. And because the EU (with or without the UK) is so powerful and influential, any developments in English/ELF use within its institutions and member states are likely to spread out first to the whole of Europe and then beyond, to English users in other parts of the world for whom the language functions as a lingua franca, such as East and South East Asia, and Latin America. If this happens, ELF, this 'hybrid of similects', as Mauranen calls it, will move further and further away from native English, but continue to maintain mutual intelligibility across its users by virtue of their accommodation skills. Native speakers of English will then be still further disadvantaged in ELF communication settings. Not only will the English they hear become still more distant from the English to which they are accustomed at home, but their already often weak accommodation skills will be still further challenged. Added to this, those who are monolingual will increasingly find themselves left behind in supposedly 'English' interactions in which their conversation partners translanguage in and out of other languages.

For those monolingual British who engage in transcultural communication, Brexit will undoubtedly prove to be a linguistic lose–lose situation. On the one hand, they will only be able to communicate in English at a time when their need to be able to speak other languages, following Brexit, has never been greater. On the other hand, the kind of English used in its lingua franca role, first in the EU, and subsequently around the rest of the world (probably led by Chinese ELF users because of their vast numbers) will diverge increasingly from native English, and its native speakers will find themselves at a growing disadvantage in transcultural settings even though using their mother tongue. As the world's English users defer less and less to the conventions of native English, not only will its monolingual speakers need to make the effort to learn other languages, but they will also need to work hard to improve their transcultural communication skills so as to understand and make themselves understood by the majority of the world's English users.

The situation post-Brexit, in effect, will present a reversal of what Van Parijs (2011) has described as the 'free riding' of Anglophones, by which he means that all other Europeans and much of the rest of the world have to learn English at a cost to themselves in time and money, whereas Anglophones do not. He has therefore proposed that the UK pay a linguistic tax to be distributed to non-Anglophones. This, he argues, would help to remedy what he sees as the current global linguistic injustice relating to English. However, with Brexit, the situation is reversed. It is now the Anglophones who will need to pay to learn other languages or become left behind in an increasingly mobile, multilingual world. They will also have to spend time improving their ELF communication skills as ELF moves ever further away from native English.

Meanwhile, for non-native English speakers—who form the vast majority of multilingual ELF users—it is a win–win situation. Although it has long been said in the ELF and World Englishes literature that the 'ownership' of English resides with all its users regardless of whether they are native or non-native speakers, this has never been widely accepted in practice: a lurking sense that native English is somehow better, purely because it is 'native', has continued to prevail, even among those who tolerate non-native English. But with ELF moving ever further away from native English norms and towards multilingual ELF users' preferred ways of using ELF, it is the non-natives who will have all the advantages. Not only will English be less time-consuming for them to learn once a raft of superfluous grammatical rules that add nothing to international intelligibility are no longer considered necessary to defer to, but they already have at least one other language than English, as well as being more effective communicators in transnational settings than the majority of native speakers. Trouble with English indeed. But only for those that Brexit is leaving behind in the UK!

Fig. 3.1 HIDDEN CONSEQUENCES will Brexit give an unexpected boost to English as a lingua franca? (Chris Duggan, cee-dee.com, adapted by *EL Gazette*)

Acknowledgement With thanks to Chris Duggan and *EL Gazette* for permission to reprint the cartoon 'Hidden consequences'.

References

García, O., & Wei, L. (2014). *Translanguaging. Language, Bilingualism and Education*. Houndmills, Basingstoke: Palgrave Macmillan.

Jenkins, J. (2015). Repositioning English and Multilingualism in English as a Lingua Franca. *Englishes in Practice*, 2(3), 49–85. Available on De Gruyter Open at: http://www.degruyter.com/view/j/eip.

Mauranen, A. (2012). *Exploring ELF. Academic English Shaped by Non-Native Speakers*. Cambridge: Cambridge University Press.

Seidlhofer, B. (2011). *Understanding English as a Lingua Franca*. Oxford: Oxford University Press.

Sweeney, E., & Zhu, H. (2010). Accommodating Toward Your Audience. Do Native Speakers of English Know How to Accommodate Their Communication Strategies Toward Nonnative Speakers of English? *Journal of Business Communication, 47*(4), 477–504.

Van Parijs, S. (2011). *Linguistic Justice for Europe and for the World*. Oxford: Oxford University Press.

Vertovec, S. (2007). Super-Diversity and Its Implications. *Ethnic and Racial Studies, 30*(6), 1024–1054.

4

A Language-Rich Future for the UK

Maria K. Norton

I am writing with the goal of contributing to a language-rich future for the people of the UK. The sociopolitical change ushered in with the UK exiting from the European Union provides an opportunity for rebirth, to reconstruct a sense of identity and replenish values. As part of that identity, the English language—spoken, written and signed—is a tremendous asset to the UK both in-country and internationally. The opportunities available to English speakers are great and, I would suggest, go hand in hand with a responsibility to learn the languages, cultures and customs of

Maria Norton is a member of the British Council, which is recognised as an authority on English-language-policy development by governments worldwide. The Council works in partnership with many European, national and regional partners such as EUNIC (European National Institutes of Culture), English-interest associations abroad such as AISLI (Italian Association of English Language Schools), IATEFL (International Association for the Teaching of English as a Foreign Language), UK universities and UK ELT (English language teaching/ training) providers including exam boards and publishers—to deliver on the UK's cultural relations agenda. The British Council's mission is to work with people around the world to increase friendly knowledge and understanding. This work covers the fields of the arts, education and society, creating educational opportunities for the people of the UK and other countries.

M.K. Norton (✉)
British Council, Milan, Italy

© The Author(s) 2018
M. Kelly (ed.), *Languages after Brexit*,
https://doi.org/10.1007/978-3-319-65169-9_4

others, not only in the spirit of mutuality but also in the interest of guaranteeing prosperity.

The UK economy is already losing around £50 billion a year in contracts missed due to a lack of language skills in the workforce, as estimated by the APPG Manifesto for Languages in July 2014.[1] Is this price worth paying for the language skills gap in the UK? How interculturally aware are locally based businesses when representing Great Britain and Northern Ireland in a multilingual world? Improving these skills will have a positive impact on the number of opportunities we can take up, as well as enriching our lives. Positive attitudes regarding language learning in the UK need to be stimulated and greater opportunities to learn and dabble in a range of languages provided for. My analysis is that in order to ensure continued trust in the UK and to stimulate trade, the importance of teaching and promoting English goes alongside the need to engender intercultural skills, and to implement an explicit language-learning policy. Let's raise awareness of the joy of language learning and bring about a positive change in perceptions regarding the language landscape of the UK.

The learning of English as a second language is one of four principle mechanisms that contribute to increased trust in the UK. The building of connections with people in and/or from the UK, and the direct experience of UK culture also contribute to that trust-building. Lastly, there is the widely acknowledged principle that people from the UK are open, tolerant and respectful of difference. Cultural relations work involves demonstrating the range of backgrounds, opinions and beliefs that people from all four nations of the UK represent (British Council 2012).

Of course, the development of trust works both ways and it is an aspect that has suffered following the referendum vote to leave the European Union. Data demonstrates that EU students undertaking courses of study in the UK are concerned by a perceived erosion of the welcome offered them (British Council 2016). Feedback from European participants in the British Council's *As Others See Us* programme shows a clear Brexit-related deterioration in the perceived attractiveness of the UK across a number of reputational and values dimensions. These risks to reputation cover three overlapping areas: the standing and attractiveness of the education system in the UK, especially higher education; 'Brand

UK' as a global leader in openness, tolerance and welcome to international visitors; and the global standing of UK English and the associated qualifications which recognise both English language and UK education and skills.

Trust can involve friendship, notions of respect, recognised commitment and consistency of relationship through good times and bad (British Council 2012: 20). The early signs of the erosion of trust in the UK may well have wider reverberations. Let us act to mitigate any risk that an erosion of trust might lead to potentially reducing the volume of international trade, limiting future prospects on the global stage and damaging levels of well-being at home as a result. Compare the 3.5% of GDP represented by the UK's £50 billion loss, mentioned earlier, with the 9% boost to Switzerland's GDP arising from multilingualism: 'English is not enough … it's very useful to draw on a rich linguistic repertoire'.[2] Our recent report, *A World of Experience*, shows that the relationship between skills development and international activity is perhaps clearest in terms of language learning; a lack of intercultural awareness and foreign language skills are a barrier to companies conducting business abroad (British Council 2015: 8). These claims are substantiated by research carried out with 2000 small and medium-sized enterprises in 29 European states. The ELAN study found that the lack of language and intercultural skills amongst employees resulted in a *significant amount* of missed business opportunities (CILT and InterAct International 2007). A decade on from now we need the picture to be brighter if we are to thrive in the global market. The proposal I support is that investing in language learning and promoting intercultural skills can help shore up international trade and relations for the UK in the choppy waters ahead, to enhance Brand UK and demand for our services.

To establish a place for the UK in what will become an increasingly complex economic and social environment, there needs to be a more robust approach to language education and an assertion of the value of intercultural skills. At a strategic level, what is called for is a new conceptualisation of the inter-relationships between languages. As outlined in the *Language Rich Europe* report, the current model of language learning assumes progression through the acquisition of one or two new languages rather than the development of intercultural competence involving different levels and uses of language (Extra and Yağmur 2013). The Saphir-Whorf hypothesis posits that every language, by its structure, presents a unique vision of the world. Accepting linguistic human rights leads us to actively promote respect for diversity as being preferable to a stance that sees diversity as an inconvenience (Maurais and Morris 2003: 50–56). In response to commentators like Robert Phillipson and critics of the UK as 'a country that is notoriously monolingual' (Phillipson 2015: 11), I believe there is much to be said for growing awareness that the notion of *mother tongue* 'has lost its meaning; it would probably be more appropriate to speak of people's first language or even first languages' (European Commission 2007: 6). With this current view of the language landscape we can effect positive developments in the realm of language learning and I would suggest a focus of energies and resources on three elements.

Education

The uncertainty brought about through Brexit has been linked to changing perceptions of UK education, and a knock-on effect on behaviours, especially around mobility, has been identified in the EU Referendum Impact Report. The potential for negatively impacting Brand UK might be allayed by rebuilding trust in UK education, particularly with regards to language policy and classroom practice.

Modern foreign language provision in the UK comes with a chequered past, yet I would like to argue that more time needs to be allocated to language learning in the school week. The recent International Summit on the Teaching Profession argued that 'students need to learn to interact with people from different cultures, to be prepared to live and work in different geographical areas', and 'the teaching profession needs to undergo a profound transformation ... incorporating socio-emotional skills, and promoting team work, critical thinking and complex problem-solving' (Gomendio 2017: 18). Looking ahead, there is a range of models for increasing (foreign- or second/third-) language provision that are currently in use in education systems worldwide and I will illustrate two specific examples here to provide food for thought.

Bilingual education is a model where learners are taught in the medium of two languages. With a reliance on language acquisition rather than explicit language learning, it is related to *immersion* models. Close to 1 million school pupils in Spanish state schools are studying through the provision of a bilingual education model that the British Council, in partnership with the Ministry of Education in Spain, formulated in 1996 (Reilly 2012: 225). Forty per cent of the school timetable is dedicated to teaching through English, as outlined in a structured curriculum framework, and teachers are provided with continuing professional development support.

A variation of this model was first piloted in primary schools in Italy in 2009, where the British Council support included a scheme of mentoring and developmental classroom observations. An independent evaluation study carried out in 2015 of the Italian bilingual programme (IBI/BEI: Istruzione Bilingue Italia/Bilingual Education in Italy) highlighted the students' greater capacity for problem-solving and tolerance for ambiguity. It also evidenced advanced Englishlanguage skills amongst the primary-school pupils involved in the bilingual track, some of whose first languages were not Italian; these included among others Arabic, Czech, German, Romanian, Tagalog, Tamil and Spanish. This model actually provided 7 hours or 25% of the weekly timetable through the medium of English, in the school subjects of history, geography, science and art. In both countries the teachers involved have been local staff, some of whom had already studied English to an upper intermediate level of competence, others who had studied English intensively over a few years to gain confidence in the bilingual classroom. Compare this with the bi- and trilingual schooling on offer in the Basque Country and a collection of Spanish case studies that demonstrate a net benefit for participants (Lasagabaster and de Zarobe 2010). Overall outcomes of this model included creating a pioneering spirit, intensified mental activity, higher frustration tolerance and greater student motivation to learn. More research needs to be done into the content outcomes, as these were less conclusive than the language outcomes.

The CLIL approach (CLIL: Content and Language Integrated Learning) has been found to be particularly effective in sustaining motivation in the realm of *using languages to learn and learning to use languages* (European Commission 2007: 10). According to the Graz Group, CLIL is a 'pluriliteracies approach', which 'helps learners become better meaning-makers, able to draw on content knowledge to communicate successfully across languages, disciplines and cultures. In this way it promotes deep learning and helps develop responsible, global citizens'.[3]

It is widely accepted that language study is most successful when studied for a specific purpose or function. CLIL's strength in this is undeniable since with this approach learners need to be equipped with the language necessary to think about subject content. In applying this methodology teachers need to break down the content to be covered into accessible chunks and also need to reconfigure the language specific to the subject matter in order to optimise comprehension and what Lev Vygotsky called 'scaffolding', so that learners can engage with increasingly complex concepts. Yes, there is a simplification of sorts required by the teacher as they break down content in their lesson planning and delivery, but this does not mean banalisation. As the learner gains confidence and proficiency they are required to draw on more complex cognitive processes, deploying higher-order thinking skills and therefore deep learning. Subject teachers are more likely candidates to become CLIL teachers than language teachers due to their expert content knowledge. After all, in some sense every teacher is a language teacher.

CLIL methodology can be beneficial in both primary and secondary school; what changes is the balance or amount of time allocated to literacy in the programme of study. There needs to be greater focus on literacy in the second/third language for the primary-school age group by virtue of the differences between their first language and their second or third languages. Take for instance the Italian model, where learners in mainstream Italian education need a greater focus on English literacy since English has far more sounds and spelling combinations than Italian, which is a transparent language/more phonetically consistent language and is spoken as it is written.

The Community

The cities of the UK have some of the most ethnically and culturally diverse populations on the planet, and away from the cities there is a social diversity that presents a reservoir of talent waiting to be tapped. The make-up of the school population is increasingly diverse throughout the UK and one calculation suggests that one in six school pupils' first language is not English, more than a million pupils.[4] Look to their parent(s) to find an array of mother tongues and first languages. All learners should be given the support they need to master the language(s) of schooling, to acquire the academic competence that is essential for knowledge-building and school success. The *Language-Rich Europe* report recommended that everyone should have the right to learn the official language of her/his country of residence to the level of academic fluency, with additional support being provided by authorities (Extra and Yağmur 2013: 4). This means there are adults in need as well as youngsters, many of whom are literate enough to offer up their first languages as a resource. This linguistic capital—'the gold mine of immigrant languages' is generally neglected and yet represents an opportunity to dabble in such a variety of tongues! We could solve our language skills gap in just one generation if we could harness the potential through judicious facilitation of intercultural exchange in the community. The success story of the revival of the Welsh language merits acknowledgement here. The renewed vitality of Welsh depended not only on the official status it enjoyed and the public support for it, but also on the motivation of members of the communities in question to learn and use the language.

This linguistic capital is also social capital and the evidence points to the value of personal networks and relationships as being contributors to lower crime rates, better health and higher educational achievement (British Council 2012: 7). On the flipside, a potential source of inequity arises from differing capabilities to build and benefit from social capital. In other words, let us arrange the community space to nurture existing social bonds and stimulate the creation of new ones so that individuals can learn, live and work with others in our pluralistic society to achieve their potential, respect others and contribute to producing an equitable society.[5] By acknowledging the value of all languages present in the community and providing conduits to channel their dissemination and use, we can provide identity-affirming experiences that shine a light on the beauty of being plurilingual. Indeed, there are entrepreneurial youngsters already active in this space, such as the developers of the Ruby Rei app, which promotes language learning through gaming.

How about initiatives that involve communities in sharing and exchanging skills, with corporate social responsibility (CSR) investment, which organisations can flex to obtain benefits in the realm of increased intercultural skills amongst their workforce?

The Workplace

The ELAN report identified the workplace as one of the most effective areas of learning in which languages can be acquired and developed in meaningful contexts. The Confederation of British Industry has found that nearly two-thirds of firms identified a need for foreign language skills, which is likely to increase as ambitious firms look to break into new, fast-growing markets.[6] Another recent survey found that only 1 in 15 employees responsible for international activities were willing to be involved in tasks that required them to speak a foreign language. However, 1 in 3 employees who had previous international experience were willing to engage in such tasks (British Council 2015: 23). Consider that around 72%of Britain's international trade is done with non-English-speaking countries and yet 75% of the UK's adult population are unable to hold a conversation in any of the 10 languages identified as most important for the UK (British Council 2014). Fear of moving out of one's comfort zone into a foreign place where the local language is unfamiliar does present an obstacle to many, yet it is precisely the experience of trying to integrate in a host society that will develop key language skills and provide the opportunity for new learning, including language learning.

The experience of living and working overseas contributes to building confidence, creativity and problem-solving skills, as well as knowledge of foreign countries and international affairs, which in turn stimulates the desire to explore other countries and cultures. An internationally aware workforce is crucial to the UK if we are to realise our ambitions for economic growth.

The British Academy provides evidence that 'the UK is suffering from a growing deficit in foreign language skills at a time when global demand for such skills is expanding … much more needs to be done to tap the supply of multilingual skills within UK society' (British Council 2013: 8). Enhancing such intercultural skills is an ongoing task since not all life-relevant competencies can be provided by initial education. Competencies develop and change throughout our lifespan, and as a result of transformations in technology the demands on us change, with our ability to act reflectively (thinking about thinking) growing with maturity.

Conclusion

There is an urgent need to close the language skills gap in the UK. Improving the outcomes of education and training by investing in competence-based approaches in general—and promoting language skills in particular—are prerequisites to achieving the UK government's goal of fostering growth, enhancing employability and increasing competitiveness. By formulating a strategy to increase language learning opportunities and enhance our motivation to broaden our intercultural competence we can aspire to maintaining our relevance in the fast-changing pace of global affairs. Our well-being as a society can be augmented, since language learning enhances cognitive functions such as attention, memory, concept formation, critical thinking and problem solving, supporting both the mental agility of older people and the development of children.

The UK needs to beware of relying too heavily on English and indeed English services offered by the UK risk facing a reduction in demand in these uncertain times. Foreign language skills are essential for the UK to compete on the global stage and to ensure we continue to learn from and engage with people from other countries and cultures. Learning languages helps raise awareness of our own culture and values, encourages openness to other cultures and attitudes and stimulates willingness and the ability to communicate and co-operate across language and cultural boundaries. This is one of the most powerful ways to build trust and friendly understanding.

Notes

1. See 'APPG Launches Manifesto for Languages', https://www.britishcouncil. org/education/schools/support-for-languages/thought-leadership/appg/ news/manifesto-for-languages.
2. See the Swissinfo report by François Grin from November 2009, cited in (Graddol 2010: 59).
3. See the European Centre for Modern Languages website, 'A Pluriliteracies Approach to Teaching for Learning', available at http://www.ecml.at/F7/ tabid/969/Default.aspx.
4. See the website of NALDIC, the National Association for Language Development in the Curriculum, which is the UK subject association for English as an additional language: https://naldic.org.uk.
5. See the OECD website on Definition and Selection of Competencies (DeSeCo), at: http://www.oecd.org/education/skills-beyond-school/definitionandselectionofcompetenciesdeseco.htm.
6. See the CBI/Pearson Education and Skills Survey 2015: http://www.cbi. org.uk/news/cbi-pearson-education-and-skills-survey-2015/.

References

British Council. (2012). Trust Pays. https://www.britishcouncil.org/organisation/policy-insight-research/research/trust-pays.
British Council. (2013). The English Effect. The Impact of English, What It's Worth to the UK and Why It Matters to the World. https://www.britishcouncil.org/sites/default/files/english-effect-report-v2.pdf.
British Council. (2014). Languages for the Future. Which Languages the UK Needs Most and Why. https://www.britishcouncil.org/sites/default/files/languages-for-the-future-report-v3.pdf.

British Council. (2015). A World of Experience. https://www.britishcouncil. org/organisation/policy-insight-research/research/world-experience.

British Council. (2016). The Impact of the EU Referendum on the UK's Ability to Access EU Funds. https://www.britishcouncil.org/sites/default/files/ accessing_eu_funds_-_summary_version.pdf.

CILT, and InterAct International. (2007). ELAN: Effects on the European Economy of Shortages of Foreign Language Skills in Enterprise. http://www. cilt.org.uk/home/research_and_statistics/research/cilt_activities/the_economic_case.aspx.

European Commission. (2007). *Final Report. High Level Group on Multilingualism.* Luxembourg: Office for Official Publications of the European Communities.

Extra, G., & Yağmur, K. (Eds.). (2013). *Language Rich Europe: Trends in Policies and Practices for Multilingualism in Europe.* Cambridge: Cambridge University Press.

Gomendio, M. (2017). *Empowering and Enabling Teachers to Improve Equity and Outcomes for All.* Paris: OECD Publishing.

Graddol, D. (2010). *English Next India.* India: British Council. http://englishagenda.britishcouncil.org/continuing-professional-development/cpd-researchers/english-next-india.

Lasagabaster, D., & de Zarobe, Y. R. (Eds.). (2010). *CLIL in Spain: Implementation, Results and Teacher Training.* Cambridge: Cambridge Scholars Publishing.

Maurais, J., & Morris, M. A. (Eds.). (2003). *Languages in a Globalising World.* Cambridge: Cambridge University Press.

Phillipson, R. (2015). Linguistic Imperialism of and in the European Union. In H. Behr & J. Stivachtis (Eds.), *Revisiting the European Union as an Empire.* London: Routledge.

Reilly, T. (2012). An Early Years Bilingual Schools Project: The Spanish Experience. In C. Tribble (Ed.), *Managing Change in English Language Teaching: Lessons from Experience* (pp. 225–230). London: British Council.

Part II

What the UK Needs in Languages

5

This Post-Brexit Linguanomics

Gabrielle Hogan-Brun

Languages are an economic resource. If deployed wisely, business benefits. If ignored, opportunities will be missed. History shows that trade and languages always go hand in hand, offering opportunities for expansion and development. The rise of ancient civilisations such as China, Egypt, Greece and Rome came down to success in trade across cultures. Early traders already knew that they needed to understand their clients to produce a good economic return across language divides. As markets grew, more communication was needed to attract buyers and to be understood by them. So traders learnt the languages of their clients in order to sell. They understood that the customer is king.

There are contemporary parallels with language use in international business, on both sides of the Atlantic. Top US economist Larry Summers

---

The book *Linguanomics* (Hogan-Brun 2017) outlines a framework that explains the historical importance of the relationships between languages and economics today. This chapter links selected *linguanomic* aspects with the implications of Brexit. A summary of some key points raised here was published in the online magazine *The Conversation*: 'How Britain's Monolingualism Will Hold Back its Economy after Brexit' (31 March 2017).

G. Hogan-Brun (✉)
University of Bristol, Bristol, UK

© The Author(s) 2018   **49**
M. Kelly (ed.), *Languages after Brexit*,
https://doi.org/10.1007/978-3-319-65169-9_5

recently tweeted the following message regarding the commercial relationship between the USA and the UK following the election of President Trump:

1) [LHSummers] Britain is now a small economy. If Trump's strategy is to make trade agreements w/ only people who speak English we will be lesser nation

This tweet suggests that trading in English only is not an effective economic strategy. In other words, the economic impact on the USA of closing off its trade barriers with non-Anglophone countries would be enormous. Similarly, post-Brexit Britain will need a language strategy as it aims to connect with fresh markets overseas.

Mind that Gap

It is 29 March 2017. Britain has triggered Article 50 to begin the process of leaving the European Union (EU). Whether a hard or soft Brexit results, the UK now has to deal with the consequences of distancing itself from, or even totally quitting, the world's largest single market. Brexit means that the UK has to use its own linguistic resources to negotiate with every new partner. As we shall see, the UK has not got a language policy that can deal with this outcome. Soft Brexit would mean that the UK could rely on the multilingual capabilities of the EU to retain its access to the single market to some extent. But any non-EU partner agreement would require the deployment of UK-based linguistic resources, which will become depleted as a result of government policy. Hence post-Brexit trade agreements are more likely to be more difficult to achieve because of an absent language policy.

We know already that one of the biggest challenges facing the UK economy is a skills shortage. The recent headline 'Hammond Puts Aside £500m to Fill Post-Brexit Skills Gap' (Helm 2017) hints at funding for technical (or hard) skills training. Clearly, UK business also requires people with language (or soft) skills to achieve sales in fresh markets. So, is the UK ready to mobilise this resource?

The EU takes about 44% of Britain's exports. Hard Brexit leaves the UK with a serious trade gap. But with any Brexit, British businesses have to reach out to countries beyond the remit of the EU. They will be on the lookout for experts able to speak the languages of new trade partners and understand the cultures of overseas contacts to negotiate and seal deals. In responding to this challenge, the UK will need to invest in soft skills training to grow its own resources. The associated costs, a kind of covert 'language tax', are the other side of the coin of Brexit.

Going It Alone

Current government statistics show that the UK already loses about 3.5% of its GDP every year because of a lack of language skills and cultural awareness in the workforce. Such losses appear to be symptomatic of a chronic condition of underachieving in British business. More than a decade ago, the British Chambers of Commerce found that linguistic and cultural barriers led to loss of contracts, turnover and profitability, and also to a reluctance in tackling new markets (2004). This lack of language skills in the workforce suggests that the UK is already overdependent on Anglophone export markets. Moreover, many British people claim that they are bad at speaking foreign languages (British Council 2015). So, without a strategic language policy, post-Brexit trade relations and export performance will suffer more.

Clearly, now more than before, this economic fallout caused by communication barriers has to be addressed by policymakers. The need to promote means for effective multilingual negotiation when establishing links with new markets outside the EU is a powerful argument for more, sustained investment in languages education. At the corporate level, a case could be made for government-sponsored initiatives, perhaps in the form of tax breaks, to complement organisational support of internal language training. Such funding would likely need to be responsive to changes in the market, but could also help foster greater commercial productivity for overall national economic gain.

Now some might argue that, in reshaping a new economic approach, Britain will draw on the former Commonwealth, through English. But proponents of (what has been dubbed as) Empire 2.0 will come up against the reality that the rest of the world has moved on: Australia, New Zealand and Canada only take 3.1% of the UK's exports. The USA is entering a phase of trade protectionism. The global economy is infused with expanding markets in other parts of the world. Among areas of economic growth are the BRIC economies (Brazil, Russia, India and China) that represent some two-fifths of the world's population. Here, the demand for Mandarin Chinese and Portuguese is firmly set in the global market, alongside Russian. Then there are the CIVETS (Colombia, Indonesia, Vietnam, Egypt, Turkey, South Africa) and others as counterparts to the EU, or the ASEAN (Association of Southeast Asian Nations). These developments suggest that more languages than ever are used in the global marketplace.

On Good Practice

Current educational approaches to foreign language learning in the UK appear alarmingly deficient. Since 2004, the UK school system has had no compulsory foreign language requirements at GCSE. Hence, interest in studying foreign languages is waning. By contrast, in France for example, students learn two foreign languages up to their equivalent of A levels. What is more, as Eurostat data showed in 2016, the UK figures among those countries with the lowest share of secondary education students taking two or more languages. So, what foreign language acquisition practices can we observe elsewhere?

In many countries around the world, schoolchildren are learning a second language at an early age. Across the EU member states, more than 80% are already doing so in elementary school. Also in English-speaking regions, Australia and New Zealand, the trend is to learn additional languages at a young age. There is a move in numerous countries to offer a greater number of languages, too. In many cases, a compulsory second language is added by the age of 10 and a third one before pupils finish compulsory schooling. This move in education reflects recognition that early exposure to different languages exploits young children's natural curiosity and that this may, in turn, aid their cognitive development and adaptability in life. More specifically, scientific research on cognitive benefits for bilinguals shows that they have better memories and are more mentally creative and flexible than monolinguals (Mackey 2014). These are additional resources that can be deployed to stimulate economic growth.

Nowadays, attention is often given to market forces in the selection of foreign languages for the school curriculum. So, in the West, Mandarin Chinese has been gaining ground among the range of languages offered. But initiatives that stimulate the learning of economically viable languages in schools may not succeed in attracting sufficient interest, despite the market incentive. Looking at a country's GDP as an indicator of a language's 'worth' has backfired in Australia. Here, the take-up rate of widely promoted Asian languages has remained low, because they were found to be culturally distant and difficult to learn. Another approach that has taken root in different parts of the world (and across the EU) is to offer a three-languages curriculum in schools. This aims to promote the learning of two languages (a global and a neighbouring one), in addition to the local language. In Britain, this could be French and Spanish, besides English.

Declining enrolment numbers for language degrees show that studying languages is less attractive in higher education, too. Many tertiary establishments, not just in the UK, have by now variously reshaped the means by which they are offering languages. Packaged as joint degree courses of the 'French with Business' type, languages are marketed more as a skill today. Alongside technical subjects, too, languages are routinely offered as an add-on to a degree to help bolster career prospects, whether for engineers, doctors or scientists. In this way higher education institutions, striving to reposition themselves like any other enterprise in the global marketplace, are pursuing a market opportunity to increase their student intake. Let us now look at means of language training that can be employed to capture the middle ground of the workforce.

Vignette: Vocational Training

How do school leavers moving to sales, manufacture and services go about acquiring their specialist language skills? One country that is successful in this respect is Switzerland, whose economic value of multilingualism has been estimated to amount to 10% of its national GDP (Bradley 2008). There, employees in many businesses and organisations can easily operate in several languages. So, a bank clerk or train conductor will be able to serve you in, typically, German, French, Italian and English. Their multi-language skills are a resource with exchange value in the overall economy. But, whilst Switzerland has four national languages, most Swiss people grow up as monolinguals. Like myself decades ago, now too, my Swiss compatriots are learning additional languages at school, both during compulsory and further education.

A recent article on 'How Switzerland Exports its Pride in Craftsmanship' (Lettau 2017) explains how Swiss vocational education works for apprentices. On choosing to learn a particular trade, they join a dual-track professional training system, where technical and academic subjects are taught in tandem for three years. Trainees spend three days a week working at their hosting enterprise and two days at a vocational college with technical and general subjects (that include post-school-level foreign language training) on the curriculum.

The Swiss federal government and industry organisations work together on vocational training, which means that the business world is not just a 'recipient' but also a contributor in the continual evolution of this scheme. This system was recently reformed with the aim of making it permeable and to link it with further education at the 'vocational baccalaureate' level. This route in turn opens the door to universities of applied sciences as well as general ones. Around 40% of students currently choose to go through this application-oriented training mode, and the number is rising (Lettau 2017: 7).

Vocational training enjoys great prestige in Switzerland. It links with craftsmanship and, ingrained as it is with the country's value system, it ensures social status. This explains why so many young Swiss people prefer the apprenticeship route to entirely school-based pre-university education (ibid.). The apprenticeship system is one of Switzerland's competitive advantages. It turns out highly employable professionals (as are required for example in the precision tool industry) rather than university graduates with no applicable work skills who fail to find appropriate professional jobs.

This dual-track system has been adopted as a template for further education in a range of other countries, too. Whether an exported educational model meets with success elsewhere (or not) depends to some extent on the nature of the big players in industry. Germany, with its strong engineering base, is also using it (*Berufsschule*; 'Make it in Germany'). Showcasing this system, Angela Merkel's recent visit to the USA included a lunchtime round table with apprentices of Siemens and BMW, who provide dual vocational training in the USA (Oltermann 2017).

Contrast the vocational system in Switzerland and Germany with the UK. The UK seems to be skirting round the need for a wholesale language education policy. Yet history shows that, with political changes currently under way, this will lead to an economic downturn. There have been recent calls to equip the UK workforce for life after Brexit. But the only concession so far is that students who opt for a technical education in order to develop specific workplace skills will be offered maintenance loans (see Helm 2017). More profound reforms that include both hard and soft skills training would be required to release the real potential of an outward-looking vocational system.

Harnessing Existing Resources

Most of Europe's countries, for example Germany, France or Poland have an official language. This tends to convey the idea that their citizens are monolingual. However, in any political unit, there is a linguistic Pandora's box lying buried under the veneer of apparent language uniformity. So, whilst English is de facto the common language in Britain, we know that it is not the first language for many citizens. In fact, over one-fifth of London's residents have another primary language, with more than 300 languages represented across the city's boroughs. Surely, tapping into this diverse language resource would yield economic benefits if fostered through education and training.

Clearly, schemes that draw on the primary language skills of individuals are an effective way of putting existing resources into practice.

Organisations have strong economic incentives to ensure that their hiring strategies are in line with their corporate strategies and goals. A pragmatic, time-honoured approach is for workplaces to improve on-site communication using the skills of bilingual staff. As well as being immediate and cost-effective, having to hand the language resources associated with a cosmopolitan society will be a big positive post-Brexit.

Organizations that realise their employees' full potential in this way may, in turn, transform the way in which they work. If properly managed through education and training in the workplace, this clearly serves economic interests, as well as strategic and security needs. The London Metropolitan Police, for example, has recently been recruiting bilinguals capable of forming a rapport with the city's diverse citizens to 'help boost confidence, solve crime more effectively and support victims and witnesses'. The languages sought after range from Arabic and Punjabi to Yoruba. The British Army's Languages Strategy survival-level competency for sub-unit command appointments and the British Academy's recent call to phase in incentives to boost multilingual skills across the British government could draw on this approach, too (2016).

A range of grass-roots initiatives has sprung up in urban areas with hotspots of multilingualism. For example in Birmingham and Manchester, and other cities, members of various major language communities are taking it into their own hands to pass on their languages to groups of school-children. They are running supplementary classes (notably in Punjabi, Bengali, Somali, Hindi, Gujarati, Arabic and Chinese) to complement mainstream education. Given the political will to fund such initiatives, local practices that bring together ideas and use talents from across different language communities could well provide a model for inspired policymaking. But only drawing on the UK's existing language diversity will not be enough to make post-Brexit a success, as we see below.

Return on Investment

In a situation where fresh markets are sought in different parts of the world, growing a multilingual skills base must be a priority. The project of reskilling a nation requires strategic long-term investment in affordable and high-quality vocational education, including language and cultural training. But basic second language ability is not sufficient in business. Companies require professionals with operational efficiency in a range of additional languages for a good return on investment. This will be a standard that is usually reached after higher education, whether at a general, advanced or more specific business level. Moreover, headhunters tend to seek professionals able to offer bilingual skills alongside other (hard) skills that are in demand on the market.

But, while multilingual skills are important, they are by no means the only requirement in intercultural communication. Anyone engaging with people from various language backgrounds also needs an awareness of how cultural differences can affect social relationships and outcomes. As Richard Hardie, chairman of the investment bank UBS, put it: 'A deep understanding of foreign languages is often essential to the combination of cajolery and seduction many companies require in their international negotiations.' However, he stressed that businesses need graduates with more than conversation skills and a good technical vocabulary. The really valuable negotiators, in his eyes, are those able to produce subtle phrasing to 'persuade someone from another culture to do something they would not otherwise want to do' (in Reisz 2014: 12).

The UK is about to embark on a series of trade negotiations with foreign countries post-Brexit. If Hardie is right, the negotiating teams will have to be packed with foreign language experts. But his full message is that the functional benefits of multilingual expertise are only part of the story. Anyone employed to ease negotiations overseas also needs an intercultural awareness. In the words of KPMG's French executive, Isabelle Allen: 'I've met a lot of people who are totally monolingual and can't read a room of speakers [from different language backgrounds] … they do not know what people are [actually] saying' (Hill 2015). Clearly, intercultural sensitivity is a bonus at the negotiating table. This means that native English speakers cannot simply take advantage of the rest of the world's desire to learn their language. Just as monolingual Britons will not grasp the subtleties of interactions in international business, they do not know what gets lost in translation either, whether this is carried out by humans or electronically. To ignore this leads to greater misunderstandings and lost opportunities.

The Future Is Now

Brexit is a wake-up call for a positive languages strategy in the UK and in particular to mobilise the already rich bilingual resource that the cosmopolitan UK represents. Bilingual agility combined with intercultural astuteness is key when trying to access fresh markets across the globe. This is a strong economic incentive for support with language training across all levels of society. Required at the policy level is commitment to, and long-term strategic investment in, languages education at school, and in further and higher education. Companies too will benefit from funding for language skills training, which in turn will be a means to generate more revenue. Here is a golden opportunity for government to support cross-sector language initiatives to ready the UK's functioning in a new set of aspired trade constellations across the globe.

Language and cultural know-how are fundamental in dealing with diverse growing economies represented in the global marketplace. But, given the unpredictability of economic developments, connecting trade forecasts with particular language training needs requires a far-sighted perspective. A prerequisite therefore is to strategically invest in a range of foreign languages in order to flexibly match the changing language needs generated by the market. This will help secure a competitive edge and grow the UK's intellectual capital.

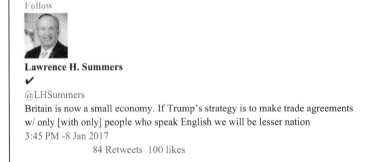

Fig. 5.1   Tweet from Lawrence H. Summers

References

Bradley, S. (2008, November 20). Languages Generate One Tenth of Swiss GDP. *Swissinfo.* http://www.swissinfo.ch/eng/languages-generate-one-tenth-of-swiss-gdp/7050488.

Foreign Language Learning Statistics. (2016). *Eurostat.* http://ec.europa.eu/eurostat/statistics-explained/index.php/Foreign_language_learning_statistics.

Helm, T. (2017, March 5). Hammond Puts Aside £500m to Fill Post-Brexit Skills Gap. *The Guardian.* https://www.theguardian.com/uk-news/2017/mar/05/hammond-budget-brexit-skills-gap.

Hill, A. (2015, December 3). Rise of the Multilingual Boss Creates a 'Monoglot Ceiling'. *Swissinfo.* http://www.swissinfo.ch/eng/language-advantage_rise-of-the-multilingual-boss-creates-a--monoglot-ceiling-/41816480.

Hogan-Brun, G. (2017). *Linguanomics: What Is the Market Potential of Multilingualism?* London/New York/New Delhi/Sydney: Bloomsbury Academic.

Lettau, M. (2017). How Switzerland Exports Its Pride in Craftsmanship. *Swiss Review, 1*, 6–8.

London Metropolitan Police Recruitment Drive. (2016). http://www.metpolicecareers.co.uk/newconstable/.

Mackey, A. (2014, September 4). What Happens in the Brain When You Learn a Language? *The Guardian.* https://www.theguardian.com/education/2014/sep/04/what-happens-to-the-brain-language-learning.

Make It in Germany. Federal Ministry of Labour and Social Affairs. http://www.make-it-in-germany.com/en/for-qualified-professionals/training-learning/training/vocational-training-in-germany-how-does-it-work.

Oltermann, P. (2017, March 16). Merkel's Goal for Trump Meeting: Selling German Cars, Not Saving Global Order. *The Guardian.* https://www.theguardian.com/world/2017/mar/16/angela-merkel-trump-meeting-cars-trade.

Reisz, M. (2014, December 11). Language Degrees: When the Words Are Not Enough. *Times Higher Education*, 12.

Summers, L. H. (2017, January 8). @LH Summers 7:45 AM. https://twitter.com/LHSummers/status/818121551501467648.

The Impact of Foreign Languages on British Business. (2004). Language Survey, British Chambers of Commerce.

UK Adults Regret Losing Language Skills from School Days. (2015, November 16). British Council. https://www.britishcouncil.org/organisation/press/uk-adults-regret-losing-language-skills-school-days.

6

Speaking to a Global Future: The Increasing Value of Language and Culture to British Business Post-Brexit

Bernardette Holmes

In Wonderland, Alice came to a fork in the road and saw the Cheshire-Cat
sitting on a bough of a tree.
'Would you tell me, please, which way I ought to go from here?'
'That depends a good deal on where you want to get to,' said the Cat.
'I don't much care where ...' said Alice.
'Then it doesn't matter which way you go,' said the Cat.
Lewis Carroll[1]

And so we reach the fork in the road. Britain is set to leave the European Union without a clear sense of where it is heading.

There are some who would argue that Britain's departure from the EU opens up significant opportunities to build a stronger economy and that British business is very well placed to take full advantage of the political and economic freedoms that may arise from the Brexit process. Assumptions are made that the direction of travel post-Brexit is entirely a matter of choice. Britain will prosper by virtue of its current status in

B. Holmes (✉)
Speak to the Future, Ipswich, UK

© The Author(s) 2018
M. Kelly (ed.), *Languages after Brexit*,
https://doi.org/10.1007/978-3-319-65169-9_6

world affairs, the position of London as the global capital of finance and the soft power afforded by speaking the global language of English.

There is a counterargument that advises strongly against overreliance on the continuing influence of English alone. Current research does, indeed, show that English has become the language of personal adoption of one in four of the world's population and the figure rises exponentially year-on-year.[2] Plainly there is an initial advantage in setting out on a global journey speaking a global language. Yet, as a growing number of the global elite speaks one and often several other languages in addition to English, the unique selling point of speaking English as a first language diminishes in relevance. As Britain sets out to meet the demands of a global market, the case for more and better language skills in addition to English and greater cultural intelligence and understanding becomes compelling.

Assessing Challenges and Opportunities Post-Brexit

There can be little doubt that the outcome of the British referendum to leave the EU marks a critical turning point in the nation's history. The UK faces the real prospect of losing free access to the largest trading block in the world, comprising 500 million consumers, in favour of mapping out fresh territory in other markets. Britain's withdrawal from the EU may well be perceived as diminishing the role of the UK in areas of international diplomacy, substantially reducing our influence on the world stage. Issues relating to the future residency status for those EU nationals already living and working in the UK economy remain as yet unresolved, straining relations with member states and compromising the recruitment of EU citizens to skills-shortage areas across all sectors of the labour market. Among many unknowns is one certainty: the contours of the economic, social and cultural landscape for the UK have fundamentally changed and will require fresh definition.

As the negotiations over the terms of the exit agreement begin between UK and EU officials, there is considerable ambiguity surrounding the kind of deal under discussion. It is unclear whether the future of trade agreements will feature at this stage of the negotiations, or whether there will be a need for a separate process. As a member of the EU, British business enjoys access to the Single European Market and trades goods and services across borders freely without the administrative burden of paperwork or the financial costs of tariffs. To leave the EU without a trade agreement would mean that British business with the EU would be subject to the rules of the World Trade Organisation. Put simply, the implications of leaving the EU with no deal would mean the likelihood of increased bureaucracy, customs checks and the imposition of tariffs on buying and selling goods with all of our existing and future trading partners worldwide. This would mean negotiations with 164 different countries involving multiple languages and multiple cultures. The nation's capacity in language skills and cultural competence will be seriously put to the test.

The choice of road to take during these negotiations will have long-term consequences, affecting businesses of all sizes. While multinational companies headquartered in the UK may find ways of absorbing the costs of a 'no-deal outcome' across their global operations, future economic expansion in the UK may become less attractive. Inward investment to the UK from international organisations may see a downturn, which could restrict economic growth and reduce opportunities in the labour market. Meanwhile for SMEs (small to medium-sized enterprises), the costs of sourcing raw materials imported from abroad will undoubtedly increase, whether SMEs are active exporters or not, and the rising operational costs of trading with international partners, including the additional costs of translation and interpreting, risk putting many smaller companies out of business.

Yet, a successful road through Brexit could lead to a wider range of opportunities. Discussion is already under way about post-Brexit trade deals with Canada, Australia, New Zealand, the USA and South Africa. Such arrangements will tend to favour existing multinational organisations and expand their global reach. SMEs may be incentivised to move forward on a new export journey, encouraging them to develop fresh international trading relationships, normally as part of a supply chain, taking advantage of the low level of sterling to export British goods and services at competitive prices. Three questions arise:

In a world that is hyperconnected and culturally diverse, should we risk restricting export opportunities outside of the EU to English-speaking countries?

To what extent will Britain's economic success post-Brexit depend on how British business handles diversity and cultural complexity?

Can we expect the labour market value of language skills and cross-cultural competence to increase?

Assessing the impact of Brexit on the economy, Mark Carney, Governor of the Bank of England, stated that the decision to leave the EU constituted a 'regime change', saying that 'in the coming years, the UK will redefine its openness to the movements of goods, services, people and capital' and emphasising that 'some of these adjustments to this new reality may prove difficult and many will take time'.[3] While alerting us to the extent of the challenge, Carney's initial analysis of the situation offered a cautious note of reassurance, saying that '[…] the UK can handle change. It has one of the most flexible economies in the world. It benefits from a deep reservoir of human capital and world class infrastructure and the rule of law.' According to Carney, the countervailing factors to redress any potential economic downturn following Brexit appear closely bound to the value of human capital.

Recognising the Value of Language Skills and Cultural Agility in a Changing Labour Market

We can agree that at a time of uncertainty economically, a country's greatest and most reliable asset is its people. It stands to reason that building a prosperous Britain post-Brexit will depend on capitalising on the knowledge and skills of the labour market, including its ability to speak multiple languages and understand diverse cultures.

Macroeconomic factors arising out of 'regime change' like Brexit will inevitably shape the nature and extent of skills demand for the future. In order to equip the current and next generations of young people with the relevant skills, aptitudes and attitudes that British business will need to operate in future markets, a helpful starting point must be to take a closer look at how business functions. A deeper understanding of the way we work now should help to forecast the potential impact of Brexit and identify key priorities for skills development, including a reassessment of the value of language skills to economic growth.

The most recent government statistics for 2016 show that there were 5.5 million private-sector businesses operating in the UK.[4] Of those, 99.9% were SMEs, of which 96% were microbusinesses operating with fewer than ten employees. Large companies with 250+ employees accounted for 0.1%. In terms of their relative significance to employment and turnover, large companies account for 40% of employment and 53% of turnover, while SMEs provide 60% of employment and 47% of turnover.

Over the last 20 years, SMEs have made a considerable contribution to job creation, innovation and economic growth. Each year the number of SMEs has increased by an average of around 3%. Figures show that there were 2 million more businesses in 2016 than at the millennium. Yet, while the overall number of businesses increases year-on-year, the number of businesses employing other people is decreasing. In the year 2000 around about one-third (32%) of businesses were employers. In 2016 the proportion of all businesses employing other people dropped to around a quarter (24%). This is due to the exponential increase in the number of businesses operating as sole proprietors, which has now risen to 76% of all businesses in the UK. The UK is becoming one of the most entrepreneurial countries in the world.[5]

The changing demographic of British business grows in relevance as we assess the skills profile that will be required in the labour market in 2020 and beyond. If business trends continue to move in the current direction, young people in the Born Global generation[6] will be entering a labour market for the private sector that is significantly different from anything that has gone before. If we base our forecasts on current statistics we can predict that:

Close to one person in every five (17%) is likely to be self-employed at some point in their working life and will be operating as a sole proprietor/trader.

One in every three (32%) is likely to start up or will be working for a microbusiness with fewer than nine co-workers.

Six out of ten people overall will be working in SMEs and four out of ten will be working in large organisations employing more than 250 people.

With a higher proportion of people likely to be working alone or in microenterprises, entering the labour market with the requisite skills assumes greater urgency. The smaller the business, the greater the need for each employee to be equipped with the widest range of knowledge and skills, including language skills, which take a significant investment of time to develop. School-leavers and graduates entering employment cannot afford to be underprepared for the world of work. In post-Brexit Britain, business will need to hit the ground running and the ground that it will be covering could be virtual or real anywhere in the global market. In fact, technological advances mean that once an organisation, however small, develops an online presence, it becomes an 'inadvertent exporter'[7] to anyone in the world with a high-speed internet connection.

Employers are becoming increasingly aware that language skills are an asset. Recent large-scale language policy research, funded by the British Academy,[8] investigated employer behaviour and attitudes toward language skills. The study involved large businesses and multinational organisations and a nationally representative sample of SMEs. There was general agreement among employers that school-leavers and graduates who only speak English will be at a disadvantage in the future jobs market. Seven out of ten large organisations and more than one-half of all SMEs agreed with this view. Seven out of ten SMEs also felt strongly that future executives will need language skills and international experience to succeed in business. There was a strong consensus across businesses of all sizes and sectors (nine out of ten) that young people who speak a different language in the home should regard their bilingualism as an asset. As the frontiers of British business extend and the internet connects us to consumers worldwide, every language assumes a higher asset value.

Predicting Future Demand for Language Skills and Intercultural Understanding

The changing profile of sector distribution in the UK also has significance in our assessment of the future demand for language skills. Over the last four decades, there has been a shift away from manufacturing and construction toward service industries. These include professional, scientific and technical industries, ICT, finance and insurance, administrative and support services, health and social work, education, arts and recreation, tourism and hospitality and the largest of the service industries, retail. All of these industries involve human relations and interaction. To be successful in service industries, a business must be responsive to the needs and preferences of its consumers. Diversity means that today's consumers will speak multiple languages and represent a wide range of different cultures. Even if transactions are carried out in English, intercultural understanding and cultural agility will be essential if a product or service is to match the cultural norms and consumer preferences of a diverse global client base.

Findings from the British Academy research into the nature and extent of the use of languages other than English in business showed that while there is little doubt that English is the most commonly used language in international transactions, organisations of all sizes and across sectors operate in a wide range of other languages. The world of business is functionally multilingual and culturally diverse.

The most frequently used European languages in large organisations and in exporting SMEs based in the UK are French, German, Italian and Spanish, reflecting the languages spoken by some of the UK's largest trading partners outside of the USA. There is a stable demand for Japanese, responding to the long-standing trade and export relationship between the UK and Japan. It is only to be expected that as organisations extend their global reach, a range of other languages become strategically important. Insight studies carried out as part of the British Academy research show that larger organisations are increasingly using Chinese Mandarin (48%), Arabic (43%), Russian (43%), Chinese Cantonese (34%) and Turkish (31%). A similar, but considerably smaller-scale, increase in language use is taking place in SMEs. While SMEs overall use other languages less frequently than larger organisations, one in five SMEs (17%) are 'language active', using predominantly Spanish, French, German and Polish. They report some use of a widening range of other languages: Arabic, Bulgarian and Lithuanian, both Chinese Cantonese and Mandarin, Italian, Portuguese, Russian, Turkish, Hindi and Urdu and many more. These languages can be seen to reflect the diversity of local languages spoken in our communities. They are the languages of the high street.

Changing Choreography of Demand and Supply of Language Skills

There are differences between large organisations and SMEs in how languages are used and how language skills are sourced.

In larger organisations, it is common to find a significant proportion of multilingual staff who are native speakers of languages other than English. Many of these staff are EU nationals. Normally, they have been recruited for professional, technical or sector-specific reasons and the fact that they also speak one or more other languages and have international experience offers a significant additional benefit to their employers.

Over the last 20 years, the mobility of highly skilled multilingual staff coming from the EU has contributed to a certain complacency in British business about the importance of language skills in home-grown employees. More than half of employers from larger organisations said that while they prefer recruits with language skills, it is not a requirement of the job specification. This is because the workforce in larger organisations is multinational and is recruited globally. For larger organisations, multilingualism is normal. Colleagues work virtually and face to face on a daily basis in culturally diverse teams and have ready access to native-speaker language skills in the most commonly spoken languages, and often in less commonly spoken languages.

Over recent years, a false dichotomy has developed between languages and sciences, which merits detailed scrutiny. There has been a popular view that the world of business prioritises sciences over languages at recruitment, which has led schools to guide students toward science and technical options and away from arts and humanities, including languages. The reality is rather more complex. Government research[9] predicting the skills that British business requires for the future shows that employers prioritise a range of sector-specific, technical and creative skills and in addition, there is an evolving demand for generic employability skills, including communication skills, problem-solving and teamworking, particularly in international contexts. In the long term, employers will continue to value *hybrid* skill sets including technical and generic skills drawn from more than one discipline. Recent studies from the

British Academy reveal that employers value both sciences and languages. Eight out of ten employers in large organisations and more than half of all SMEs agreed that language skills are equally as important as qualifications in science, technology, engineering and mathematics (STEM) subjects. We can conclude that language skills and cultural agility must position themselves, alongside STEM subjects, in a broad matrix of employability skills for the future.

It makes logical sense that employers will generally tend to prioritise professional, technical or sector-specific skills over language skills in setting out job specifications. To summarise the words of global talent recruiters, a candidate who speaks five languages but who cannot fulfil the technical brief is of little use to the company. However, all things being equal, a candidate who fulfils the technical brief and speaks five languages will have a distinct competitive advantage over the candidate who only speaks English. In a value-added economy, global talent scouts will seek out the value-added recruit. Post-Brexit, the added value of language skills may well be in the ascendancy.

Critical Skills Shortages Post-Brexit Impacting on Trade

There are clear risks post-Brexit that British business will face critical and wide-ranging skills shortages through the restricted mobility of EU nationals coming to live and work in the UK. What is less widely publicised is that restricted mobility of EU nationals will not only adversely affect the deficit in professional, technical and sector skills but will also significantly reduce ready access to language skills and international cultural awareness across businesses of all sizes and sectors. The imperative to fix the fractures in the pipeline supplying language skills from UK schools and universities assumes an even greater priority. Given the lead time necessary to develop language competence of an appropriate level deemed by employers to be useful in professional contexts (CEFR B2 to C1[10]), there is no time to lose in strengthening the implementation of language policy and provision across the UK.

Larger organisations are set up to develop strategies to mitigate risk. Post-Brexit Britain may see larger businesses relocating all or part of their operations to countries outside of the UK. If this is the case, pressure from the Treasury urging SMEs to export will intensify to shore up British business and drive the economy forward. Are SMEs ready for the challenges ahead?

Research from the Federation of Small Businesses (FSB) shows that UK SMEs are reluctant exporters.[11] The FSB reports that only one in five of FSB members export and 16% are part of exporters' supply chains. Of those SMEs that are currently exporting, nine out of ten are trading with EU countries. There are strong reasons why exporting SMEs trade within the EU. SMEs are less familiar with markets outside of the European Economic Area (EEA) and have less confidence in dealing with different regulatory environments. One of the distinct advantages of trading within the EEA is that regulations for trading adhere to common standards; once a product or service meets those standards, it can be traded across the whole of the EEA without further negotiations.

While the largest export market for small businesses within the UK is the EEA (93%), the FSB notes some signs of increasing interest in exporting to Asia (56%) including the Middle East (23%). One of the principal factors that inhibits SMEs from expanding outside of the EU is fear of entering into new and complex negotiations with unknown markets. SMEs overall cite[12] language and cultural barriers as one of the persistent problems accounting for the reasons why they do not wish to trade internationally. If there were greater access to a wider range of languages and knowledge of other cultures among their employees, SMEs may be more willing to overcome their reluctance to begin the export journey.

SMEs tend to be reactive rather than proactive in their business strategy. The FSB Exports Survey 2016 shows that 76% of SME exporters choose to trade with particular markets because of direct contact from local customers/clients in those countries. One in five SMEs that currently export says that the ability to speak the local language and knowl-

a are strong reasons why they export to the chosen
ɪalf (51%) of those SMEs considering exporting in
ᴇ ability to speak the local language will be a crucial
decision to export.

ɡuages other than English need no persuasion that
ˡue to their operation. The Born Global survey of
..ₚₒᵣₜₛ that seven out of ten 'language active' SMEs believe that
language skills are essential for economic recovery in the UK. Eight out
of ten of these SMES are calling for the return of compulsory language
learning up to the school-leaving age. There is a growing sense of agreement across all SMEs (52%) surveyed that additional languages would be
helpful to extend business opportunities in the future. Nevertheless, there
is still a perception among a large number of SMEs (six out of ten) that
English will be enough to operate in international markets. Unsurprisingly,
these SMEs only deal with English-speaking clients. It seems clear that
there is still considerable work to be done by the Department for
International Trade to prepare SMEs, if we are to maximise export opportunities in the future. While English may take British business some of
the way forward, the journey will be smoother and faster if negotiations
can be skilfully conducted in a range of languages and draw on a deeper
understanding of different cultural preferences.

There is sufficient compelling evidence from employers showing that
the success of Britain's future business strategy will rely in no small measure on Britain's access to language skills and cultural intelligence. Yet,
without the boost from native speaker recruitment, these skills are in
short supply. Less than one-third of GCSE candidates[13] achieves a grade
C or above in a modern language and less than half of the cohort enters
a GCSE at the end of KS4. Over the last 20 years, the overall numbers of
students taking Advanced level have fallen by 46%, and the drop in entry
figures for French and German (63% respectively), two of the most strategically important languages for the future, is acute. The decline is keenly
felt at university level, where the number of departments offering graduate degrees in modern languages has plummeted with the loss of 46
departments since the millennium.

Women with Language Skills Shaping the Future of British Business

There is some encouraging news for British business as it sets out along the journey toward Brexit and that is the growing presence of women in leadership positions. Business statistics show that 20% of all current SMEs are led by women, and in October 2015 it was announced that 26% of FTSE 100 board members were female. Serendipitous, perhaps, but there may be lucrative advantages in the expanding influence of women in business leadership post-Brexit, since, traditionally, there are more female school-leavers and graduates entering the UK labour market with language skills. Post-Brexit, the UK may see more multilingual female entrepreneurs come of age.

Investing in Our Multilingual Capital

If the future of the UK rests in large part on the value of human capital, as Carney suggests, it seems self-evident that there should be concerted action at national level to ensure that more young people leave formal education with the ability to speak at least one other language and be conversant with other cultures. Support for the effective development of home languages to levels of operational literacy using a formal register appropriate to professional use should be guaranteed. Language learning in schools should be prioritised for the majority of learners. Languages should be given sufficient resources in terms of time in the curriculum, professional development for teachers and access to native speakers. Incentives for undergraduates to continue language learning and to use languages in interdisciplinary and applied contexts should be explored. Greater co-operation between employers and education will be of considerable benefit in designing appropriate curricula for the future.

For the UK economy to flourish independently of the EU, we must set even greater priority on developing our home-grown talent and investing in our assets. To support a world-class infrastructure requires the foundation of world-class education and training. There needs to be enhanced provision of learning and training opportunities in school, college, higher education and in the workplace. Provision for high-quality academic and vocational routes must be expanded to ensure that every person has access to the education and training they need to fulfil their potential. The quality of education and training in language and culture matters for the economy and, of greater importance, it matters for the kind of society that we want to be.

Britain must now begin to redefine itself. It must review its business strategy and reassess its core values and beliefs. For the UK to renew or create connections with trading partners, there is a need to start afresh. Rebuilding future partnerships will rely on a delicate process of restoring trust and confidence in client relations. We must develop a generation of young people with the relevant skills, aptitudes and attitudes to operate in a global labour market. They will hone such skills most effectively through opportunities to study and work abroad, developing intercultural competence and cultural agility through lived experience. They will need to think differently and flexibly, adapting to multiple perspectives and avoiding the expectation that everyone interprets the world through an Anglocentric prism. What becomes abundantly clear, now more than ever, is that to negotiate new deals with global partners successfully and to initiate and sustain strong networks internationally, the next generation must have a global mindset and be equipped to communicate effectively in English and in other languages.

Redefinition is about questioning and understanding one's own identity while remaining open and curious about diversity, recognising and respecting the identities of others. It is through sharing language and culture that we transcend borders and begin to redefine the contours of new and shared landscapes. Being outward-facing and culturally literate are equally as important to creating a thriving business community as they are to building and sustaining cohesive and peaceful societies.

There is an Arabic proverb that seems particularly apt as Britain prepares for its global future:

يد واحدة ال تصفق.

One hand doesn't clap.

Accomplishing the complex task that lies ahead will rely on co-operation from all sides. In the new reality post-Brexit, renewing or establishing relations with international partners will require multilateral co-operation and understanding. The ability to converse and negotiate in a partner's language and the ability to understand and respond to different cultural norms will be needed to smooth the path to greater, long-lasting relationships. Success will mean speaking to a global future in as many languages as there are cultures.

Notes

1. Lewis Carroll, *Alice's Adventures in Wonderland* (1865), p. 56 Penguin Classics 2009.
2. British Council, *The English Effect* (2013): https://www.britishcouncil. org/organisation/policy-insight-research/research/the-english-effect.
3. See http://www.independent.co.uk/news/business/news/interest-rate-cut-decision-brexit-eu-referendum-bank-of-england-mark-carney-a7171596.html.
4. Chris Rhodes, *Business Statistics*, House of Commons Library, Briefing Paper Number 06152, 23 November 2016.
5. The UK is ranked 8th in the Global Entrepreneurship Index 2017, behind the USA, Switzerland, Canada, Sweden, Denmark, Iceland and Austria but above Germany in 12th position and France in 13th.
6. The Born Global Generation is the term coined by the author to describe the generation of people born from 1995 to 2009. See more at: http://www.cambridge.org/it/education/news/are-you-ready-global-future/.
7. Lord Young, *Growing Your Business: A Report on Growing Micro Businesses* URN BIS/13/729, Crown copyright 2013.
8. British Academy, *Born Global: A British Academy Project on Languages and Employability*, 2016: www.britac.ac.uk/born-global.
9. UKCES, *The Labour Market Story: Skills for the Future*, Briefing Paper, July 2014.
10. *Common European Framework of Reference for Languages: Learning, Teaching and Assessment (CEFR)*. The Framework describes levels of competence in languages and is widely used in Europe and increasingly in other countries across the world. See: https://www.coe.int/t/dg4/linguistic/Source/Framework_EN.pdf.
11. FSB (Federation of Small Businesses), *Destination Export: The Small Business Export Landscape*, July 2016.
12. *Thinking Global: The Route to UK Exporting Success*, Research by Cebr for World First, October 2016: https://www.worldfirst.com/downloads/Think_Global_WorldFirst.pdf.
13. Teaching Schools Council, *Modern Foreign Languages Pedagogy Review*, 18 November 2016.

7

Science and Languages

Charles Forsdick

The need for a lingua franca in scientific research is widely accepted, not least because a shared language permits the collaborative working and associated circulation of knowledge on which progress so often depends. The implications of the monolingual assumptions that the acceptance of such a lingua franca implies are, however, rarely considered, even though it is only recently—and indeed over the past century—that English has begun to fulfil this linguistic function. This contemporary cultural dominance often eclipses any awareness of the diversity of languages on which the development of science has historically depended. At the same time, scientific monolingualism disguises the ways in which the development of knowledge depends (and has always depended) on complex processes of translation—of concepts, terms and ideas—which reveal the inherently multilingual nature of scientific research. In very practical terms, without translation, teams of multiple national origins or scientists working transnationally across multiple sites cannot communicate. In addition, translation permits the sharing of ideas without which certain forms of knowledge are privileged, while others are denied existence beyond

C. Forsdick (✉)
University of Liverpool, Liverpool, UK

© The Author(s) 2018   **75**
M. Kelly (ed.), *Languages after Brexit*,
https://doi.org/10.1007/978-3-319-65169-9_7

their immediate context, in a process of non-translation known in its extreme form as 'epistemicide' (the killing of knowledge systems). This chapter considers the interdependency of science and languages, underlining the extent to which scientific research as a fundamentally human endeavour relies on, and is often enhanced by, a recognition of linguistic diversity.

The relatively recent rise to dominance of English as the global language of science is explored by Michael D. Gordin in his *Scientific Babel* (2015). The core argument is encapsulated in the book's subtitle: *The Language of Science from the Fall of Latin to the Rise of English*, but the study tracks a set of dynamics much more complex than this narrative of rise and fall: geopolitical struggles, the pressures of nationalism and numerous other considerations have led to the emergence of what Gordin dubs 'the most resolutely monoglot international community the world has ever seen—we call them *scientists*' (p. 2). The role of non-Western languages in the early history of science is well recorded, with the translation of Galen's work into Arabic preceding its appearance in Latin and revealing the ways in which the circulation of scientific knowledge across cultures has long contributed to its evolution. Gordin also tracks the more recent languages in which science has been published between 1880 and 2005, and describes a shift from an initial situation in which English, French and German were all relatively common, to the current context, in which English totally eclipses any other means of expression. This is in some ways a wider story of globalisation—and of the rise of global English (and relative decline of other world languages) that has accompanied this process. What this narrative of progressive dominance disguises, however, is the persistent presence of other languages. This is true historically, since Latin once played the role that English fulfils today, at certain points eradicating other tongues apart from Greek. And other languages such as Russian have also been historically dominant in the scientific community. It is also true in the patterns of contemporary usage, for despite the often overwhelming presence of English in publication and other forms of scientific communication, other languages continue to be essential to everyday practice.

With the decline of Latin as vehicular language of science in the early modern period, French, German and Russian emerged as being as important as English across the sciences, a reflection of the ways in which core debates, relating for instance to chemical nomenclature, were actively transnational and translingual. As the nineteenth century progressed and as modern scientific research—often published in the language of the scientists conducting it—proliferated, there was indeed growing anxiety that multilingualism would become detrimental to scientific progress. Not only would scientists have to keep up with developments across multiple languages, but there was also a risk that with growing nationalism they might retreat into the increasingly monolingual enclaves of their own nation states. With efforts to create a universal language of science proving fruitless, world historical events—not least two World Wars and the advent of the Cold War—impacted on the languages used in science. The decline of German was, for instance, matched by a steady consolidation of Russian, a development to which the USA responded with considerable investment in the emerging possibilities of machine translation, a by-product in the scientific arena of post-war ideological battles. This linguistic rivalry now seems somewhat quaint. Machine translation continues to be the focus of significant research efforts, but English has become the dominant and often exclusive language of scientific research. This is evident in publications, in the delivery of conference papers, in everyday communication in multilingual, multinational laboratories and—increasingly—even in the teaching of the science curriculum in a number of non-Anglophone countries.

Many—particularly amongst native speakers of English—would argue that the current situation is a wholly positive one. There is no denying that, in numerous ways, a shared language allows the circulation of (certain) ideas and the (relatively) efficient conduct of research. The assertion that English—in the area of scientific activity—is 'enough' brings with it, however, clear drawbacks and may even be detrimental to developments across the sciences. For instance, there are significant negative implications of monolingualism for science education, especially in countries where delivery is not in English. In those countries, budding scientists might be lost because of their weak linguistic skills. More generally, the power of the Global North in scientific research is perpetuated not only as a result of distribution of resources but also of the deployment of its dominant languages. The assumption that all scientific knowledge circulates in English is, however, deeply flawed, as just two examples attest. A recent survey of over 75,000 scientific documents on biodiversity conservation published in 2014 revealed that over a third were not published in English. And scientists in Brazil currently publish around 50,000 articles a year, of which about 60% are in Portuguese.

Notwithstanding this persistent multilingualism, the rise and fall of languages of science in the past makes it clear that such any complacent narrative of dominance is not simply linear. In a twenty-first century seen by many as 'post-monolingual' (and crucially, by extension, post-Anglophone), it is feasible that another language—such as Chinese—might in due course take over from English, and there are still certain pockets of activity—mathematics, for instance, where French is still relatively common—that could challenge currently dominant linguistic trends. At the same time, post-Brexit, it is possible that rapid advances in research culture in France and Germany, countries that remain European centres of the sciences, might lead to other changes in the languages in which scientific investigation is conducted. Finally, a return to more multilingual practices of scientific research might be accelerated by the rapid improvements in machine translation.

In a context of increasing investigation of the benefits of multilingualism (including cultural, social, economic and cognitive) as well as of the limitations of monolingualism, the place of languages in science deserves close scrutiny. Despite the long and complex linguistic histories outlined above, research exploring the place of languages in scientific collaboration has been rare. Recently, an AHRC-funded research project on 'Researching Multilingually at the Borders of Language, the Body, Law and the State' has included among its case studies one on global mental health.[1] This project has begun to question the often-hidden monolingual assumptions that underpin many disciplinary fields (including in the sciences), both in their core methods or concepts, and in their everyday practices. The work is complemented by another AHRC-funded project, on 'Listening Zones of NGOs', the aim of which is to explore the role that languages and cultural knowledge play (or often do not play) in the policies and practices of humanitarianism and development (including regularly in healthcare contexts).[2] Both of these projects raise key questions about the risks of approaches and understandings that are alinguistic or linguistically indifferent, i.e., that fail to acknowledge the extent to which any lack of recognition of the importance of language might impact on the conduct of research or the delivery of services.

Much scientific activity is conducted in richly bilingual or multilingual contexts. This is true, of course, of many laboratories staffed by international scientists, a fact made clear during the European Union referendum campaign in the UK by cancer researchers who focused not only on the reduction in funding that departure from the EU is likely to cause, but also on the parallel loss of highly qualified, multilingual scientists from outside the UK on whom research in this area is so dependent. It is also apparent across a range of other scientific disciplines in which researchers work outside the laboratory and use languages daily to interact with human subjects (in psychology and across the medical sciences), or rely on indigenous knowledge about, for instance, local fauna, flora and crops (as is the case in biology, zoology and agronomy). In all of these cases, scientists with access to a range of languages are at a distinct advantage, sensitive to contextual nuance and able to operate directly with their subjects or informants. It is also apparent that in situations of clinical research, openness to a repertoire of languages is increasingly prized, not least because in-depth knowledge of the context under scrutiny is often greatly enhanced by the knowledge of one or more languages in addition to the researcher's own. In such situations, there is often a reliance on interpreting, but when provided professionally, this can not only prove expensive but also limit analytical accuracy if the translatability of terms is in doubt.

There is already an increasing interest in the ways in which qualitative cross-language research of this type, reliant on translators or interpreters, must systematically acknowledge their presence in investigations, and explore the implications of the negotiation of language barriers that this implies. For instance, translators' qualifications and experience may have an impact on the accuracy of findings, and their role in a study may significantly affect research design. To take a particularly striking example, it is arguable that in qualitative research in the healthcare field, participants or focus groups in multilingual communities benefit greatly from facilitation by researchers with shared language skills. Such researchers are often much more able to solicit information not freighted via ungrounded assumptions or passed on via a third-party translator. Increasing attention is also paid to the concept of 'culturally competent care', an approach that pays attention to the needs (including, significantly, linguistic ones) of different communities. However, it is apparent that, given the reliance of much healthcare research on English, there is a deficit in the scholarship on some ethnic groups as a result of the relative lack of research staff with appropriate linguistic skills. With the rise of non-Western medicines and an increasing recognition of their potential efficacy for mainstream healthcare, the need for cross-cultural and cross-linguistic research on alternative practices is also increasingly apparent. In such situations, in the clinic, in the laboratory and in the field, English is patently no longer 'enough'.

Similar issues impact on the practices of multilingual research teams, for whom the stipulation of English as a working language may be seen to impose particular linguistic and cultural norms onto the framing of questions, data and results as it becomes increasingly clear that concepts do not exist universally across cultures and languages. There is a growing literature on both of these areas, but additional implications of multilingualism in scientific research are becoming apparent in our current political context. A cross-national co-operation is increasingly encouraged by funders, ranging from the European Research Council to national bodies such as the Wellcome Trust, and a greater sensitivity to the challenges of such modes of working is required, as is an acknowledgement of the often implicit challenges relating to cultural and linguistic diversity addressed from the earliest stages of research design. This is particularly true in forms of qualitative research that may generate multilingual datasets. But it also has implications for the conduct of research—especially in a European frame—when consensus around English as the language of scientific research post-Brexit should not be assumed. It is also possible that the funders of transnational research may begin to complement investment in Open Access with funds for multilingualisation, including the active recognition and negotiation of language barriers as a criterion for funding. Although this has not yet been made explicit in calls of the UK Global Challenge Research Fund, the logic of that initiative suggests that researchers should be encouraged to translate the findings of their work into the national and local languages of the developing countries in which they work, a reminder that the linguistic dimensions of what in medicine is known as 'translational' research are yet to be fully explored.

This renewed openness to bilingualism and even multilingualism has clear implications not only for the production of scientific knowledge, but also for its dissemination. In one of the most striking recent illustrations of the limitations of monolingualism in recent years, research highly relevant to the outbreak of the H5N1 flu in 2004 and its cross-species spread to pigs was available only in Chinese-language journals. The findings were only disseminated to a wider international audience when one of the authors on the paper presented them some months later at an international symposium on SARS and bird flu in Beijing. An earlier case relates to research published in German in the 1930s on the links between lung cancer and smoking, findings largely ignored as a result of language barriers until they were rediscovered three decades later by scientists in the UK and USA. These examples show the very real limitations of reliance on English as the dominant if not on occasion sole language of scientific communication. The dependency on English also prevents knowledge flowing in the other direction, for much scientific research is now not available in local languages, impeding access to it by scientists, practitioners and policymakers whose knowledge of English is limited. The evolution of academic publishing in recent years means, however, that increasing numbers of papers appear in English, with the result that the scientific multilingualism (albeit one limited to major European languages) mooted in Europe in the years following the Second World War has increasingly lost any purchase. In this context, there is a need to recognise the extent to which translation is not only a social good, ensuring the widening of access to science on a global scale and integrating scientists seen as peripheral into a multilingual worldwide scientific community, but also offers an opportunity to open up fields of reference beyond their often-narrow Anglophone focus. Research shows that 31 nations out of a total of 191 contribute 98% of citations in scientific research, an Anglocentric situation central to understanding the global challenges relating to the technological underdevelopment of emerging societies and economies. There are proposals in response to this situation for the creation of bi- or trilingual scientific publications, which would allow the visibility of work that originates in languages such as Arabic, Chinese, Portuguese and Spanish, and also encourage the acknowledgement of perspectives often restricted to work in languages other than English.

Some scientific journals now encourage non-Anglophone authors to include the original version of their article as supporting material alongside its English translation. Such initiatives would at the same time break away from the tendency of papers published in a certain language to reference research published in the same language. They would also challenge the linguistic imperialism of recent journal 'twinning' initiatives that tend to privilege English to the detriment of other languages.

One consequence of these developments in the conduct, framing and dissemination of research in actively multilingual terms is that they would encourage more (Anglophone) scientists to learn and use languages other than English. Such a move would not only underline the clear complementarity of science and languages, but would also stress their shared contribution to a range of national interests. The strategic value of STEM subjects (science, technology, engineering and maths) has long been recognised. Modern languages has also been characterised in England and Wales as a 'strategically important and vulnerable subject'. The link between the two areas has rarely, however, been properly explored, and there are even cases (outside the UK) of a direct antagonism between them. For example, the Florida legislature recently approved a proposal to permit high-school students to count credits from computer coding as a modern languages course, in an attempt to enhance the state's commitment to education in technology. There is an increasing movement to advocate not for STEM but for STEAM (the additional 'A' referring to the arts and humanities), but a growing awareness of the importance of languages leads to what another commentator (integrating more particularly the 'L' of 'languages') has dubbed MELTS. Far from being a burden, the association of languages with scientific knowledge provides many new opportunities.

The importance of languages in scientific research relates to dimensions that are both national and transnational, domestic and global. In healthcare research, for instance, there is a pressing need to understand the implications of the growing linguistic diversity of the UK in the delivery of effective services for all. But scientists are also increasingly tackling global issues, such as climate change, disease prevention and antimicrobial resistance, all of which require knowledge about the world, including its different languages and cultures. Languages are a vehicle of the proactive internationalisation of scientific research in the twenty-first century. We must increasingly acknowledge the need to conduct and publish research across a range of languages in a number of areas of scientific research, and, equally importantly, to investigate the potential limitations imposed more generally on scientific research by Anglophone monolingualism and the silencing of linguistic difference.

Scientific research is just one of a range of areas faced with marked uncertainty in the current political context, in which the urgent need to learn additional languages (for scientific as well as general purposes) is becoming increasingly apparent. Such an extension of linguistic skills, and of the intercultural awareness that accompanies these, is only part, however, of a wider acknowledgement of the importance of multilingualism in an understanding of scientific research that does not privilege certain languages and cultures over others, but aspires instead to being genuinely global.

Notes

1. See the project website: http://researching-multilingually-at-borders.com.
2. See the project website: http://www.reading.ac.uk/modern-languages-and-european-studies/Research/mles-listening-zones-of-ngos.aspx.

Further Reading

Amano, T., González-Varo, J. P., & Sutherland, W. J. (2016). Languages Are Still a Major Barrier to Global Science. *PLOS Biology, 14*, 12.

Gordin, M. (2015). *Scientific Babel: The Language of Science from the Fall of Latin to the Rise of English*. New York: Profile Books.

Johnson. (2017, February 2). The Giant Shoulders of English. *The Economist*. Available at http://www.economist.com.

Meneghini, R., & Packer, A. L. (2007). Is There Science Beyond English? *EMBO Reports, 8*(2), 112–116.

Montgomery, S. (2013). *Does Science Need a Global Language?: English and the Future of Research*. Chicago: University of Chicago Press.

8

Languages in the Eye of the Law

Ann Carlisle

Introduction

An essential for any society to function fairly is equality of access for all individuals to the country's legal system and support services. It is also essential to assure effective service delivery by providers, including the ability to communicate effectively with the multilingual communities they serve. The ethnic and cultural mix of people residing in the UK, and the mix of languages they speak, is rich and diverse. This mix has evolved over centuries, with waves of migration from different regions of the world and the establishment of whole communities within the UK displaced due to war, natural disasters, economic or political exigencies. There are now well over 350 languages spoken in the capital city, but London is not alone in facing the linguistic challenges of such diversity. Whilst some peoples have arrived in great numbers, put down roots and established communities within our cities, others have come to find work and ways of supporting better the families that they leave behind in the home country. Within any one of these communities there will be

A. Carlisle (✉)
Chartered Institute of Linguists, London, UK

© The Author(s) 2018
M. Kelly (ed.), *Languages after Brexit*,
https://doi.org/10.1007/978-3-319-65169-9_8

speakers who have adopted English as their language of habitual use, others who select their heritage language or English according to the social or professional context of interaction and some who remain monolingual in their first language. All will need access to and an understanding of the public services that we take for granted such as education, health, social services and in some cases police and the criminal justice system.

There has been much debate about whether people choosing to live or work in the UK should be obliged to learn the language of the country. There is value in both sides of the argument, on one hand from the perspective of ensuring equality of opportunity and on the other, of respecting their human rights. However, language is a highly complex tool, which can take many years to learn and even more to perfect. Add to that the highly specialist nature of the public service environments and services from which people need to draw benefit and the problem of communication is far from quick to resolve. The workaround is to draw on the expertise of professional linguists trained in communicating the most complex of messages faithfully and without bias through the means of translation or interpreting between English and another language. This gives speakers of other languages the same level of understanding and confidence in their interactions with public services as those whose first language is English. Sourcing sufficient numbers of trained and qualified linguists in both the range of languages and specialist fields required is a constant and far-reaching challenge, particularly when policy in language education remains focused on the languages of our closest European neighbours. So what is the scope of the requirement in policing, courts and the justice system?

There are multiple and complex acts of legislation that govern, though not always directly, how the needs and rights of foreign nationals in the UK are to be respected. They are also there to prevent discrimination against speakers of other languages and help to determine the language requirement in both police and criminal justice settings. The European Convention on Human Rights is in force at a European level, while at a national level the Equality Act 2010 ensures that public services in the UK consider the needs of all individuals, whatever their first language. More specific to policing and the justice system, there is the Police and Criminal Evidence Act (PACE) 1984 (most recently revised in Code C 2014), the

Ministry of Justice's Code of Practice for Victims (2015) and the Witness Charter: Standards of Care. Most significantly, European Directive 2010/64/EU directly governs the rights of citizens to experience legal proceedings in a language which they can understand. All the above pieces of legislation work together to support defendants, witnesses and victims who find themselves in contact with the UK criminal justice system.

The Police

PACE sets out the 'code of practice for the detention, treatment and questioning of persons by police officers' in England and Wales.[1] With regard to persons in Wales, nothing in this or any other Code affects the application of the Welsh Language Schemes produced by police and crime commissioners in Wales in accordance with the Welsh Language Act 1993. At the point of detention, the custody officer is tasked with determining whether or not a detainee requires the services of an interpreter and in which language. The detainee must be told clearly at this early stage of their right to interpretation and translation. Arrangements put in place must comply with the minimum requirements of the European Parliament and Council's Directive 2010/64/EU. This serves to 'safeguard the fairness of the proceedings, in particular by ensuring that suspected or accused persons have knowledge of the cases against them and are able to exercise their right of defence'.[2]

In addition to the formal requirement for interpretation and translation in evidential work— that which is directly related to a prosecution, such as the interviewing of detainees, victims and witnesses—there are many instances where language can either hinder communication or prevent understanding in other, non-evidential areas of police work. Such work might include frontline policing on the streets, community relations, public order management, for example at football matches and large-scale events or support work for investigations.

The Metropolitan Police Service (MPS) has the largest language requirement of any police authority in the UK and is used as an example here to demonstrate the nature and diversity of demand. In the year to March 2014 over 75,000 requests were made for language services and included—in order of level of demand—telephone interpreting, interpreter deployment (face-to-face and remote), translations and specialist deployments (language support for operations). Telephone interpreting and interpreter deployment accounted for approximately 95% of demand. The languages most in demand were Romanian and Polish for which 30% of requests were made in total. Polish also topped demand for specialist deployments providing support for operations.

A typical month sees the MPS make arrangements for interpreter deployment at the rate of 80–90 per day and calls put through to telephone interpreting providers at the rate of approximately 120 per day. In October 2016 the languages most in demand for interpreter deployment, in decreasing order, were Romanian, Polish, Bengali, Turkish, Spanish, Arabic, Punjabi Indian, Portuguese, Lithuanian and Urdu. Punjabi and Urdu did not appear in the high-demand languages referred for telephone interpreting but were replaced by Bulgarian and Mandarin. Only one language commonly taught in our schools, Spanish, is consistently high in the demand profile for interpreting services. Other languages reflect key population concentrations in the capital city, both established and those that have more recently arrived, particularly through European enlargement. Demand is also driven by the likelihood of communities of other language speakers having acquired bilingual skills or high levels of language capability with English.

There are a number of strategies that have been implemented to service this demand. Telephone interpreting is the first line of support, with all police officers now able to call this up through the MPS Airwaves radio system, thus providing easy access to language support to speakers of other languages when on the streets, without the need to return to a police station. Such support will also play a critical part in the MPS's future engagement with London's diverse community. For face-to-face interpreting, the MPS holds a register of trained and qualified interpreters who are deployed by a command centre which matches language with location of requirement across the boroughs of London. To provide a faster and more efficient service it has set up a video-interpreting facility which links interpreter hubs at the command centre with police stations and interview suites across London. The MPS also holds a Specialist Deployments register of MPS officers and staff with language capability who can be called on to give assistance in non-evidential work. The officers and staff are tested and accredited with a nationally recognised qualification from the Chartered Institute of Linguists (through its associated awarding organisation, the IoL Educational Trust). This provides assurances for the MPS on the quality of service that officers and staff provide, as well as gaining trust from the members of the public being supported. Lastly, and more recently, the MPS has proactively recruited officers from the communities of London who already possess heritage language skills in areas of high demand, so that these skills can be put to use by the service through the Specialist Deployments register.

The challenges of providing the service are significant. In one month alone last year interpreting was required in 75 different languages, several of them classified as a rare language. Education policy focuses on provision in our schools for three main languages—French, Spanish and German. Universities have falling numbers of language undergraduates and postgraduates and current funding arrangements are forcing many departments delivering lesser-taught languages to close. University language centres are faring somewhat better, with student numbers increasing and a greater capacity to cater for a wider range of languages, but demand is often at lower levels of proficiency and accreditation is not always provided. Those providing interpreting services such as for the MPS are mostly foreign nationals with English as a second language, and where they do not already hold an interpreting qualification, a professional qualification and/or registration with the NRPSI (the National Register of Public Service Interpreters) is required.

The Criminal Justice System

The concept of public-service interpreting as it is known and referred to today and its application within the legal framework of the UK dates back to the early 1980s. Development of the leading professional interpreting qualification in the field, the Diploma in Public Service Interpreting, resulted from a minor incident in Cambridge when a 14-year-old French girl was picked up for shoplifting. There was no procedure in place to secure adequate interpreting for the child, revealing a communication gap in ensuring the rights of the child to understand the process happening around her. Representatives of the various public services—education, legal services, health services and local government—formed a taskforce and project, funded by the Nuffield Foundation, to bring about change.

In October 2010 the European Parliament and Council of the EU passed Directive 2010/64/EU on the right to interpretation and translation in criminal proceedings. The Directive supports the EU's aim to 'develop an area of freedom, security and justice' and to secure mutual recognition of decisions. The Council of Europe's European Convention for the Protection of Human Rights and Fundamental Freedoms and the Charter of Fundamental Rights of the European Union enshrine the right for all citizens to a fair trial and guarantee the rights of defence. Interpretation and translation fall within the 'rights of individuals in criminal procedures' where minimum rules are established to meet the linguistic needs of defendants and others who are unable to understand the language of the court. The Directive 'should ensure that there is free and adequate linguistic assistance, allowing suspected or accused persons who do not speak or understand the language of the criminal proceedings fully to exercise their right of defence and safeguarding the fairness of the proceedings' (2010/64/EU).

Current arrangements for the provision of interpreting services within the criminal justice system flow from a National Agreement in 2002, which determined arrangements for securing interpreting services. In particular it set out minimum levels of qualification, vetting, professional registration with the National Register, fees and terms and conditions. In January 2012 the interpreter booking system of the Ministry of Justice switched from a system of individual bookings being made directly with independent interpreters to an outsourced, centralised model organised through a framework agreement with suppliers. The ensuing confusion and disorder which arose, with costly abandoned trials, highlighted the highly specialist and complex nature of legal interpreting.

The Ministry of Justice requires interpreting resources to cover over 150,000 deployments per year. While many of these are in major towns and cities there are cases where rare languages may be required at very short notice in more remote areas of the UK. The Ministry's report on interpreting and translation services for the first two quarters of 2016 shows that just over half (51%) of completed service requests were for criminal cases (including Crown Court and magistrates' courts), about a third (32%) were for tribunal cases and about a sixth (16%) were for civil and family court cases. Between 2013 and 2016 the criminal court requirement for interpreting and translation services remained at a fairly stable 20,000–22,000 deployments each quarter. Tribunal requirement dropped significantly through 2014 from just under 20,000 to around 12,000–13,000 deployments in each quarter, and has remained steady since. The civil and family courts have a clearer upward trend, with the requirement rising steadily since 2013 from 2000–3000 to 6000–7000.

Services are contracted in 217 languages, 41 of which form a grouping of 'standard' languages with a further 176 listed as 'rare languages'. The vast majority of deployments (88%, or 34,100 in Q2 of 2016) were for languages in the standard language group. Nine per cent of deployments (or 3700 in Q2 of 2016) were for languages in the rare language group. Standard-group languages are wide-ranging and include many that elsewhere might themselves be considered as 'rare'. The listing shows European languages such as French, Spanish, Dutch and Polish as well as less common languages such as Dari, Latvian and Vietnamese. The rare language listing recognises Bilen (Horn of Africa), Hazaragi (a Persian dialect), Fujianese (China/Taiwan) and Sindhi (Pakistan).

The Language Challenge

For both the police and the criminal justice system, finding the resources to satisfy demand is a constant challenge with such large numbers of languages involved and a countrywide requirement that cannot readily be forecast or anticipated. For interpreters and translators there is a robust system of training, qualification, registration and vetting that can ensure that language professionals deployed by the police and within the criminal justice system are competent to offer the specialist nature of services required. Professional standards are maintained for public service interpreters through qualifications that ensure they have the skills necessary to deal with all aspects of legal proceedings in whichever of the four nations of the UK they operate in. The Diploma in Public Service Interpreting has set the professional standard in this area since the 1980s. A specialist Diploma in Police Interpreting qualifies interpreters in the specifics of servicing police interviews and statement-taking activities in other languages. Interpreter registration with the National Register of Public Service Interpreters, the UK's independent voluntary regulator of public service interpreters, guarantees to end users that interpreters are properly qualified, accountable and have fulfilled minimum levels of experience.

Matching linguistic resources geographically to requirement can be costly and time-consuming. A 'rare language' requirement in Newcastle may necessitate someone travelling from London or further afield to fulfil a deployment. Here, advancements in technology have helped. This is likely to expand further with the main revision to PACE Code C, which is to expressly permit the use of live-link communications technology for interpreters. The changes enable interpretation services to be provided by interpreters based at remote locations and allow access to be shared by forces throughout England and Wales. This will avoid interpreters having to travel to individual police stations, and will improve the availability of interpreters for all languages. By reducing delays in the investigation, it will enable a more streamlined and cost-effective approach to the administration of justice.

The outsourcing of interpreting and translation services by the Ministry of Justice in recent years, driven by government budget reductions and the need to streamline services previously contracted on a job-by-job basis directly with individual interpreters, has resulted in the severe depletion of the public service interpreter and translator resources available to the police and justice system. This is largely attributable to the falling rates of pay and worsening of terms and conditions that have accompanied the above changes. These terms and rates of pay were previously laid down by the National Agreement on arrangements for the use of Interpreters in the Criminal Justice System, which also stated that all interpreters for spoken languages must be registered with the NRPSI. The Ministry of Justice has since disregarded the NRPSI's potential to assist with the assurance of quality in court interpreting.

Public service interpreters provide an essential service to people who are at risk and who are vulnerable, but most importantly they provide equal access for people, whatever language they speak, to a system which we want to be fair and open to all. In December 2016 the government published a draft Public Service Ombudsman Bill, which would create a single Public Service Ombudsman for all UK reserved matters that would absorb the existing remits and responsibilities of the Parliamentary Ombudsman, the Health Ombudsman and the Local Government Ombudsman. The Bill would hold public services to account and offer a route of redress for citizens who felt public services had failed them. With numbers studying languages falling dramatically in our schools and universities and fewer language specialists entering the professional fields of interpreting and translation, there is a real risk that public services will find themselves unable to fulfil their obligations under the legal frameworks and directives which govern their work.

A departure from the European Union under Brexit will certainly result in some of these frameworks changing. However, the UK will remain bound by common law affecting fundamental rights such as the European Convention of Human Rights (now incorporated into primary UK legislation under the Human Rights Act 1998). The outcome of the Brexit negotiations will determine what other, if any, European legislation may regulate UK activities in the future. Where jurisdiction over the UK no longer applies, the government will have to decide what should replace it. The requirement for languages within public services will not disappear, though the scope may be very different. If I were to take a view, I believe the relevance, importance and status of languages are more than likely to be accentuated by our exit and there is therefore all the more urgency to act to protect and safeguard our national capability.

Notes

1. See the website for Police and Criminal Evidence Act 1984 (PACE) codes of practice: https://www.gov.uk/guidance/police-and-criminal-evidence-act-1984-pace-codes-of-practice.
2. See the Directive 2010/64/EU of the European Parliament and of the Council of 20 October 2010 on the right to interpretation and translation in criminal proceedings: http://eur-lex.europa.eu/legal-content/EN/TXT/?uri=celex:32010L0064.

Further Reading

Corsellis, A. (2008). *Public Service Interpreting: The First Steps*. London: Palgrave.

Giambruno, C. (Ed.). (2014). *Assessing Legal Interpreter Quality Through Testing and Certification: The Qualitas Project*. Alicante: Publicaciones de la Universidad de Alicante. Available at http://www.qualitas-project.eu/sites/qualitas-project.eu/files/the_qualitas_project_web.pdf.

Guide to Language Interpreter and Translation Services in Courts and Tribunals 1 January 2013 to 30 June 2016, Ministry of Justice. https://www.gov.uk/government/statistics/use-of-language-interpreter-and-translation-services-in-courts-and-tribunals-statistics-1-january-2013-to-30-june-2016.

Inside the Met. *The Linguist*, Edition 52/3, June/July 2013, pp. 8–9, Chartered Institute of Linguists. http://www.ciol.org.uk/archive#ufh-i-31017-the-linguist-52-3.

Lost for Words: The Need for Languages in UK Diplomacy and Security, The British Academy, 2013.

NRPSI Annual Review of Public Service Interpreting in the UK 2015, National Register of Public Service Interpreters. http://www.nrpsi.org.uk/downloads/AnnualReview2015.pdf.

9

Language Plenty, Refugees and the Post-Brexit World: New Practices from Scotland

Alison Phipps

O wad some Power the giftie gie us
To see oursels as ithers see us!
It wad frae mony a blunder free us,
An' foolish notion:
What airs in dress an' gait wad lea'e us,
An' ev'n devotion!

Robert Burns, 'To a Louse: On Seeing One on a Lady's Bonnet at Church', 1786, http://www.scottishpoetrylibrary.org.uk/poetry/poems/louse-seeing-one-ladys-bonnet-church

Introduction

On the day the Brexit result was announced, 24 June 2016, the spokesperson for the Scottish National Party in Westminster, the MP Angus Robertson, appeared on the media in Europe, speaking fluent German. As

A. Phipps (✉)
University of Glasgow, Glasgow, UK

© The Author(s) 2018
M. Kelly (ed.), *Languages after Brexit*,
https://doi.org/10.1007/978-3-319-65169-9_9

resignations and disarray gripped the UK Government, one of the leaders of the Scottish National Party in Westminster was using one of the symbols of Europe—a foreign European language—to engage in politics with those the UK had just voted to leave. The use of German by Angus Robertson was both strongly pragmatic and political. It was an effective, symbolic way in which the government of Scotland could make its 62% 'Remain' vote palpable in its communications with its European partners.

This was not exceptional. Other members of the Scottish Parliament also regularly display their language skills with relative frequency. At the opening of the Scottish Parliament in 2015, the MSP Humza Yousef took his oath in Urdu. In the Parliament, Gaelic, sign-language, German, French and Norwegian feature, alongside regular use of Scots. Scots is not a language simply of the domestic sphere but in comfortable use across much of Scottish life. Rather as Te Reo is scattered with ease across the English of Aotearoa/New Zealand in public discourse, so Scots is found in inflection and turns of phrase as well as its lexicon in everyday speech. Languages are present and used as strong symbols of an inclusive nationalism by the ruling party in Holyrood, and, as I shall argue, increasingly so post-Brexit and in the wake of the political crisis in Europe affecting refugees. This symbolic use means that different languages are seen, heard and experienced as part of the daily public and political discourse in Scotland.

Multilingual Scotland

Scotland has three 'home' languages, which are officially recognised as such by the Scottish government: English, Gaelic and Scots. It is, consequently, officially a multilingual country and has been since 2005. This marks a difference in Scotland when viewed in terms of the maturity of the multilingual policy debate across the UK. It also connects, I would argue, to devolved policies of education, of linguistic inclusion and to its indigenous language polices (Gaelic language Act of 2005) and the Sign Language (Scotland) 2015 Act. The latter requires sign-language planning to be undertaken by public bodies and the development of an awareness-raising strategy for sign language in Scotland. Furthermore, the policies of integration for refugees and asylum seekers have included ever greater focus on languages as essential to the provision of bonds and bridges for integration (Ager and Strang 2008). In addition, in the political discourse relating to the hosting of refugees, there has been a marked difference in leadership to that offered by the UK Parliament in 2016: Scotland has embarked on the development of language support for refugees.

Language Delivery and Educational Policies

Until very recently language policymaking in Scotland continued to operationalise the communicative language learning and skills focused model of delivery, which connect the learning of language to general education policy, and to employability more specifically. Like the learning of modern foreign languages, the language learning for refugees has been entirely linked to the use of human capital in the service of the labour market and productivity. Equally, the languages taught in school until revisions to *A Curriculum for Excellence* (the national curriculum for Scottish schools), remained the traditional European choices of French, German and Spanish or Italian, until the adoption in 2012 of the European 1+2 languages policy (Phipps and Fassetta 2015). In an explanation of the policy, relating to language-learning outcomes and experiences for parents of children in Scotland, Education Scotland offers this distinction:

> There are two parts to learning in languages. The first is about the language your child needs to be fully involved in their society and in learning (English, Gàidhlig). The second is learning additional languages.
> Your child will develop a secure understanding of how language works, and will use language to communicate ideas and information in English and other languages. They will develop their ability to communicate their thoughts and feelings and respond to those of others.[1]

The languages listed in the outcomes and experiences framework for modern languages are: French, German, Spanish, Italian, Gaelic (for learners), Urdu, Mandarin and Cantonese. Scots is also listed as a minority language, recognised officially as such by both the European

Commission and the Scottish government. With the coming of changes such as the Sign Language (2015) Act, Scotland, and consideration in the Scottish Parliament of the idea of adding Polish to the list of modern languages offered in schools, it's clear that multilingualism is developing apace in the varied, devolved policy contexts of Scotland.

Languages, Migration and Refugee Integration

The expansion of the multilingual space in Scotland is perhaps best exemplified by a comparison of refugee integration policies between Scotland and England and Wales.

The policies in Scotland already demonstrate multilingual, integrating ideas, which are not yet present in this context in England and Wales. Scotland was one of the first jurisdictions worldwide to develop an integration strategy for refugees. For example, it wasn't until January 2017 that the All-Party Parliamentary Group for social integration began to make recommendations for an integration strategy for England and Wales which would include an extension of English for Speakers of Other Languages (ESOL) support, and that applicants should learn English overseas first before they were granted a visa to allow them to live and work in the UK.

There is an important distinction to be made between integration and assimilation. When integration is understood as 'assimilation' there is a strong belief that new migrants will strive to become as much like the host communities as is possible, in language and cultural mores. In Scotland, however, the policies point to an understanding of integration as a multilateral and ongoing social process with onus on all parties—host communities and 'New Scots'—to work towards the formation of new intercultural, multilingual communities.

However, language policymaking is at a relatively early stage in Scotland when it comes to thinking beyond a simple English-language/ESOL/EAL (English as an Additional Language) college-delivery model. Since the Syrian Vulnerable Persons Resettlement Scheme was announced in 2015, and Scotland took a leading role in resettlement, local authorities and

NGOs as well as the Refugees Welcome civil-society movement have become involved in language-learning activities. Languages are no longer an add-on to discussions about education or employment or health in Scotland, but rather there is active consideration of the place languages and multilingual realities might play in questions of integration.

It's a typical refugee integration forum gathering. The room is packed with great intentions and considerable experience of policy-making and policy-delivering. There are, thankfully, and after several earlier interventions in meetings, members of the group who are refugee-background themselves and therefore represent what is now termed 'experts by experience'. The meeting format is not conducive to such expertise, produced and choreographed as it is for middle-class civil servants and those with high levels of meeting-literacy. For the past two years I've served as a Commissioner with the Poverty Truth Commission and the experience has radically reformed all my assumptions about how to make policy in a way which is inclusive, formulated under the Poverty Truth Commission's own borrowed slogan: 'Nothing about us without us is for us.'

We are listening—and it's is good we've got this far and are doing so directly—to Congolese refugees resettled years previously in the Greater Glasgow area. It doesn't make for happy listening and it's clear that we need to do better. But the crunch comes, the one which will have us making new policies, when we are challenged directly and with the kind of words which come as poetry, cracking open a space in the density of policy talk.

'You are stingy with your languages; you do not speak to us in the street.'

In the room there is a sharp intake of breath. *'Genuine thinking is by nature poetic'* says the philosopher Martin Heidegger, *'it reveals the unconcealedness of being.'*

There has, at some level, been a breach and an important one.

Hospitality has been given and received and now we are receiving the gift in return, desired by Scotland's national Poet, Robert Burns: O wad some Power the <u>giftie</u> <u>gie</u> us

To see oursels as ithers see us! [oh the gift that God could give us, to see ourselves as others see us.]

Whilst these words created a discomfort there was also gratitude and, importantly, a recognition of the courage shown by a new Scot in naming with such frank openness and honest humour, his experience. The refugee was a native speaker of French, so in this meeting, in response to what he has told us, I broke the hegemony and expectation of a seamless discussion in English, by responding first in French and then in English.

In previous discussions of refugee policies at local government level in Scotland, I had witnessed Scottish ministers carefully performing language integration through their leadership. On one memorable occasion when a refugee stood in a gathering to address the government minister responsible he did so through an interpreter. Before responding, the minister in question paused and turned to his audience and to the interpreter directly explaining that he would now speak in shorter sentences in order to allow the interpreter to do her important work. It was a small thing, but it was a piece of policy being enacted, which enabled a moment for integration work to be experienced at the level of the pace and tone of, and care for, the languages; and for language work to be undertaken in the room.

To get to a place where a minister can work multilingually in these ways does not come by accident. It requires ministers to be briefed by those who know how to interpret and translate, to gain an ease in multilingual settings, and, most significantly, not to be fazed by being addressed in languages they do not understand. To create conditions from which a refugee-background resident of Scotland can shift the register and attitudes of civil society groups, NGOs and public sector workers with a challenge to this 'stinginess with languages' is also only possible if a policy environment can sustain and embrace multilingualism, and has already begun this work in the past.

This, for me, is at the core of the policy initiatives developing, many in embryo, in Scotland at present. It stands in stark contrast to integration policies in England and Wales, and in much of the largely monolingual Western world. In short, in Scotland there is an attempt to overcome the fear people have come to associate with other languages by enabling language contact and language learning which does indeed, and rightly, focus primarily on English, but goes beyond this into democratising multilingual experience, language awareness and language access.

In England and Wales the policies have been marked by outsourcing and segregation, and by cuts to ESOL provision, and they have operated a monolingual model of integration. They stand in contrast to the multilingual policies being experimented with in the multilingual jurisdiction of Scotland. Many of the policy and educational research initiatives in Scotland are focused on 'mapping exercises'—discovering who is offering what, in terms of language provision, to whom, where and when. Civil society groups like City of Sanctuary, or the Refugee Integration Networks, have all contributed by offering activities such as ESOL classes but also language learning events where the deficit model of language integration does not dominate. In other words, where the focus is not simply on migrants or refugees becoming functional in English, but also on allowing others in the welcome movement and community to learn some new words and phrases of Arabic or Tigrinya or Pashtu, for example. There has been a discernible shift in this regard, which can be seen not only in the range of languages offered by a Curriculum for Excellence, but also with the refugee language cafes and clubs and gatherings that are taking place in community centres, museum basements, sports halls and even gardens, all with the aim of working towards a more inclusive linguistic landscape. This represents a break with the previous educational model, which focused only on learning the languages of Europe, and a shift into the wider global language learning of a world in conflict, a world of migration, and of a world which respects varieties of indigenous speech.

When observing many of the models being adopted there are two distinct approaches, which are to be noted for our purposes here. Firstly, much of the refugee language policy in Scotland is contained in the kinds of technocratic, learning-outcomes discourse which promises a linear flow towards the goal of fluency. It mirrors directly the kinds of discourse used in applied linguistics and language-pedagogy research, with models and levels and a sense of a linear flow towards ever greater heights on a language ladder, delivered with ever diminishing resources of time and contact in the classrooms. This is what forms the policy-delivery bedrock for the funded ESOL and EAL classes and for the communicative learning, and is also reflected in the language statement for parents, 'A Curriculum for Excellence', cited above.

Secondly, in the informal community-language classes, there is an adoption and continuation of communicative language teaching by those trained in it; but also now volunteers, or those who have experienced language learning themselves, are using the methods they have been schooled in already. This gives a wide teaching ecology, from grammar-translation and audiolingual models through to communicative approaches, depending on the age and experience of those facilitating and teaching. In addition, and where I find the greatest divergence from the dominant communicative or even intercultural language education models, is in the development of language learning through other activities—language in sewing classes, in shopping expeditions, in gardening or dance and theatre and arts classes. Languages are still predominantly being taught in classrooms, with a formal focus on language learning as the activity, but other activities are also being used as vehicles for language exchange and conversation and development.

Repeatedly, in the context of discussions relating to integration, the question of languages surfaces. However, in the detail of the 'New Scots' integration strategy of 2014, reference to language was sparse and was focused on ESOL classes and support for refugees learning English. It did, nonetheless, recognise refugees' language contributions, within the neoliberal frameworks of globalisation:

> Refugees have a range of skills, experience and resilience which can be utilised. Their language skills can inform Scotland's position in a globalised market and their potential for entrepreneurialism can be harnessed. (Scottish Government 2013: 38)

Between 2014 and 2017 a paradigmatic shift in understandings of languages can be traced through the policy documentation on refugee and migrant integration in Scotland, which reflects the developments in multilingualism. As the final evaluation report on the New Scots Strategy 2014–2017 was published, the central place of multilingualism for integration was fully recognised as being of mutual benefit under the heading: 'Recognising Scotland's Linguistic Diversity'. In the report, Sharing Lives, Sharing Languages mention is made repeatedly to the interpreting and translation of policy and practice guides, and other documents, into at least 11 languages, together with a strong focus on the importance of bilingualism, bilingual training and a role for the language-befriending activities of the pilot programme:

> The Scottish Government is funding Sharing Lives Sharing Languages, a peer education pilot, which aims to build connections between refugees and those whose first language is not English, and the host community, by developing a participative approach to language learning. (Scottish Government 2017: 55)

A pilot policy Sharing Lives, Sharing Languages was announced by the Scottish government in 2016 to develop complementary language learning activities in communities. This grew out of a number of initiatives at NGO, civil society and local authority level as the Syrian Vulnerable Persons

Resettlement programme was announced and Scotland volunteered to take a large share of the refugees. The funding model allowed for support of the new arrivals over the initial five years of their settlement and, as many new organisations came to engage statutorily with the newly arrived Syrians, the level of language needs on all sides was sufficient for the pilot to be proposed and implement. The proposal came from Education Scotland and from two academics—Alison Strang, who led the integration strategy for Scotland and proposed a peer-education model, and myself. It was clear that the number of hours offered by structured ESOL classes needed a firm complement and that for good integrating practices to be forthcoming, a mutual effort at language engagement was needed, not least as a way of working with the 5:1 ratio of volunteers to refugees in Scotland.

These new language befriending programmes were in no way seen as replacing structured classroom ESOL provision. The Scottish Government this as a key way in which the indigenous Scottish communities (many of whom are also New Scots and migrants themselves) could volunteer support for newly arrived refugees and asylum seekers, notably through language learning activities:

> Syrian refugees will be encouraged to share their cultures and practise English with their new neighbours through a pilot scheme aimed at helping them settle into Scottish communities.[2]
>
> Speaking at the Parliamentary Debate on Syrian Refugees, Equalities Secretary Angela Constance confirmed £85,000 funding for the new scheme which will build on the English language training all Syrian refugees have received.
>
> The pilot project, which will be trialled in four local authority areas, will bring together refugees with members of their new communities, to practice their English and swap information about their different cultures. Volunteers help refugees learn more about local life by involving them in walking groups, coffee mornings, choirs or through sports activities.

This represents a shift in the multilingual landscape of Scotland's language education and integration strategy, and it can be traced to the intervention by the refugee from the Democratic Republic of Congo and his challenge to 'language stinginess' in Scotland. Sharing Lives, Sharing Languages is entering the evaluation phase at the time of writing

(May 2017) and has been delivered, not by the language education specialists in the further education sector, but as a complement to their work, through the Scottish Refugee Council. The Scottish Refugee Council has acted as the main hub for the volunteer movement Scotland Welcomes Refugees, and has galvanised its volunteers into a great deal of 'language-befriending activity', as this is now being described. This locates language befriending activities within the same frameworks as integration-policy delivery in communities and international networks, and as arts-based approaches to integration, such as the Refugee Festival Scotland—a three-week-long series of activities which focus on celebrating Scotland's refugee and host communities.

These environments are a long way removed from ESOL classes or the jobcentre requirements for English language learning, with their ever present threat of benefits sanctions. Already these safe spaces outwith formal testing or threat are proving to be conducive to language practice.[3]

Language Plenty

A key feature in the shifts, which I have traced in this chapter, is an approach which adopts the dominant discourse of a language deficit model in learners, and speaks of 'barriers, competence, levels' to one which operates according to a psychosocial narrative paradigm. Telling and celebrating stories of language plenty, in contexts of befriending, which normalise multilingual relationships and bilingualism across Scotland are all part of this change. Frimberger (2016) has been one of the first to document this shift. In her work she has observed the way arts-based methods of language teaching can enable a movement into multiple relationships and expressive forms, which expand the space available for interpretive resources across society. In her descriptions of her practice-based research with young asylum-seeker and refugee learners she speaks of 'language plenty'. This concept allows for a reversal in the traditional language power dynamics by acknowledging the many languages spoken by refugees, versus the few that are often present in encounters with the indigenous population in Scotland. Those schooled in Scotland will often have access to at best one or two languages, whereas New Scots are often functionally multilingual in three or four languages.

In policy framings too, the discourse matters and if integration is to be real and meaningful and not simply assimilationist, then the discourse of policymaking will have to bend to the poetics of such a challenge. 'Language pals'; 'language befriending'; 'language plenty'; 'sharing lives, sharing languages'; all these phrases are relative newcomers in the language-policy landscape, and even in the research tropes in applied linguistics and foreign language pedagogy. But they point to a dynamic shift towards multilingualism, and beyond even the language learning which was developed from the Council of Europe. As the old certainties of multiculturalism, of European language policies of 1+2 and of intercultural communicative competence all begin to crack under the strain of what I and others now see as the end of peacetime policymaking in the European context, it is in the poetics of such a challenge that we might begin to make policies which can serve all. The policies developed for Europe during over 60 years of relative peace are being tested by the arrivals of those fleeing conflict. The presence of speakers and learners who have not grown up in days when European peace was a given, brings new challenges to language policymaking. Lessons need to be learned from those contexts worldwide which operate different models of multilingualism. And policymaking itself needs new language. Terms such as 'integration and cohesion' are used with critical caution and wariness at present.

In Scotland, we find emergent language policies which are shifting the discourses, even if we are all 'beginners' in the practices of 'language plenty', are overcoming a certain language 'stinginess' and have only come to this realisation through the power: '*the giftie gie us, to see oursels as ithers see us!*'

Notes

1. See 'Languages in Curriculum for Excellence': https://education.gov.scot/ parentzone/learning-in-scotland/curriculum-areas/Languages%20in%20 Curriculum%20for%20Excellence.

2. See 'Language Boost for Refugees', *Scottish Government News*, 8 September 2016. https://news.gov.scot/news/language-boost-for-refugees.
3. See 'Sharing Lives, Sharing Languages', Scottish Refugee Council, 20 January 2017. http://www.scottishrefugeecouncil.org.uk/news_and_events/blogs/3062_sharing_lives_sharing_languages.

References

Ager, A., & Strang, A. (2008). Understanding Integration: A Conceptual Framework. *Journal of Refugee Studies, 21*(2), 166–191.

Frimberger, K. (2016). Enabling Arts-Based, Multilingual Learning Spaces for Young People with Refugee Backgrounds. *Pedagogy, Culture, Society, 24*, 285–299.

Phipps, A., & Fassetta, G. (2015). A Critical Analysis of Language Policy in Scotland. *European Journal of Language Policy, 7*(1), 5–28.

Scottish Government. (2013). New Scots: Integrating Refugees in Scotland's Communities, 2014–2017.

Scottish Government. (2017). New Scots: Integrating Refugees in Scotland's Communities. 2014–2017. Final Report.

10

What Every Policymaker Needs to Know About the Cognitive Benefits of Bilingualism

Dina Mehmedbegovic

Introduction

The *Manifesto for Languages* produced by the APPG (All-Party Parliamentary Group on Modern Languages 2014) argued that the UK needs to have a strategy for 'national recovery in language learning'. The *Manifesto* calls for a set of important commitments to be made by the political parties in the next general election, which would form a Framework for National Recovery in Language Learning. In this document it is suggested that £48 billion could be added to the UK economy if 'national competence in languages is revived'. The *Manifesto* exposes the severity of language-learning decline at different levels.

My intention for this chapter is to present the case for an approach that can be applied at individual, institutional and national level, as a national strategy, based on interdisciplinary research evidence. My approach is conceptualised as a Healthy Linguistic Diet approach and every policymaker and leader in education, health and economy willing to take it on board could confidently expect to see short-term and

D. Mehmedbegovic (✉)
University College London, London, UK

© The Author(s) 2018
M. Kelly (ed.), *Languages after Brexit*,
https://doi.org/10.1007/978-3-319-65169-9_10

long-term benefits in terms of educational attainment, cognitive enhancement, well-being throughout different life stages, health benefits, especially in advanced age and a boost to the economy.

In the British Academy's report on the state of the nation (Tinsley 2013), the deficiency of language skills was identified as being so severe amongst the available and incoming workforce that some large companies had started deleting language requirements from their adverts and staff profile requirements, having to focus their business strategies on English-speaking countries only. The report terms this phenomenon the 'creation of a vicious circle of monolingualism' (Tinsley 2013: 11).

Without any doubt this vicious circle of monolingualism rests on the dominance of the English language, unrivalled by any other language in our history: 'no other language has been spoken by so many people in so many places … one in four of the human race is competent in English' (Crystal 2002: 10). Current British Council estimates also strongly suggest that this figure result in a false feeling of 'English is enough', reflected in the decline of language learning and skills (British Council 2014). Therefore, I would like to advocate that current attempts to promote language learning in the UK need to use new and different arguments than the ones used in other countries and contexts, such as globalisation, mobility and employability. In this chapter I will outline cognitive benefits linked to language learning within my Healthy Linguistic Diet approach, which are entirely intrinsic and therefore liberated from the burden of having to prove useful in the context of English language dominance.

Key Concepts: Bilingualism, Multilingualism, Plurilingualism

The definition of bilingualism encompasses huge variations across different contexts. The common feature of all definitions available in theory and in practice lies in the recognition that bilingualism at the individual and societal level refers to the existence of two languages—meaning the recognition that a number of individuals and communities use two languages in their everyday lives. In some cases, like the definition that is used in mainstream schools in England, the 'existence' of two languages is defined as 'exposure to two languages; living in two languages' (Eversley et al. 2010). This is a very inclusive definition, which avoids complex and in some cases hard-to-measure aspects of language use: competency, proficiency, fluency and literacy. The reasons why it is essential for schools to have a broad, inclusive definition of bilingualism are explored below.

The criterion of 'living in two languages' allows for the inclusion of a variety of profiles of bilingual pupils. These different profiles can be divided into three main categories, discussed here in the context of England and its mainstream education.

First are bilinguals born and educated in England. They are children from well-established immigrant communities, mainly originating from the Commonwealth countries: India, Bangladesh and Pakistan. Second are recent immigrant bilinguals. They come from many different European, Asian, African and South American countries. They are mainly new to English and have various degrees of literacy in their first language. The third group consists of settled immigrant bilinguals. These children were not born here, but have been immersed in an English speaking environment for different lengths of time. They are at different stages of developing bilingualism depending on their backgrounds, support and abilities. They differ from bilinguals born here mainly by having had some of their formal education in a language other than English. Therefore, in many cases, they have higher levels of literacy and background knowledge in that other language (Mehmedbegovic 2011).

Having a definition that enables teachers and practitioners in mainstream education to identify all these different cases as types of bilingualism is essential in order to collect data that: accurately reflect the full range of societal bilingualism; recognise experiences and language practices which children engage with outside school; identify a variety of needs in terms of language development and language support that these children may have; and can inform the allocation of funds available for language development, either in English or in their home language.

The term multilingualism is used widely by practitioners and policymakers within the education system in England, especially London. In the context of schools, practitioners and policymakers in England refer to 'multilingual schools', 'multilingual classrooms' and 'multilingual communities of learners'. In reality this is in recognition of the fact that some or many students in these schools have a language other than English as a part of their lives, mainly outside their mainstream school. In educational literature, multilingual schools and classrooms are defined as having the curriculum taught in different languages—for example in international schools.

On the other hand, the Council of Europe's policies promote a vision and a discourse of plurilingualism, as explored below. Often the question is asked: what is the difference between multilingualism and plurilingualism? The main distinction for the Council of Europe is that a multilingual approach is about having many different languages co-exist alongside each other, but separately, within individuals or society, with the ultimate aim of achieving the idealised competency of the native speaker in each language (Council of Europe 2001: 4). A plurilingual approach, on the contrary, places emphasis on the development of effective communication skills which draw on all of our linguistic and cultural experiences in an interactive way. This is promoted as a lifelong activity, a process of learning the language of home, society, other peoples; developing communicative competencies throughout our lifetime; and in different situations flexibly calling upon different parts of this competence in order to achieve effective communication. Plurilingualism recognises an all-encompassing communication competence that is made up of different languages that one person has been exposed to and acknowledges the partial nature of the knowledge anyone can have of one language, be it their mother tongue or not. Therefore plurilingualism removes the ideal of the native speaker as the ultimate achievement and replaces it with the aim of an effective pluralistic communicator who draws on his/her varied repertoire of linguistic and cultural knowledge in a flexible, creative and individual way (Council of Europe 2001: 4, 5, 169). The emphasis in this process is on attitude formation and language and cultural awareness as essential to one's understanding of social and physical environments and ability to function effectively in local, national and international environments (Tosi and Leung 1999: 17). Plurilingualism provides a true qualitative leap in terms of understanding, conceptualising and developing models of practice, which include home language support. My Healthy Linguistic Diet proposal is underpinned by the understanding of language learning and language competencies as defined by the plurilingual approach.

Cognitive Advantages of Bilingualism and Language Learning

Clinical research studies carried out in the second part of the twentieth century involving bilinguals (those who use two languages) and monolinguals (those who use one language) provide a significant body of evidence which covers differences in a wide range of variables:

* visual presentation and processing,
* audio processing,
* brain activity and engagement.

Jim Cummins lists 160 studies focused on bilinguals in education from different countries and contexts, all of which provide evidence that bilingual children perform better than monolingual children across the curriculum (Cummins 2001).

Studies conducted with early-years and school-age children have found that bilingual preschool children demonstrate better focus on tasks while ignoring distractions than their monolingual peers. A similar enhanced ability to concentrate has been found in bilingual adults, particularly those who became fluent in two languages at an early age. Managing two languages helps the brain sharpen and retain its ability to focus while ignoring irrelevant information (Bialystok 1999).

More recent studies with adults have provided insights into physical changes, which happen in the brain when two languages are used, demonstrated as the enhancement of brain matter. Bilingual adults have denser grey matter (brain tissue packed with information-processing nerve cells and fibres), especially in the brain's left hemisphere, where most language and communication skills are controlled. The effect is strongest in people who acquired a second language before the age of five and in those who are most proficient at their second language. This finding suggests that being bilingual from an early age significantly alters the brain's structure, and that proficiency and intensity of use result in the same benefits (Kovelman et al. 2008). This type of evidence is crucial in raising awareness that language learning is a valuable lifelong activity. It also shows that it is wrong to think that older learners do not gain cognitive benefits from it. The 'Never Too Late?' study provides evidence that although earlier and later language learners enjoy a different range of benefits, they all have significant advantages in comparison with people who only have one language (Bak et al. 2014).

Bilinguals also show significantly more activity in the right brain hemisphere than monolingual speakers, particularly in a frontal area identified as the source of the bilingual advantages in attention and control. This expanded neural activity is so consistent on brain scans that it has been labelled as a "neurological signature" for bilingualism (Kovelman et al. 2008).

The latest evidence is even more significant in terms of one's wellbeing. The most recent research studies conducted in Canada identify bilingualism as a big hope in equipping ourselves better to engage with the threat of dementia: 'Executive brain power', developed by the use of two languages, has been identified as a key factor in prolonging quality of life in later life and fighting off the onset of dementia by three to five years (Bialystok et al. 2012; Freedman et al. 2014).

Similarly, researchers from the University of Edinburgh examined the medical records of over 600 people in India. They found that people who spoke two languages did not show any signs of dementia for more than four years longer than those who used one language (Mortimer et al. 2014; Freedman et al. 2014).

Based on this evidence bilingualism is increasingly appreciated as successful brain training, contributing to a cognitive reserve which can help delay dementia. Dr Thomas Bak, the principle researcher at University of Edinburgh, states that: 'These findings suggest that bilingualism might have a stronger influence on dementia than any currently available drugs. This makes the study of the relationship between bilingualism and cognition one of our highest priorities.'[1] What implications do these findings have on our priorities concerning bilingualism in education? And what evidence do we have that bilingualism enhances academic achievement? This is addressed next.

Bilingualism and Academic Achievement

The cognitive advantages of bilingualism, specifically in terms of academic achievement, are linked to the processes of being exposed to two languages and therefore having broader linguistic experiences and access to a wider range of thinking modes. Switching between the two languages has been identified as a good 'brain exercise' resulting in more flexible thinking. The comparison of two languages and using the knowledge of one language to advance the other result in enhanced higher-level linguistic skills known as metalinguistic skills. These findings confirm ideas first promoted by one of the most recognised development psychologists, Lev Vygotsky. He viewed bilingualism as key in enabling a child to approach language in a more abstract way and in more general categories (Vygotsky 1962: 110).

The evidence of bilingual children approaching language and other academic content in a more abstract mode is clearly outlined by two Canadian researchers, Lambert and Tucker, who observed and tested a group of six-year-olds educated mainly in their second language. In this longitudinal study the observed children demonstrated a high level of interest in comparing their two languages; approaching their second language as a code; and using their first language as the basis for relating and translating both academic content and linguistic input. Therefore, the researchers were proposing that the acquisition of the second language had benefited not only their competence in their first language, but also their mastery of the academic content (Lambert and Tucker 1972: 82).

It is also important to reflect on the fact that some studies have identified minor disadvantages of bilingualism, while there are also studies that provide both types of evidence. For example, Ben-Zeev (1977) reports a delay in recalling certain words, while at the same time participants in this study showed advantages in terms of more analytical tasks, for example word classification.

However, it can be said with certainty that there is a consensus amongst researchers who strongly support bilingualism as a source of cognitive advantage. The following quote from Bialystok captures what can be seen as the agreement in this area of research:

> … bilingualism never confers a disadvantage on children who are otherwise equally matched to monolinguals and the benefits and potential benefits weigh in to make bilingualism a rare positive experience for children. (Bialystok 2006: 598)

This concludes a brief overview of select relevant studies and their key findings. Next, I will outline my approach: the Healthy Linguistic Diet.

Educational Priorities

The research evidence presented in this paper underpins my argument that bilingualism is a source of cognitive advantage so significant at the individual and societal level that it is not only an education imperative to promote it, but a moral one too. According to the Alzheimer's Society, delaying the onset of dementia by five years would reduce deaths directly attributable to dementia by 30,000 a year. Dementia costs the UK £23 billion per year, yet the government has no plan on how to deal with dementia now or in the future.[2]

If bilingualism is identified currently as the most promising strategy known in terms of prolonging a dementia-free life there certainly should be no delay in working on timely and necessary changes throughout the education system in order to benefit from its advantages.

For these changes to happen it is necessary to shift the thinking throughout the education system, from that of policymakers to school leaders, practitioners, learners and parents. The first imperative is that all the stakeholders should be aware of what qualitative difference bilingualism can make to their cognitive functioning in general, and specifically in later life. The second imperative is that all stakeholders need to be equipped with strategies that can transform school practice and independent learning.

This shift in policy and practice needs to start with school leaders and the school workforce. By promoting the development of school policies and practices which are crucial for an extended, dementia-free life, we are at the same time offering enhanced cross-curriculum performance for bilingual children and all those eager to learn other languages. Enhanced school performance is a key aspect in this shift, which will be of interest to every school leader and teacher.

New Strategy: Healthy Linguistic Diet

My concept of a Healthy Linguistic Diet is based on the principle that all languages used by schoolchildren need to be supported in order to be maintained and developed further for the purposes of cognitive benefits. These benefits are not only needed by individuals from bilingual backgrounds; they are needed by schools too, as well as governments. For schools they mean better results in league tables; for governments they mean billions of savings in later life care.

The same applies to all languages used and spoken by adults and all approaches to lifelong learning.

I envisage my Healthy Linguistic Diet as a strategy which would, in the first instance, provide structured spaces for children and adults to discuss 'being bilingual' with the aim or raising awareness of bilingualism and its benefits. The reason I start with explicit discussions about bilingualism is derived from a 'critical incident' moment I had in a London school, which led to my conceptualisation of a Healthy Linguistic Diet. While facilitating a discussion group focusing on exploring reasons for underachievement with a group of Bangladeshi boys, one participant stated: 'We underachieve because we speak two languages'. His friend replied: 'It is not true, I read in a scientific journal that bilingualism improves your brain' (Mehmedbegovic 2011). What struck me here as a critical incident was realising that 14-year-old bilingual children were not given opportunities to learn about bilingualism in terms of research evidence and the impact of bilingualism on cognitive functioning. From this example it is clear that some children internalise a deficit model of bilingualism through a lack of any other model or explicit information on what it means to be bilingual, while those who are looking to gain knowledge about bilingualism have to do their own research for literature outside of expected interests and reading for young people in secondary education.

Based on this first-hand experience from an inner London school I have been working on developing principles and strategies which can be used for an approach conceptualised as similar to thinking about a healthy diet—in this case it is a linguistic diet. Considering the big push for healthy lifestyles and healthy eating under the umbrella initiative Healthy Schools, I would like to suggest that the concept of a Healthy Linguistic Diet should be integrated into this Healthy Schools initiative.[3] A Healthy Linguistic Diet has real potential to contribute to the aims outlined by the government: raise achievement across the curriculum, improve long-term health, enhance well-being and improve inclusion. The following are suggestions for the key whole-school strategy.

Providing Regular and Rich Opportunities for Engagement and Use of Both or Several Languages

Teachers and school leaders need to find regular opportunities to provide a consistent flow of affirmative messages with the aim of eliminating misconceptions about bilingualism as a problem and bad practices based on these misconceptions. These messages should also highlight that most cognitive benefits of bilingualism apply also to those who learn another language in school/university/outside of school.

Teachers need to be provided with examples of good practice, guidance and training to develop the essential skills for integrating home languages across the curriculum. This shift in practice should be led by the awareness that where home languages are a part of teaching and learning, the impact of this will be evident in improved results across the curriculum as a whole. This approach, which includes home and foreign languages, should start with early-years learning and continue throughout compulsory and lifelong education. The overall aim should be to support bilingual children in developing their full potential, and to encourage positive attitudes towards this specific intellectual potential that they have. At the same time, approaches used to support children in maintaining their home languages should also be utilised for all children in order to develop interest and enthusiasm for learning other/foreign languages.

A recent EU-funded project, LUCIDE (Languages in Urban Communities for Integration and Diversity in Europe), has produced a set of toolkits: guidance documents with examples for educators and other professionals in public services, which can be a very useful starting point and be used as ongoing support in developing good practice. These toolkits are based on research evidence and examples of good practice collected from a network of 13 European multilingual cities including London, and in partnership with cities from Canada and Australia.[4]

Providing Access to and Sharing Relevant Knowledge on the Values and Advantages of Bilingualism

Bilingual children and their parents need to be given clear, affirmative and consistent messages by schools and their teachers in terms of the benefits of bilingualism and home language support. Students (and parents) should be given advice on what they can do themselves in order to support their own bilingual development. These messages should include raising awareness on the cognitive advantages of bilingualism, which are applicable to all languages.

Bilingualism Matters Centres, whose mission is to provide evidence and advice to all stakeholders (parents, educators, policymakers) in order to help them make informed decisions regarding bilingual children, would make excellent partners to schools and school leaders in securing access to the latest research evidence.[5]

Providing a Framework Which Supports Lifelong Development of Bilingual Competencies

All children (monolingual and bilingual/plurilingual) and adults (monolingual and bilingual/plurilingual) in schools and other educational contexts should be encouraged to develop behaviour and habits that would support lifelong development of bilingual/plurilingual competencies. These practices need to become an integral part of efforts to bring up children, in the spirit of the Healthy School Initiative, with the aim of leading children towards a healthy lifestyle.

The Council of Europe places particular importance on the lifelong development of plurilingual competencies: plurilingulism is defined as competencies in different languages, and their varieties which individuals engage with in their lifetime. EU language policy is based on the principle that all individuals 'are entitled to develop a degree of communicative ability in a number of languages over their lifetime in accordance with their needs'.[6]

Raising Awareness Among Adults

In my own experience I have found that there is very little understanding about dementia amongst professionals in public services, nor in general amongst the adult population I encounter through my work and privately. Except for those with a family member sinking into dementia, there is a lack of understanding that dementia is not only about forgetting names or dates; it is about irreparable loss of one's overall mental capacity. In practical terms, that means: loss of the ability to read, write, speak, eventually even walk, eat and swallow. It is a slow death of one's brain and all its functions. Understanding it fully, for most people, means accepting it as a terrifying prospect, as well as accepting the swiftly increasing probability that it may happen to oneself. This is especially true for people who live longer in the developed world.

Dementia is often diagnosed too late—this is due to a lack of awareness, the stigma around mental health and the medical fraternity's inability to prevent or reverse the illness. If we want to change any of this we need to work closely with medical professionals and adult educators. The approach would first of all involve raising awareness amongst these key professionals on the benefits of bilingualism in terms of extending dementia-free life by several years, as the research shows. These professionals would then use opportunities to promote the importance of learning other languages as a lifelong activity. In the same way that a GP would ask patients about physical activity and highlight that for a healthy heart one needs to walk, swim and be active in different ways, he/she would also highlight the increasing risk of dementia and promote language learning as a way to maintain a healthy brain. Indeed, parallels can easily be drawn between physical activity and keeping our heart strong and healthy on the one hand, and mental engagement and having a brain that can fight off dementia for a few years longer, on the other hand.

Also, strategies of wider engagement such as publicity and education through available media need to be used—for example, in the same way that healthy eating is promoted in different ways amongst different age groups. News items, documentaries, adverts, films, TV programmes, language clubs and activities—policymakers should consider all available media in order to raise awareness and motivate the adult population to engage in lifelong language learning.

Conclusion

Health and social care costs for dementia patients in England are currently around £8.2 billion according to the National Audit Office. Alzheimer's Research UK has estimated that the overall cost of dementia to society as a whole is £23 billion a year. They also estimate that savings of £80 million could be made every year by improving hospital care. My question is: what savings can be made by promoting bilingualism, for example through a Healthy Linguistic Diet?

Loss of a home language is often presented as a natural language shift or freedom of choice, as evidenced in my study on attitudes to bilingualism (Mehmedbegovic 2011). Evidence shows that underprivileged communities suffer more language loss than affluent ones. Therefore, by not equipping underprivileged communities with awareness on the equal benefits of all languages we are widening the rich–poor gap in yet another way. Every effort needs to be made to ensure that children from minority groups do not drift towards language loss, in the form of loss of their home language.

Language loss is a loss for all who aim to achieve:

- Better attainment across the curriculum;
- A better-equipped workforce for a globalised world;
- Better self-esteem at an individual level;
- Longer dementia-free lives and significant cost savings for society.

Therefore the maintenance of home languages and learning of other languages should be positioned in education and lifelong learning as a basis for enhancing human cognitive potential and equipping oneself for a better quality of life in later life. The equal value of cognitive benefits linked to bilingualism and language learning/use, regardless of what combination of languages is in question (English–French or English–Bengali or English–Welsh) needs to be promoted and explicitly communicated to all stakeholders: children, parents, carers, teachers and school leaders. In my research and engagement with stakeholders in different contexts I have identified one big obstacle in utilising the existing linguistic diversity in the UK: hierarchy of languages. By hierarchy of languages I mean the outcome of processes and perceptions which result in a small number of select languages being considered high status, desirable to learn and 'have' such as French and Spanish, and a much larger number of languages which are not seen as an asset and have a very low status value, resulting in language loss at the individual level (Punjabi is one example I identified as such in my research) and language death at the societal level (Cornish is one of the languages which, in recent years, was identified as endangered and then dead, although there are attempts under way to revive it).

The dichotomy of high- and low-status languages, underpinned by historic factors such colonialism and/or economic dominance, prevent minority groups from being aware of the value of their languages. Hence my plea that a sharp U-turn needs to be made in terms of presenting and promoting the cognitive benefit rationale for developing bilingual skills. The rationale embedded in the cognitive benefits of bilingualism overcomes the issue of language hierarchy and this is the winning card that I suggest should be used to promote language learning in the UK. The cognitive benefits rationale also overcomes the 'English is enough' fallacy discussed at the beginning of this article.

This Healthy Linguistic Diet approach promotes the equality of all languages in terms of their impact on our well-being and cognitive functioning. It makes every individual aware that no matter what languages they have the opportunity to learn and be exposed to—French, German, Bengali, Polish or any other—they are making an equally valuable effort and investment in their own long-term well-being, and consequently also the long-term well-being of the wider society as a whole.

Notes

1. See the website of Bilingual Matters: http://www.bilingualism-matters. ppls.ed.ac.uk.
2. See the website of the Alzheimer's Society: http://www.alzheimers.org.uk/ site/scripts/press_article.php?pressReleaseID=90.
3. Information on this is available at: http://dera.ioe.ac.uk/6798/1/ Introduction.pdf.
4. These can be accessed at: http://www.urbanlanguages.eu/.
5. In the UK there two Bilingualism Matters centres: in Edinburgh and Reading. Information about their mission, activities and possibilities for partnerships can be accessed on the website: http://www.bilingualism-matters.ppls.ed.ac.uk/branches/branch-network/.
6. Information about Council of Europe work in this area can be found at: http://www.coe.int/t/dg4/linguistic/Division_EN.asp.

References

All-Party Parliamentary Group on Modern Languages. (2014). Manifesto for Languages. https://www.britishcouncil.org/sites/default/files/manifesto_for_languages.pdf.

Bak, T. H., Vega-Mendoza, M., & Sorace, A. (2014). Never Too Late?: An Advantage on Tests of Auditory Attention Extends to Late Bilinguals. *Frontiers in Psychology*. http://journal.frontiersin.org/article/10.3389/fpsyg.2014.00485/full. Accessed 26 May.

Ben-Zeev, S. (1977). The Influence of Bilingualism on Cognitive Strategy and Cognitive Development. *Child Development, 48*(3), 1009–1018.

Bialystok, E. (1999). Cognitive Complexity and Attentional Control in the Bilingual Mind. *Child Development, 70*, 636–644.

Bialystok, E. (2006). The Impact of Bilingualism on Language and Literacy Development. In T. K. Bhatia & W. C. Ritchie (Eds.), *The Handbook of Bilingualism*. Oxford: Blackwell.

Bialystok, E., Craik, F. I. M., & Luk, G. (2012). Bilingualism: Consequences for Mind and Brain. *Trends in Cognitive Sciences, 16*, 240–250.

British Council. (2014). Languages for the Future. Which Languages the UK Needs Most and Why. https://www.britishcouncil.org/sites/default/files/languages-for-the-future-report-v3.pdf.

Council of Europe. (2001). *Common European Framework of Reference for Languages: Learning, Teaching, Assessment*. Cambridge: Cambridge University Press.

Crystal, D. (2002). *Language Death*. Cambridge: Cambridge University Press.

Cummins, J. (2001). *Language, Power and Pedagogy*. Clevedon: Multilingual Matters.

Eversley, J., Mehmedbegovic, D., Sanderson, A., Tinsley, T., Von Ahn, M., & Wiggins, R. D. (Eds.). (2010). *Language Capital: Mapping the Languages of London's School Children*. London: CILT.

Freedman, M., Alladi, S., Chertkow, H., Bialystok, E., Craik, F. I. M., Phillips, N. A., Duggirala, V., Raju, S. B., & Bak, T. H. (2014). Delaying Onset of Dementia: Are Two Languages Enough? *Behavioural Neurology, 2014*, Article ID 808137, 8 pages.

Kovelman, I., Baker, S. A., & Petitto, L.-A. (2008). Bilingual and Monolingual Brains Compared Using fMRI: Is There a Neurological Signature of Bilingualism? *Journal of Cognitive Neuroscience, 20*(1), 1–17.

Lambert, W. E., & Tucker, G.R. (1972). *Bilingual Education of Children: The St. Lambert Experiment*. Rowley: Newbury House.

Mehmedbegovic, D. (2011). *A Study in Attitudes to Minority Languages in England and Wales*. Saarbrucken: Lambert Academic Publishing.

Mortimer, J., Alladi, A. S., Bak, T. H., Russ, T. S., Shailaja, M., & Duggirala, V. (2014). Bilingualism Delays Age at Onset of Dementia, Independent of Education and Immigration Status. *Neurology, 81*(22), 1936–1944.

Tinsley, T. (2013). *Languages: The State of the Nation*. London: British Academy. http://www.britac.ac.uk/publications/languages-state-nation.

Tosi, A., & Leung, C. (Eds.). (1999). *Rethinking Language Education: From a Monolingual to a Multilingual Perspective*. London: CILT.

Vygotsky, L. (1962). *Thought and Language*. Cambridge: MIT Press.

Part III

Where the UK Stands in Language Capacity

11

Languages in English Secondary Schools Post-Brexit

Teresa Tinsley

'Language learning on the brink of crisis.' This was the headline in the *TES* in November 2002, reporting on how English secondary schools were intending to respond to government plans to remove languages from the statutory curriculum for 14–16-year-olds. A decade and a half later, with that measure still in place, fewer than half of 15–16-year-olds take a language at GCSE, down from 76% at the time of the headline. Neither a 10-year National Languages Strategy, nor the inclusion of a languages GCSE in the English Baccalaureate (EBacc) measure of school performance, have come anywhere near making good the shortfall, equivalent to more than 160,000 pupils in 2016.[1] Crucially for the supply of linguists, A-level entries for languages have also declined: numbers sitting French have dropped by a third and those for German by nearly half since 2002. This in turn has had a baleful impact on university provision for languages at degree level, where there have been widespread closures and shrinkages.[2]

Although the declines in participation in languages beyond the age of 14 have affected all types of school, there is plentiful evidence to show that this is increasingly associated with socio-economic disadvantage,

T. Tinsley (✉)
Alcantara Communications, London, UK

© The Author(s) 2018
M. Kelly (ed.), *Languages after Brexit*,
https://doi.org/10.1007/978-3-319-65169-9_11

poverty and areas of the country affected by economic decline. Entry rates for GCSE languages are highest in London and the south-east and lowest (and falling) in the north-east of England. Schools with high proportions of pupils eligible for free school meals have the lowest GCSE entry figures and are more likely to exclude some children from language learning by setting up the curriculum in ways which make it impossible for certain groups to continue with a language after just two or three years at secondary school.[3]

It is into this fragile and fractured context for languages in schools that the challenge of leaving the European Union has been hurled. At time of writing, the consequences of Brexit, intended or otherwise, are not yet known, nor is it known to what extent they will affect languages in schools either directly or as part of a chain reaction. What we do know is that there will certainly be a readjustment of the UK's relationships with the countries whose languages are most commonly taught in schools: France, Spain and Germany. The juncture provides a good opportunity to review the shifts which have taken place over the last decade or more, what further changes are to be expected and what now needs to be done to bring health to a much misunderstood and undervalued element of the curriculum.

Historical Picture

It is important to recognise that the high point of 76% of pupils taking a GCSE in a language was not a long-established trend, but the crest of a wave, which peaked following the introduction of a national curriculum which made languages a compulsory subject for all pupils up to 16. This new curriculum was introduced successively from 1989 and the first cohort completed their GCSEs in 1998.[4] Three-quarters of them sat a language.[5] This, the first national curriculum for England, can be seen as complementary to the then almost complete process of comprehensivisation, and was underpinned by the same vision of achieving equality of opportunity in education. It was widely recognised that if language study was to become an essential strand of mainstream education rather being studied only by an academic elite, teaching would need to make the subject relevant, accessible and enjoyable for all. The wider context, with a growth in travel, international exchange, technology and popular culture, favoured this and there was a wave of activity designed to make language learning 'real' for pupils. No longer was language learning conceived as an entrée only into great works of literature; now music, film and the internet brought language classrooms alive, and there were business links, international projects, competitions and opportunities for work experience. Schools were given greater autonomy and encouraged to find creative ways of overcoming disadvantage and disengagement. More than 300 Specialist Language Colleges were created, offering pupils enhanced opportunities to learn languages and reaching out to primary schools and local communities. The 2002 National Languages Strategy set out a ten-year plan for improving language competence with the development of language teaching in primary schools as a core aim.[6] There was widespread support for language teachers through national centres, regional hubs and local authorities. Celebrations of language learning included not only those subjects taught as part of the curriculum but also the languages children brought into school from their international backgrounds. With the creation of tools like the Languages Ladder, a more diverse range of qualifications started to be developed, and an innovative Languages Diploma was developed to form a strand in the intended reform of education for 14–19-year-olds. We glimpsed, for a moment, a vision of the UK as a more multilingual nation, eagerly embracing the opportunities of the Single Market with its citizens well-equipped to benefit from the rapid globalisation which was increasingly bringing the world to our doorsteps.

So, what went wrong? Why did we fail to realise this vision? And to what extent will the Brexit vote mean a further step backwards for language learning?

Reasons for the Entrenchment of Monolingualism

Many hands have been wrung and many column inches dedicated to the reasons why English teenagers have failed to embrace language learning with enthusiasm since it stopped being a compulsory subject for those over 14. One immediate reaction is to identify learners as the root of the problem. Surely, if only pupils were made aware of the opportunities, for jobs, travel and a brilliant international future, they would more pleasantly disposed towards the intricacies of pronouns and the pluperfect tense? Careers advice is of course part of the picture, but there are other factors at play. Some attribute the problem to bad teaching: a perceived lack of rigour which accompanied attempts to popularise the learning of languages, a focus on fun and supposed 'relevance' at the expense of the nitty-gritty of verb endings and adjectival agreements. Maybe pupils simply weren't given the basic tools for getting to grips with the language? Others see the problem as a wider one for English native speakers and point to an underlying 'island mentality', in which the point of language learning is not self-evident or obvious. They draw attention to how, paradoxically, globalisation has reinforced the use of English as an international lingua franca, with a consequent decline in the value attached to foreign language skills.

None of these explanations is sufficient, since they fail to take into account the educational context: an exam-dominated curriculum within which languages has to struggle for a place alongside a host of other more or less popular subjects. In 2004, the government did not 'make languages optional', as is sometimes claimed; it allowed schools to do so as part of the strategy of granting them greater autonomy. At the same time, it demanded more accountability from schools for 'delivering' successful outcomes for pupils, and it did so through the examination system. This meant that not only were schools responsible for deciding which subjects beyond the core should remain compulsory, if any, but that they could manipulate the ways that options were presented to pupils in order to achieve the most beneficial outcomes in school league tables. With languages regarded by pupils and curriculum managers alike as a 'difficult' subject, the only way was down for numbers studying the subject. In a recent national survey of languages in secondary schools, teachers were vehement in their criticism of both the GCSE and A-level examinations. They reported that languages are not only harder than other subjects, but more unreliable in terms of achieving the high grades needed for university entrance, and that neither the form nor the content of the exams are conducive to inspiring teaching.[7] Whilst learners may be put off languages by the thought of having to work harder for the same results as they might achieve in other subjects, the pressure upon schools to achieve good GCSE outcomes means that schools have a built-in incentive to steer learners towards other subjects. In addition, strong public advocacy for STEM subjects (science, technology, engineering and mathematics) has created the impression that languages are less critical to success in terms of university applications or subsequent careers. The introduction of the EBacc as a performance measure for schools in 2010–2011 gave an initial boost to numbers taking languages (from a low point of 40%), but this has flattened out since the introduction of a new measure, Progress 8. This is widely seen as a watering-down of the EBacc since although it includes a language, this is not an essential element.

Current Policy

The Conservative government which was elected in May 2015 came into office with refreshed ambitions for its education policy. It saw languages as a 'traditional academic subject' and articulated its concern around an observation that children from poorer backgrounds are less likely to opt for these subjects, which include the humanities, sciences and ancient as well as modern languages. It has therefore proposed 'EBacc for all'—an aspiration for at least 90% of pupils to take all EBacc subjects—including a language—to GCSE. At the same time, new GCSEs and A levels are being introduced which are intended to address some of teachers' concerns about the content and assessment regime of the current exams, but also to be more rigorous and challenging. Schools are thus caught in a pincer movement between the pressure to boost participation and the risk of increased failure. There is public concern about the number of additional language teachers that would be needed to fulfil the increase in demand if 90% of pupils were to take a language to GCSE. At time of writing there has not yet been a government response to its 'EBacc for all' consultation, held in summer 2016.

How Membership of the EU Affects Language Learning in Schools

Lower numbers of pupils taking a language to GCSE and A level has meant fewer graduates in languages emerging from UK universities. Those that do so have a wide choice of career pathways open to them and are in no way disposed to go into teaching in large numbers. The consequent shortage of language teachers has, for more than 20 years now, been made good through recruitment from abroad. Teacher-training places have increasingly been filled by candidates from France, Spain and other European countries eager to spend some time living and working in the UK. No figures are kept on how many language teachers are nationals of other EU countries but it is certainly a very significant proportion, accounting in some schools for the whole languages department.

Schools have, for decades now, taken advantage of European funding programmes to provide opportunities for teachers to refresh and update their language skills abroad and for pupils to take part in exchanges, international projects or even work experience in another European country. School-to-school links provide opportunities for the whole school, not just the languages department, to engage internationally and recognise the importance of speaking another language. On 26 September each year, the European Day of Languages is enthusiastically celebrated with careers fairs, competitions, special events and assemblies in schools up and down the country. With languages an unpopular and potentially risky choice for pupils, efforts to promote the subject have focused on the opportunities for study, employment and cultural enrichment emanating from the UK's membership of the European Union. Initiatives such as Routes into Languages have highlighted the opportunity for all students, whether studying languages or another subject, to spend a year or a term at a university in another EU country, funded through the Erasmus scheme. Returning undergraduates from the programme have acted as ambassadors in schools, and inspired pupils with stories of their experiences. Raising awareness of the opportunities to live, work or study in other European countries, to earn a better salary and do a more interesting job, has been used to counteract some of the more negative perceptions of language learning.

Likely Impact of Brexit

It is easy to see then, how the departure of the UK from the European Union might have a devastating effect on the fragile position of languages in secondary schools, especially if this were to include withdrawal from all of its funding programmes. If conditions for trainee language teachers from other European countries become more difficult, this source of supply is likely to dwindle. Potential recruits will be less likely to consider the UK as a potentially agreeable destination once it is no longer a member of the EU and we are not yet in a position to make good this supply from home-grown sources. Although it seems unlikely that serving languages teachers from other EU countries would be forced to return, many may decide to leave if their status deteriorates, if they feel that the UK becomes a less welcoming place to live or if their efforts to teach their language seem to fall on stony ground. A major teacher-supply crisis is already looming, and in these circumstances the EBacc for all may well be put on the back-burner as a long-term ambition rather than treated as a policy to implement with all possible speed.

The departure of the UK from the European Union will clearly reduce opportunities for UK nationals to work in other European countries and in European institutions. Whether this reduction will be compensated for by new opportunities arising post-Brexit in Europe or beyond, it is not yet possible to say. Our departure will surely send a message to learners and their parents that European languages will be less valuable for employment purposes and schools will therefore have a harder job to promote the subject. The prospect of a wider climate of xenophobia, mistrust of foreigners and an all-pervading emphasis on the speaking of English would hardly be propitious for language learning, to say the least.

Of perhaps greatest concern is the risk that the social and cultural divide which the Brexit vote exposed will be widened. Many young (and now middle-aged) people have already become that outgoing, internationally confident generation envisaged decades ago, beneficiaries of years of free movement and funding programmes. They have friendships across borders, they are able to work internationally, they expect to travel: they are in a relatively good position financially and will find a way to ensure that their children enjoy similar experiences. On the other hand, those who only see threats from globalisation and the world beyond our borders will be easy prey for unthinking populism and exclusionary nationalism. These are the people most likely to be excluded from language learning but paradoxically those who have most to gain from it. So far policy on language learning (and, indeed it may be argued, education policy generally) has done little to cater for their needs. Casting languages solely as a traditional academic subject may even be counterproductive in this regard.

It is still early days, and language teachers do not yet report any great impact from the Brexit vote. However, the most recent Language Trends survey shows that there are considerable concerns both about the status of current language teachers who are nationals of other EU countries, and the supply of future teachers from abroad. Teachers are also worried about opportunities for exchanges and, were the UK to withdraw from the Erasmus+ programme, concerned about the impact this would have on pupils considering taking language degrees, for whom the lure of a year in another European country is a strong incentive. In a few schools, negative attitudes have hardened and pupils and parents have questioned the point of learning languages, particularly European languages. However, many teachers and schools see their role as even more important than before and are determined to continue to open up a world beyond English to their pupils.[8]

What Needs to Be Done?

In this context, it is even more important that languages are made relevant and accessible for all, not just for an academic elite. The role of schools in promoting openness, tolerance and friendship across borders will become even more critical. They must ensure that all pupils not only achieve their best academically, but also develop the confidence and skills to engage with others from outside their communities. This will matter perhaps even more for the less academically gifted than for those with the intellectual capacity to tackle the new GCSEs and A levels successfully. The cultural and intercultural learning which takes place through friendly contact with speakers of other languages benefits all pupils and society at large, and must be given value alongside academic success in language learning as measured through the exams. We may need to find ways other than the current exam system to support, recognise and value this. Teachers must have time and space to develop exchanges and extra-curricular activities and be recognised for it. We should not necessarily look to the government to lead this, though there is much the government can do to support and enable it.

In other areas, there are actions where it is the government's clear responsibility to act. In the short term, it should safeguard the status of existing language teachers from other EU countries. Their role must be publicly recognised and applauded, and the stream of new recruits maintained. In addition, a longer-term plan for improving UK language capacity must be instituted to make good our home-grown supply of linguists, not only for the teaching profession, but for other occupations where they will be needed.[9]

The government should also ensure that UK schools, colleges and universities are able to continue to participate in international programmes which build friendship and solidarity between nations within and beyond the EU and provide young people with skills and experience they need for success in the global economy. They must ensure that no new impediments, such as visa requirements or loss of funding streams, limit young Britons from learning to play a role internationally.

Finally, there must be monitoring to measure the ongoing impact of Brexit on language learning in schools. Improving the UK's language capability has always been low on the political agenda and an uncertain vote-winner. Our departure from the European Union will create multiple challenges, many of which are as yet unforeseen. We must not allow our language capability to become collateral damage in this process; rather, let us use the opportunity to renew and revitalise language teaching in our schools, starting from a secure base in the primary phase.

Notes

1. Figures from JCQ, August 2016. The cohort was 599,600 of which 291,400 entered a language GCSE.
2. See Chap. 15.

3. Teresa Tinsley and Kathryn Board, *Language Trends 2015/16*, British Council & Education Development Trust, 2016.
4. Alan Moys (ed.), *Where Are We Going with Languages?*, Nuffield Foundation, 1998.
5. Teresa Tinsley and Kathryn Board, *Language Learning in Primary and Secondary Schools in England*, CfBT Education Trust, 2013.
6. DfES, *Languages for All, Languages for Life. A Strategy for England*, 2002.
7. Teresa Tinsley and Kathryn Board, *Language Trends 2015/16*, British Council & Education Development Trust, 2016, p. 158.
8. Teresa Tinsley and Kathryn Board, *Language Trends 2016/17*, British Council, 2017 (forthcoming).
9. See Chaps. 18 and 19.

12

Modern Languages in Scotland in the Context of Brexit

Hannah Doughty and Marion Spöring

Looking Back to Move Forward

The varying levels of disinterest in languages across the four UK nations have been well documented but in the light of the Brexit outcome on 23 June 2016 they have once again been put into sharp focus. Looking at the state of affairs from the Scottish perspective we want to take a step aside from the complex political landscape and consider the implications for languages, with a particular focus on the efforts of one particular stakeholder group: the language teaching professionals across the education sectors. No matter what the future holds following Brexit negotiations, they will continue teaching their subject—but how their subject is regarded may still depend on the kinds of steps they take now, as well as how government supports these actions. However, before we examine the present context more closely, we want to take a quick look

H. Doughty
University of Strathclyde, Glasgow, UK

M. Spöring (✉)
University of Dundee, Dundee, UK

© The Author(s) 2018
M. Kelly (ed.), *Languages after Brexit*,
https://doi.org/10.1007/978-3-319-65169-9_12

back at the language education policy in Scotland over the last 25 years or so in order to identify some key issues that may help us move forward constructively.

Just like other Anglophone countries Scotland has struggled to keep learners engaged with languages since the latter lost their status as a mandatory subject for university entrance in 1967. However, there have been a number of well-intentioned initiatives, one of which in particular—entitled Languages for All—was linked to the UK's membership of the European Union. It was introduced in 1989, in anticipation of the introduction of the Single European Market in 1992, as highlighted by James Scott (2015: 15). Additional support for languages arrived in the shape of Modern Languages in the Primary School (Scottish Executive 1992), which stipulated that young people should be introduced to a language other than English no later than the last year of primary school.

Statistics compiled by Scott (2015) show that whilst the 'Languages for All' policy was in force (up until 1999) almost 90% of all young people in their last compulsory year of secondary schooling (S4, aged 16) were entered for a language examination. However, the expectation that language learning would increase in the senior post-16 examinations did not materialise, and a major research initiative funded by the then Scottish Higher Education Funding Council investigated the issue. The report (*Foreign Languages in the Upper Secondary School*, henceforth the *FLUSS* report), led by Joanna McPake and Professor Richard Johnstone (McPake et al. 1999), found that although the majority of learners believed in the *long-term* benefits in language learning they were not convinced of the *short-term* benefits, in relation to achieving their immediate educational and career goals (McPake et al: 12). Arguably then, it appears that, contrary to expectations, students did *not* connect labour mobility within the single market to the need for language learning.

Additionally, even before the findings of the *FLUSS* report had been published, a Ministerial Action Group on Languages (2000) was set up to consider how best to secure modern language education in the curriculum. The recommendations, for the most part accepted by the government (Scottish Executive 2001), included an entitlement for each child to receive 500 hours of language learning from Primary 6 onwards. In our view, however, by focusing exclusively on the primary-school sector, the key failing identified by the *FLUSS* report, the learners' perception that language learning was irrelevant for their short-term futures was *not* addressed. Furthermore, as Scott (2015) points out, the linguistic change from 'consensual obligation' to 'legislated entitlement' had the unintended consequence that educational policy enactors (in particular, head teachers) interpreted the latter term as a 'legislated option'.

In its own response to the matter, the then Scottish Centre for Information on Language Teaching and Research (Scottish CILT, now rebranded as SCILT, Scotland's National Centre for Languages) commissioned a renowned academic from Australia, Professor Joseph Lo Bianco, to produce a language and literacy policy for Scotland (Lo Bianco 2001). It examined the relevance of languages to all areas of society and called for languages to be considered a resource. But the report went largely unnoticed.

The narrow focus on the school sector also indirectly caused policy-makers to remain unaware that a similar process of decline was happening in Scottish further education (FE). Languages in this sector had previously been thriving, again in part linked to the rationale of free labour mobility within the single market (see the report by Hall and Bankowska 1994). However, uptake of Scottish FE language modules took a dramatic downturn following a number of qualification reforms. Hannah Doughty (2005, 2011a) identified a vicious circle whereby assumptions rooted in a monolingual mindset on the part of policymakers, qualification agencies and senior stakeholders contributed to misinterpretations of statistical evidence and misconceptions in the formulation of questions designed to gauge future skill needs in the labour market. For example, to ascertain whether businesses had a need for people with language skills a local Chamber of Export's survey asked the question: 'Has the lack of language skills been a barrier to export in your company?' Ninety-two per cent had answered 'no'—but upon closer examination it was found that many had answered 'no' because they **were** employing people with language skills, i.e. there was no 'lack of (staff with) language skills'. At national level, labour market surveys focusing on identifying future skill needs repeatedly found that only 3% of businesses were training their staff in language skills and similarly concluded that language skills were not an essential—when in reality businesses were actively recruiting people who already *had* the relevant language (and intercultural) skills. However, these misleading statistics were then used by education managers as a rationale to remove language options from vocational business and marketing programmes. This, by default, reduced the number of language entries, which educational policymakers took as a sign of disinterest in language learning, and at the same time reinforced the 'English is enough' fallacy amongst younger FE students. The annual CBI reports highlighting the need for people with language and intercultural skills were simply dismissed in light of this 'evidence'.

The origins of Scotland's current language education policy can be traced to the 2007 election manifesto of the Scottish National Party (SNP) with its promise to put 'science, modern languages and technology at the heart of the curriculum' (SNP 2007: 11). In 2011, the commitment to languages was even more explicit, acknowledging EU influence at the same time:

> We will introduce a norm for language learning in schools based on the European Union 1+2 model—that is we will create the conditions in which every child will learn two languages in addition to their own mother tongue. This will be rolled out over two Parliaments, and will create a new model for language acquisition in Scotland. (SNP 2011: 24)

However, language professionals in tertiary education felt that the recommendations arising from the languages education policy published in 2012, the so-called '1+2 approach to language learning' (Scottish Government 2011), henceforth simply referred to as '1+2', yet again focused too narrowly on the school sector. In response to this repeated narrow emphasis, the idea of a much closer cross-sector involvement in the implementation of the 1+2 language policy started to take shape.

Language Provision in Scottish Universities

In the Scottish university sector there are at time of writing 13 institutions (down from 15 in 2010) which offer a diverse range of languages for study. Depending on the institution, they offer traditional Modern

Languages degrees as well as degrees with a language, Joint Honours with languages or a mix of credit and non-credit bearing provision (Institution-Wide Language Programmes, Adult Education, to name but a few). French, German and Spanish dominate provision, but a fairly wide range of other languages can be studied. Unfortunately, the geographical spread of the universities is uneven: there are four based in Edinburgh, in what we now call the 'East' hub (University of Edinburgh, Edinburgh Napier and Heriot-Watt Universities, as well as the Open University in Scotland), and four universities in the 'West' hub based in Glasgow and surrounding area (Universities of Glasgow, Glasgow Caledonian, Strathclyde and the University of the West of Scotland). The so-called 'Central' hub includes the universities of St Andrews and Dundee on the East Coast, as well as the University of Stirling, which is more accurately described as being located in the centre of Scotland. For the vast remainder of the country north of Dundee and Stirling (the 'North' hub) however, there are only two universities with which schools can link up, and in reality it is mainly just one, the University of Aberdeen, since the University of the Highlands and Islands only offers provision in Gaelic and the Nordic languages. This is a particular challenge with which we are still grappling.

There are indications that many higher education students opt for language study, not always as part of a specialist degree, but in combination with other subjects. The data sets for more conclusive evidence are being investigated by the authors, but are not yet complete. There is, however, positive evidence that the number of graduates in Scotland who have studied a language as part of their degree has indeed risen from 2830 in 2010–11 to 3145 in 2014–15 (extracted from HESA data for individual institutions' returns), an 11% increase (Higher Education Statistics, 2015). At the same time, the range of languages at specialist degree level has reduced and postgraduate provision is now concentrated in a smaller number of universities. We hypothesise that we are witnessing a trend towards a changing landscape in language learning, with some university students realising opportunities which they may not have taken up at school. It is for this reason that we maintain there is a need for continued cross-sector efforts in the languages field.

Social Networks and Cross-Sector Initiatives

The potential of social networks in policy contexts that are increasingly transient has been examined previously (as discussed by Hannah Doughty 2011b and more recently by Gallagher-Brett et al. 2014). Inspired by the Routes into Languages programme,[1] which operated in England, and later also in Wales, the Scottish branch of the University Council for Modern Languages (henceforth UCMLS[2]) decided to explore the potential of implementing a number of cross-sector (university/school) initiatives in collaboration with SCILT. The important point to note here is that implementation would need to be within existing funding allocations. In the event, four collaborative initiatives were agreed, with at least one to be held in each of the regional hubs (Table 12.1):

The above initiatives tackle different motivational and attitudinal barriers: Mother Tongue Other Tongue in celebrating all languages arguably

Table 12.1 Four cross-sector collaborative initiatives

Name	Age	Aims
Mother Tongue, Other Tongue[a]	All ages	Poetry competition designed to encourage children to write in their mother tongue or in a language they are learning. This is about valuing ALL languages
Language Linking Global Thinking[a]	11–15	Undergraduate students about to go on their year abroad are linked up with a class (in upper primary or lower secondary school) and keep in regular contact with the pupils for the duration of their stay abroad. The aim is to encourage children to consider stays abroad as part of their own tertiary study
Word Wizard[a]	11–14	Motivational spelling competition for learners of French, German, Spanish, Gaelic and Mandarin in early secondary school. The final is usually held at the Scottish Parliament
Business Brunches	14–17	Young people from up to 14 schools attend a university-based venue where they have the opportunity to meet with a range of businesses that value and employ people with language and intercultural skills. The focus here is on the employability agenda. An additional Business Brunch was held in Inverness (North hub region) to compensate for the lack of suitable university provision there

[a]Adapted from a Routes into Languages initiative

challenges xenophobic tendencies, whereas Language Linking Global Thinking is about dispelling the anxiety about living abroad in a different culture. The Word Wizard spelling competition has a strong extrinsic motivational aspect, whereas the Business Brunches help learners to 'see' the relevance of languages to their short-term career goals, as identified by the *FLUSS* report.

In addition, each university may have additional cross-sector initiatives or events specific to its own institution. For example, Heriot-Watt University runs the increasingly popular Multilingual Debate, again aiming to let secondary students experience the relevance of language learning. It doubles as an examination/showcase for their Year 4 students on the Interpreting and Translation degree programme. There are also numerous Language Ambassador Schemes, which involve undergraduate students going out to schools in order to promote their university's language-study programmes.

To 2021: And Beyond

At time of writing we are in the second phase of cross-sector collaboration and now have a cross-sector action plan in support of 1+2, which will take us to 2021, and indeed beyond. To get to this point UCMLS conducted an online survey and held a further national cross-sector conference in September 2016 to explore the views of teachers, teacher trainers and the wider business community on the status quo regarding the state (and status) of implementation with regard to the 1+2 language policy. The findings of the survey and the conference itself confirmed and supported some of the evidence collected through a study led by John Christie, conducted on behalf of the Scottish Government by the Association of Directors of Education in Scotland and the University of Edinburgh (Christie et al. 2016). A number of critical challenges were identified, but we highlight only the top two:

* Many respondents feared that other policy objectives in schools are taking over, such as 'closing the attainment gap'. *It is therefore important that we keep up the momentum through continued cross-sector initiatives on 1+2.*

- Funding remains another area of worry because monies dedicated specifically to 1+2 will likely cease in 2021. In 2016, additionally, a delayed funding announcement for local authorities meant that some councils decided to recall their 1+2 Development Officers, who represent a key level of support for schools to help them implement 1+2. *It will therefore be crucial to identify innovative and sustainable ways of building on achievements to date.*

Whilst these are substantial hurdles, overcoming them does not, in our view, hinge directly on the outcome of the Brexit negotiations, although there must be concern about the potential impact on language teacher and language specialist employee availability if freedom of movement gets restricted. They do, however, point to the need for more structural reforms and perhaps also alternative curriculum models. This is why UCMLS decided to contact Angela Scarino, Associate Professor at the University of South Australia. She had authored the research-informed shape paper for the national modern languages curriculum in Australia, and in November 2016 provided us with an insight into the different approaches taken across Australia to implement new language curriculum models (Scarino 2016). We also conducted a further consultative survey and held another set of regional hub meetings about what cross-sector collaboration should look like as we move towards 2021, the implementation deadline set for 1+2. At a national event on 10 March 2017 UCMLS introduced their analysis of the findings and launched their Cross-Sector Action Plan proposals for 1+2 up to and beyond 2021.[3]

Crucially, UCMLS is now represented on two Strategic Implementation Groups (SIGs) set up by the Scottish Government, one for education and one for wider public engagement. Whilst these SIGs operate without additional funding and in an advisory capacity only, we view UCMLS membership on these two groups in a positive light. Most importantly, it has brought our initiatives to the attention of other 1+2 stakeholders, including representatives from parents, local authorities, Education Scotland (the Scottish Government's Executive Agency for Education), Directors of Education, Initial Teacher Education, General Teaching Council Scotland, cultural organisations (e.g. British Council, French Institute, Goethe Institute) and business.

With all these various promotional and consulting activities going on it is difficult to tease out any direct cause and effect. It is remarkable, nevertheless, that since the start of the cross-sector collaborative activities, language entries for French and German at the 16+ examination level have seen a statistically significant increase, for the first time in over a decade.

Coincidentally, the most recent Scottish Social Attitudes Survey (Scottish Government 2016: 1) found to the surprise of many (including language education professionals!) that 89% of respondents, regardless of their socio-economic background or prior language-learning experience, believe that learning languages other than English in school is important, with Western European languages seen as most useful.

Despite this encouraging news we recognise that we are some way from seeing this professed positive attitude to languages translated into widespread language learning at all levels of education.

Concluding Thoughts

The fortunes of modern languages in Scotland have not been linked in the media to the outcome of the Brexit vote as they have been in other UK nations, notably England. We credit the lead taken by the Scottish Government vis-à-vis the European Union with this phenomenon. We also believe that the 'fate' of language learning in Scotland will not depend on the eventual outcome of the Brexit negotiations. However, in these increasingly straitened times some fundamental issues remain outstanding before languages in Scottish education have a chance to prosper.

There is, in our view, an urgent need for structural reforms in education, and for a strategic promotional campaign focusing on all sectors and encompassing the idea of lifelong learning, normalising the idea of language learning throughout life. Strategic planning for numbers of graduates with high-level language skills in a diversity of languages, suitably qualified for entering teacher training, and planning numbers of trained teachers in languages, including those in primary teaching, is necessary. We must find ways of getting languages to be given the same priority as STEM subjects, including in the promotion of teacher training and the expansion of a graduate and non-graduate workforce with a range of language qualifications gained in further and higher education. Strategically planned and funded research to support the implementation process is urgently needed. These are definitely areas where Scottish Government support will be crucial.

However, we take some comfort from the positive indicators about languages as evidenced in the growing numbers of language learners in schools and universities. Just maybe, the Brexit cloud in Scotland will have a silver lining.

Notes

1. See http://www.routesintolanguages.ac.uk.
2. See http://www.scilt.org.uk/BeyondSchool/UCMLS.
3. See http://bit.ly/UCMLS_ActionPlan2017.

References

Christie, J., Robertson, B., Stodter, J., & O'Hanlon, F. (2016). *A Review of Progress in Implementing the 1+2 Language Policy*. Edinburgh: ADES and University of Edinburgh.

Doughty, H. (2005). *Critical Perspectives on Modern Languages in Scottish Further Education 2000–2002, Doctoral Thesis*. Stirling: University of Stirling.

Doughty, H. (2011a). La Grande Illusion: Why Scottish Further Education Has Failed to Grasp the Potential of Modern Languages. *Scottish Languages Review, 23*, 7–14.

Doughty, H. (2011b). Modern Languages in Scotland: Social Capital Out on a Limb. *Arts and Humanities in Higher Education, 10*(2), 141–155.

Gallagher-Brett, A., Doughty, H., & McGuinness, H. (2014). Social Capital and Modern Language Initiatives in Times of Policy Uncertainty. *Scottish Languages Review, 27*, 39–52.

Hall, J., & Bankowska, A. (1994). *Foreign Languages for Vocational Purposes in Further and Higher Education*. Edinburgh: The Scottish Council for Research in Education.

Higher Education Statistics Agency (HESA) (2015). Student Records 2010–2015.

Lo Bianco, J. (2001). *Language and Literacy Policy in Scotland*. Stirling: Scottish CILT.

McPake, J., Johnstone, R. M., Lyall, L., & Low, L. (1999). *Foreign Languages in the Upper Secondary School: A Study in the Causes of Decline*. Edinburgh: Scottish Council for Research into Education.

Ministerial Action Group for Languages. (2000). *Citizens of a Multilingual World*. Edinburgh: Scottish Executive.

Scarino, A. (2016). Australia's Language Policies. Video presentation and discussion as part of a 1+2 Development Day held on 29 November 2016 at a Scottish Government venue in Glasgow. Video available at: http://bit.ly/ScarinoUCMLS2016.

Scott, J. (2015). Modern Languages in Scotland: Learner Uptake and Attainment 1996–2014. *Scottish Languages Review, 29*, 11–26.

Scottish Executive. (1992). *Modern Languages in the Primary School*. Edinburgh: Scottish Executive.

Scottish Executive. (2001). *Government Response to Citizens of a Multilingual World*. Edinburgh: Scottish Executive.

Scottish Government. (2011). *Language Learning in Scotland: A 1+2 Approach*. Edinburgh: Scottish Government.

Scottish Government. (2016). *Attitudes Towards Language Learning in Schools in Scotland*. Available at: http://www.gov.scot/Topics/Education/Schools/curriculum/LanguageLearning/ScottishSocialAttitudesSurvey.

Scottish National Party. (2007). *Election Manifesto*. Available at: http://www.politicsresources.net/area/uk/ass07/man/scot/snp.pdf.

Scottish National Party. (2011). *Election Manifesto*. Available at: http://votesnp.com/campaigns/SNP_Manifesto_2011_lowRes.pdf.

13

Speaking from Wales: Building a Modern Languages Community in the Era of Brexit

Speaking from Wales

Modern languages in Wales have been in decline for over a decade. Between 2002 and 2016, entries for GCSE modern languages fell by 48%. Welsh pupils perform well at GCSE, with 77% of pupils attaining grades A* to C in 2015, yet attainment at Key Stage 3 (ages 11–14) in modern languages is the lowest of all non-core subjects, with the exception of second-language Welsh. This is largely because teaching modern languages only begins in Year 7 (age 11). The picture is similar at A level. Between 2001 and 2016, entries for A-level modern languages dropped by 44%. The biggest declines were in French and German, the staple languages of Welsh secondary education, with French A level registering a drop of 60% and German a drop of 66%. In contrast, the situation for Spanish is one of uneven but modest growth, although figures for 2016 entries show that entries for A-level Spanish dropped by an alarming 26%. These dispiriting trends emerge despite the fact that 82% of all

C. Gorrara (✉)
Cardiff School of Modern Languages/ Ysgol Ieithoedd Modern Prifysgol Caerdydd, Cardiff/Caerdydd, UK

© The Author(s) 2018
M. Kelly (ed.), *Languages after Brexit*,
https://doi.org/10.1007/978-3-319-65169-9_13

Welsh A-level modern language students achieve grades A*to C. Such statistics also mask significant regional variations. Schools in areas of higher socio-economic disadvantage face the biggest challenges in terms of take-up and attainment. For example, in 2013, the percentage of pupils opting for a modern-language GCSE in the Blaenau Gwent region dropped as low as 12% (Miller 2013).

The extensive Welsh-medium schooling system is an important factor in the modern languages landscape in Wales. Welsh-medium schools—where Welsh is the medium of instruction—account for nearly one quarter of all schools in Wales. In more suburban areas where English is the dominant language, Welsh-medium schools are often associated with higher educational achievement and become one means for English-speaking parents to make a selective choice in the state-funded schooling system. In many Welsh-medium schools, the majority of pupils speak English at home and are immersed in Welsh at school. Anecdotal evidence suggests that the situation for modern languages in such schools is less bleak overall than for their English-medium counterparts. This may be due to greater awareness of the support needed for language learning in Welsh-medium schools and an accompanying sense of the benefits of bilingualism throughout the curriculum.

This situation is, therefore, something of a conundrum. Why are modern languages so weak in a nation with a strong cultural attachment to bilingualism? Indeed, looking at other Anglophone countries around the world, the picture for modern languages there is similar to Wales. In the USA, for example, recent research by the American Academy of Arts and Sciences shows that modern languages education is dwindling at a dramatic rate. Only 22% of elementary- and secondary-schools students enrol in language classes or programmes (Flaherty 2016). In Australia, the state of modern language learning in schools has been described as 'dire', with just 10% of High School Certificate students in New South Wales (Years 11 and 12 or ages 14 to 16) believed to be studying a language other than English (Munro 2016). In Wales, we have been able to gain valuable insights into why modern languages are in decline thanks to two recent reports into language trends in Wales. Commissioned by the British Council from external evaluators, the annual *Language Trends Wales* reports provide a detailed evaluation of the place of modern languages in the primary and secondary sectors in Wales (Tinsley and Board 2014; 2015).

These reports have highlighted two areas for concern: curriculum squeeze and pupil attitudes towards modern languages and language learning.

Firstly, modern languages occupy a precarious place in the secondary-school curriculum in Wales. Unlike Welsh, which is taught from the Foundation phase (from ages 3 to 7) onwards, modern languages are not compulsory at GCSE and begin in Year 7 (age 11). Alongside their GCSE and A levels, Welsh pupils can study for the Welsh Baccalaureate, a broad-based qualification offering transferable skills alongside traditional learning. When first launched across Wales in 2007, the Welsh Baccalaureate incorporated 20 hours of modern language learning. However, following a Review of Qualifications for 14–19-year-olds in Wales in 2012, the language requirement of the Welsh Baccalaureate was discontinued, replaced by a component devoted to global citizenship skills. There is currently no programme for primary languages in Wales, although the *Language Trends Wales* reports do show that nearly 50% of primary schools surveyed offered modern languages classroom activities. This is often in the form of short taster sessions. However, the secondary-school teachers surveyed questioned the value of such sessions as a meaningful engagement with modern languages.

The time allocated to modern languages is equally under threat, with 40% of modern-languages teachers surveyed reporting that their school does not observe the two hours per week of modern-languages teaching recommended by Estyn, the education and training inspectorate for Wales, and HM Chief Inspector of Education and Training in Wales (Estyn 2016). Pupils with special educational needs (SEN) are routinely permitted to stop studying a modern language at Key Stage 3 (ages 11–14), whilst low numbers choosing to study modern languages at GCSE have undermined the viability of modern languages in some schools where financial constraints dictate minimum group sizes for subjects to run. More generally, teachers report that the Welsh government's new Literary and Numeracy Framework has had unintended consequences for modern languages as some School Leadership Teams have not connected modern languages to their broader school attainment targets, which prioritise literacy. With the further integration of the Welsh Baccalaureate into the secondary-school curriculum from 2017, option choices at GCSE in many schools have dropped from four to three (and in a small number of schools to two). In a survey of teachers, teachers expressed fear that competition from other subjects in this context will affect modern languages disproportionately (Tinsley and Board 2014; 2015).

Secondly, teachers surveyed returned repeatedly to negative attitudes towards modern languages amongst pupils, their parents and the wider public (Tinsley and Board 2014; 2015). These concerns are shared with teachers in other parts of the UK. In the same survey, teachers commented on the widespread perception that modern languages were 'difficult' and that grading for modern languages qualifications was unpredictable, putting off more able pupils from choosing languages. As new specifications for GCSE, AS and A-level modern languages qualifications were introduced in Wales in September 2016, these concerns were particularly evident in the *Language Trends Wales* report 2015–16. There was also a strong sense that School Leadership Teams privileged performance in STEM subjects (science, technology, engineering and maths) and that this prioritisation was reflected in the reporting structures for schools devised by the Welsh government. More generally, teachers and other modern language stakeholders lamented a narrow perception of what modern languages study entailed. Pupils and parents tended to focus on transactional language skills and had poor awareness of the intercultural benefits of studying modern languages. This then led to misunderstandings about the professional opportunities modern languages could open up for pupils—beyond specialist jobs such as teaching and interpreting. Such negative messaging from parents (and sometimes careers advisors) then influenced how pupils saw the 'usefulness' of modern languages. More positively, a recent survey of 3567 Year 9 (ages 13 and 14) students in Wales indicates that 64% of those surveyed 'thoroughly enjoyed' or 'generally enjoyed' their modern-languages classes.

Making a Case for Languages in Wales and Taking Action

Since 2014, however, many in Wales have recognised the sustained efforts needed to reverse the decline in the uptake of modern languages. This renewed focus on modern languages is due, firstly, to an evolving educational context in Wales, following the recommendations for change made by Professor Graham Donaldson in his independent review of the

Welsh curriculum, *Successful Futures* (2015). It is also due to an acknowledgement, on the part of the Welsh government, that the previously centralised model of support for modern languages in Wales was not delivering the expected benefits. From the mid-1990s to 2015, modern languages in Wales was supported by a national organisation, CILT Cymru, the National Centre for Languages in Wales, funded by the Welsh government and with an annual budget, in its final years, of £600,000. In 2013–14, the Welsh government took the decision to cut CILT Cymru's funding by two-thirds and, in July 2015, the Centre was wound up. In the wake of CILT Cymru's demise, pressure increased to find alternative means for supporting modern languages in schools in Wales. Modern language communities made their voices heard, above all via the British Council in Wales and the University Council for Modern Languages. At the university level, activism centred on the Routes into Languages Cymru network, a group of modern language stakeholders in existence since 2008 and, from 2014, funded by Welsh universities with additional support from the British Council in Wales, the European Commission in Wales and two of Wales's four regional education consortia. Distinctive and different from Routes into Languages in England, Routes into Languages Cymru provided a good example of the benefits of multisectoral partnership working.

A major outcome of rethinking modern languages in schools in Wales has been the Welsh government's five-year Global Futures programme, 2015–20. This programme responds to one of the four curriculum objectives set out by Professor Donaldson; that learners in Wales be equipped to compete in the new global economy. The programme is made up of three key strategic actions: to promote and raise the profile of modern languages as an important subject at Level 2 (ages 7–11) and as a longer-term choice for career opportunities; to build capacity and support the professional development of the modern languages teaching profession; and to provide enhanced learning opportunities to engage learners. Each of the four Welsh regional education consortia has ring-fenced funding to support modern languages in their area and each has appointed a modern-languages lead responsible for disseminating effective teaching practice and developing training, networking and enrichment activities for teachers and learners. The Global Futures programme does not have targets for uptake and attainment at GCSE and A level, a choice that was questioned by some stakeholders initially as diminishing its potential impact.

The real strength of the strategy has been its impact in building a community of modern-linguist advocates in, and for, Wales. The Global Futures Steering Group brings together representatives from the four regional education consortia, the Welsh university sector, the British Council, the Alliance française, the Goethe Institute, the Spanish Embassy Education Office, the Italian Consulate, the Confucius Institutes in Wales, BBC Wales, the Open University Wales and Estyn. This partnership approach has reaped rewards in building trust and common purpose, with all stakeholders aware of where we are now, where we need to be in five years and how we might invest in long-term change and innovation. One case study of the benefits of looking afresh at supporting modern languages in Wales has been the success of a modern languages mentoring project in secondary schools, funded as part of the Global Futures programme.

Case Study: Student Mentoring and Creating Partnership

In November 2015, four Welsh universities began training modern languages undergraduates to act as mentors to pupils in Years 8 and 9 (ages 13 and 14) in partner secondary schools within the radius of their home university. The 18-month project aimed to raise the profile of modern languages in schools and to increase the number of pupils taking one or more modern languages at GCSE. The project targeted pupils less likely to opt for a modern language GCSE, for example male pupils or those eligible for free school meals, with the hope of broadening pupil horizons and showing them the career opportunities available to those with language skills. In its first year, the project placed 32 modern linguist undergraduates from Aberystwyth, Bangor, Cardiff, and Swansea universities in 28 schools across Wales to deliver a six-week programme of mentoring. Working predominantly with small groups of three to six mentees, the mentors spoke about their language journeys, why choose a language a GCSE, the career opportunities that come with languages and busted myths about the ubiquity of English. In so doing, they highlighted the value of languages for personal and professional development and stressed the importance of intercultural awareness for the world of work (Gorrara 2016). In its second full year, the project recruited and placed 52 university mentors in 47 schools. This equates to a modern linguist undergraduate mentor in nearly a quarter of secondary schools in Wales.

External evaluation of the scheme has stressed the positive impact of the project to date. At the level of take-up, 13 of 21 schools who responded to the external evaluator's survey request in the first year of the project reported an increase in numbers choosing to study GCSE modern languages, and this in a context of continuing national decline. In one partner school in an area of significant socio-economic disadvantage, following mentoring intervention, modern languages are running at GCSE for the first time in three years. On a more general level, schools have reported an impact on whole cohorts of pupils in a kind of 'pyramid effect' as word of mouth about the project has generated interest in modern languages. The evaluation report highlights three particular areas where individual pupils have benefited: mentors have provided inspiring role models and demonstrated the excitement of interacting with other European cultures; mentors have grown pupils' confidence in themselves as language learners and helped to build resilience; and mentors have raised pupil aspirations and prompted pupils from disadvantaged backgrounds to consider going to university. This has been transformative for some for, as one teacher commented, what one mentor inspired in her mentees was the idea that you can 'have your dream' and that going to university is an achievable ambition. Now confirmed with funding for a third year (2017–18), the mentoring project will develop a digital platform to increase the reach of the project beyond the radius of the partner universities.

Modern Languages in Wales in the Era of Brexit

If the Global Futures programme and the modern languages mentoring project demonstrate the benefits of partnership working, what could happen now in the era of Brexit? Firstly, developments in Wales predating Brexit will bring further changes for modern languages. Professor

Donaldson's *Successful Futures* report will have far-reaching consequences for the school curriculum in Wales. This new framework will see modern languages brought together with English and Welsh to form a Languages, Literacy and Communication cluster, one of six new Areas of Learning and Experience. This could provide a real opportunity to harmonise language teaching and pedagogy, developing 'triple literacy' as Welsh, English and modern languages come together. This approach has a record of success in Wales following schemes piloted in the early 2000s through CILT Cymru. Secondly, the possible outcome from Brexit of loss of membership of the European Single Market will focus minds in Wales on how best to develop and safeguard European and international trade partnerships. Renewed attention to languages skills, training and intercultural competency looks set to reap dividends if Wales decides to invest further in the skills needed to work for multinational (and multilingual) corporations based both inside and outside Wales. Thirdly, it seems likely that we will see greater differentiation in modern languages education and policy amongst the four UK nations. This was always a longer-term trend given devolved education policy. We can already see differences between the four UK nations. Scotland has invested £18 million to date in training and resources for a 'mother tongue plus two' policy that reaches into primary schools. England has set aside more than £35 million for teacher training and workforce development for primary languages, with modern languages one of the core academic subjects now required for the English Baccalaureate. In Northern Ireland, in the absence of a formal modern languages strategy, the Chief Inspector of the Education and Training Inspectorate Northern Ireland has recently expressed her serious concern at the fall in provision and the state of modern languages in Northern Irish schools. In Wales, the Global Futures pledge of 'Bilingualism + one', announced in 2015 by the then Education Minister Huw Lewis, suggests that Wales as a nation is aspiring to best practice models being developed in Scotland. Currently, there are no details of the funding required to deliver on such a pledge. It is, therefore, difficult to predict what this will look like in the future. However, it could be that Wales and Scotland could gain from partnership working.

In the immediate future, therefore, there will be interest within Wales and beyond in its evolving strategy for modern languages. There is impetus within the modern languages community in Wales to develop an integrated programme for modern languages, that begins in primary school and continues to university, and which offers a broad suite of qualifications, including vocational ones such as the Global Business Communication qualification currently offered by Welsh examination board WJEC. With devolved education policy, Wales has the capacity to be a laboratory for new ideas and to be sector-leading in its practice for modern languages. Yet this strategy will need to take account of how Wales voted in the EU referendum. With the exception of Monmouthshire, Cardiff and the Vale of Glamorgan in the South, Ceredigion in mid-Wales and Gwynedd in the North, Wales voted to leave the European Union by 52.5 to 47.5%. Repeatedly poor results for Wales in the PISA (Programme for International Student Assessment) league tables demonstrate the real need to combat a culture of educational underachievement in Wales. Both these contextual factors show that we cannot assume messages about the value of a more global mindset have purchase in large swathes of Wales. Indeed, there is evidence of continuing national apathy in Wales when it comes to learning languages. The modern languages community needs to work with pupils and their parents in Welsh schools to challenge a deeply ingrained monolingual mindset—even in a bilingual nation. As one teacher noted in the *Languages Trends Wales* report 2015–16, we are in 'a battle against insularity' (Tinsley and Board 2015: 70). This battle against insularity goes to the heart of the challenges not only for modern languages in Wales but in the whole of the UK. As Simon Kuper commented in his article on 'The Problem with English' for the *Financial Times*, we have a paucity of language skills in the UK compared to other European nations. This means that 'other Europeans know us better than we know them'. This language deficit risks both Brexit negotiations and our engagement with a brave new world outside the European Union.

References

Donaldson, G. (2015). *Successful Futures. Independent Review of Curriculum and Assessment Arrangements in Wales*. Cardiff: Welsh Government. http://gov.wales/topics/educationandskills/schoolshome/curriculum-for-wales-curriculum-for-life/why-we-are-changing/successful-futures/?lang=en.

Estyn. (2016). *Modern Foreign Languages, July 2016.* https://www.estyn.gov. wales/sites/default/files/documents/Modern%20foreign%20languages.pdf.

Flaherty, C. (2016, December 15). Language by the Shrinking Numbers. *Inside Higher Education.* https://www.insidehighered.com/news/2016/12/15/new-report-makes-data-based-case-building-us-capacity-foreign-language.

Gorrara, C. (2016). How Mentoring Can Improve Modern Languages Uptake in Schools in Wales. *The Conversation.* http://theconversation.com/how-mentoring-can-improve-modern-languages-uptake-in-schools-65380.

Kuper, S. (2017, January 12). The Problem with English. *Financial Times.* https://www.ft.com/content/223af71a-d853-11e6-944b-e7eb37a6aa8e.

Miller, C. (2013, April 2). Fall in Foreign Languages GCSE Prompts Fears for Wales' Future Prospect. *Wales Online.* http://www.walesonline.co.uk/news/wales-news/fall-foreign-language-gcses-prompts-2514337.

Munro, K. (2016, June 12). Why Students Are Turning Away from Learning Foreign Languages. *The Sydney Morning Herald.* http://www.smh.com.au/national/education/why-students-are-turning-away-from-learning-foreign-languages-20160610-gpg6ek.html

Tinsley, T., & Board, K. (2014). *Modern Foreign Languages in Secondary Schools in Wales. Findings from the Language Trends Survey 2014/15.* Reading/London: British Council/CfBT Education Trust. https://wales.britishcouncil.org/en/language-trends-wales.

Tinsley, T., & Board, K. (2015). *Language Trends Wales 2015/6: The State of Language Learning in Primary and Secondary Schools in Wales.* Reading/London: British Council/Education Development Trust. https://wales.britishcouncil.org/en/language-trends-wales.

14

Languages in Northern Ireland: Policy and Practice

Janice Carruthers and Mícheál B. Ó Mainnín

Introduction

Northern Ireland's geographical and political status in the United Kingdom (UK) is unique and this has a number of important consequences for questions of language learning, languages in the community and language policy. Northern Ireland (NI) is constitutionally part of the UK but it is also linked in terms of political co-operation (through the North–South bodies created by the Good Friday Agreement) to the Republic of Ireland. Crucially, post-Brexit, it will be the only part of the UK to have a significant border (of 500 km) with an EU state. At the moment, multiple aspects of daily life have an entirely normalised cross-border dimension, including business, agriculture, tourism, sport, the churches and scientific research. Indeed, many citizens live and work on

This chapter contains elements of the research undertaken on language policy for (1) the AHRC's Open World project 'Multilingualism: Empowering Individuals, Transforming Societies' http://www.meits.org/; (2) the research project (on language policy in the devolved administrations) attached to the AHRC Leadership Fellowship in Modern Languages, held by Janice Carruthers.

J. Carruthers (✉) • M.B. Ó Mainnín
Queen's University Belfast, Belfast, UK

© The Author(s) 2018
M. Kelly (ed.), *Languages after Brexit*,
https://doi.org/10.1007/978-3-319-65169-9_14

159

different sides of the border. Culturally, identities in NI are complex and fluid, ranging from those who consider themselves entirely 'Irish' to those who consider themselves entirely 'British', with a spectrum of more nuanced identities in between, including that of 'Northern Irish'. The most recent census in 2011 offered citizens seven 'national identity' options around different combinations of 'British', 'Irish' and 'Northern Irish', with the largest categories 39.89% British only, 25.26% Irish only and 20.94% Northern Irish only.[1] Northerners can choose whether they wish to carry Irish or British passports such that, post-Brexit, some citizens in NI will carry EU and others British passports.

Arising from this, the most important contextual factors for languages in NI are as follows:

- As part of the UK, the education system in which languages are taught is broadly aligned with that in England and Wales in terms of policy and assessment.
- The post-primary sector includes both selective and non-selective schools: there is an unofficial assessment at age 11 for entry to most grammar (selective) schools. Almost all post-primary schools, including grammar schools, are publicly funded.[2]
- At both primary and post-primary level, there are non-denominational schools (in practice, majority non-Catholic), Catholic schools, a very small number of schools of other denominations, integrated schools and Irish-medium schools. The majority of schools fall into the first two of these categories.
- There is a growing Irish-speaking community and a substantial number of learners of Irish, both inside and outside the school and university sectors. There are also speakers of Ulster-Scots, although this is not normally offered as part of the curriculum. Many Irish-language groups and agencies operate on an all-Ireland basis.
- The main immigrant communities, according to the 2011 census, speak Polish, Slovak, Hungarian, Latvian, Lithuanian, Russian, Chinese, Malaysian, Tagalog and Portuguese.[3] In general, the immigrant communities are small relative to those in other parts of the UK.
- A languages strategy, 'Languages for the Future', was published by the Department of Education in 2012 but only a small number of the

recommendations have been implemented, such as the creation of a Northern Ireland Languages Council.[4]

The chapter contains two main sections: first, 'Languages in the Education System' and second, 'Languages in the Community'. In both sections, we discuss both policy and practice together. A final section draws together the main issues and the implications of Brexit for languages in Northern Ireland.

Languages in the Education System[5]

The Primary Sector There is a serious problematic issue around languages in the primary schools, which was highlighted in a recent *Review of Current Primary Languages in Northern Ireland* and mentioned by the Chief Inspector of Schools in her most recent report, i.e., that 'Northern Ireland is the only part of the United Kingdom where there is no entitlement to languages provision in the primary curriculum'.[6] Policies in England, Scotland and Wales are different from each other (see Chaps. 11, 12 and 13) but all of them provide for language learning in the primary curriculum. In Northern Ireland, some primary schools offer language provision but the nature of this depends entirely on what the school is able to support; in some schools, there is simply no provision. Practice in Northern Ireland is therefore starkly out of line both with elsewhere in the UK and with elsewhere in Europe; in the latter, around 80% of children learn at least one 'second language' in primary school.[7]

The devolved Department of Education for Northern Ireland has a statutory duty in relation to the provision of Irish-medium education: 'it shall be the duty of the Department to encourage and facilitate the development of Irish-medium education'.[8] In practice, there are 28 Irish-medium primary schools and 7 Irish-medium units attached to English-medium primaries: these are spread across Northern Ireland, although Belfast, Co Armagh, mid-Ulster and the north-west have particularly strong provision. This sector is growing, with all the indicators pointing towards increasing numbers in the future.[9]

Finally, in terms of newcomer children who speak heritage languages (or 'community' languages) at home, the issues in primary school centre on language support and respect for linguistic diversity: none of the heritage languages is taught in the schools.[10] A recent report by Barnardo's highlights a number of areas of good practice, such as the need to translate key communications with parents, the use of classroom assistants who speak heritage languages, support for learning English and events to celebrate the linguistic diversity that pupils with heritage languages bring to the school environment.[11] In terms of heritage-language learning for primary-aged children, this is mainly achieved through lessons, outside the formal school environment, organised by the communities themselves (e.g. in Chinese, Arabic and Portuguese) and learners can ultimately take formal qualifications such as GCSEs and A levels.

The Post-primary Sector[12] The same legal and entitlement frameworks apply in NI as in the rest of the UK: learning a second language is compulsory at Key Stage 3 (and provision includes Irish as a language of the EU) but not thereafter and therefore not at GCSE. That said, taking a second language to GCSE is an entitlement for all pupils and remains compulsory within many of the selective schools, with French, Spanish, German and Irish the main languages on offer.[13] Amongst the foreign languages, provision in French and Spanish is stronger than in German, with some schools either closing A-level German due to financial pressures created by what are now considered 'non-viable' class sizes and other schools sharing provision across two or more schools in an Area Learning Community. Irish is only taught to GCSE and A level in the Catholic sector although here, too, there is provision for cross-school collaboration in Area Learning Communities.[14] The logistics of Area Learning Communities can vary: rural schools (of which there are many in NI) can find this more operationally challenging than urban schools, which are situated in relatively close proximity. There are two Irish medium post-primary schools and three Irish-medium units in English-medium schools: this sector is growing.[15]

There is some evidence that, with the pressure on schools to improve results, 'weaker' pupils in the selective sector may be exempted from the school's requirement to take a second language at GCSE. Uptake in the non-selective sector is dramatically low in comparison to that in the selective sector: languages are often perceived as difficult to learn and to score highly in at public examinations, with the result that they are much healthier in the stronger end of the selective sector than elsewhere in the post-primary environment. In fact, it is quite clear from the Annual Qualifications Insight for 2016 that, at both GCSE and A level, the percentage of pupils obtaining grades A*–C in Languages is higher than in STEM subjects and higher than in other 'Arts and Humanities'.[16]

In the four main languages offered (French, Spanish, German and Irish), the most interesting statistic is that the percentage proportion of the GCSE and A-level population taking a second language has remained steady over the last five years: this is clear from Figs. 14.1 and 14.2 in the 'languages as a % of total entries' line.[17] In practice, due to the falling birth rate in that period, the raw numbers taking languages have nonetheless fallen (also marked up in Figs. 14.1 and 14.2 as 'total language entries').

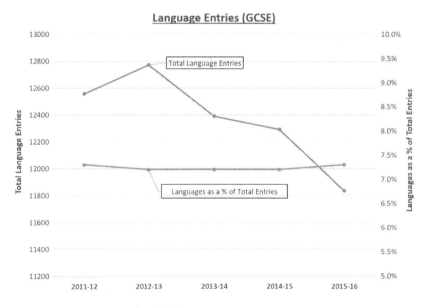

Fig. 14.1 Language entries GCSE

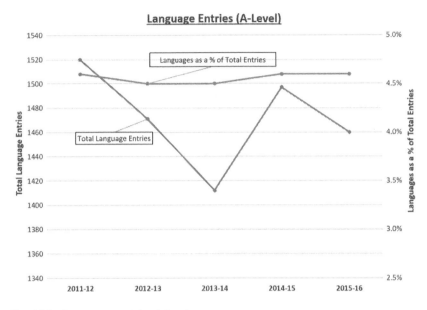

Fig. 14.2   Language entries A level

There is clear evidence of a shift of patterns within the four main languages. The proportion of pupils taking French is falling at both GCSE (Fig. 14.3) and A level (Fig. 14.4), while the proportion taking Spanish is increasing: these trends are broadly in line with those elsewhere in the UK (see Chaps. 11, 12 and 13). Numbers in Irish are increasing and numbers in German fluctuate but overall are holding steady at GCSE with a small drop at A level. The A-level drop may of course be linked to problems of provision in schools, as mentioned above. It is easy to enter a vicious circle when the numbers are too small to run an A-level class, and the lack of A-level provision means that German can be perceived as being in decline, which in turn does not help recruitment. It may also be linked to university-level provision (see below), of which there is likely in the near future to be none at Joint Honours or above for German in Northern Ireland.

Beyond the four main languages, the Confucius Institute (based in Ulster University) delivers cultural and language tuition to primary

Percentage of Total Language Entries (GCSE)

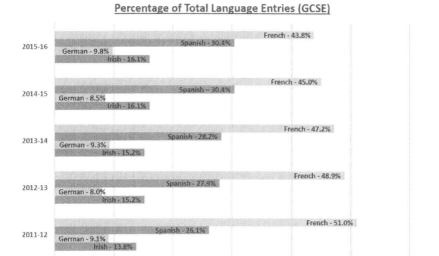

Fig. 14.3 Language-entry breakdown at GCSE

Percentage of Total Language Entries (A-Level)

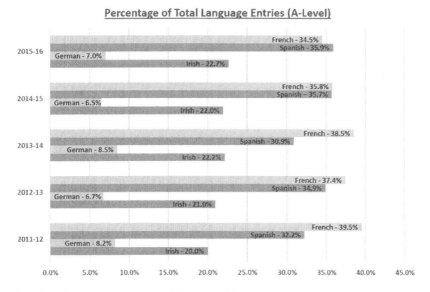

Fig. 14.4 Language-entry breakdown at A level

and post-primary schools via eight Confucius classroom hubs, with 12,000 pupils involved in their programme which includes 122 schools.

University Of the two Northern Ireland universities, only Queen's University offers entry to full degrees in Modern Foreign Languages: both universities offer Irish but Ulster University announced in 2015 that it intends to close its School of Modern Languages and has ceased entry to degrees in foreign languages. Queen's offers full degree-level programmes in French, Irish, Spanish and Portuguese; International Business with German or Mandarin; and a wide range of languages for students on other degree programmes through the Language Centre. While the teaching and research programmes in the languages offered are thriving, it is unfortunate that it is no longer possible to take a degree at Joint Honours level in German in NI, the language that consistently appears as the second most important (after French) for Business in the CBI's Skills Survey.[18]

Languages in the Community

Irish and Ulster-Scots Northern Ireland differs from the other devolved regions of the UK (and from the Republic of Ireland) in not having specific legislation which seeks to protect indigenous minoritised languages, in this case Irish and Ulster-Scots. Both Wales and Scotland have enacted legislation to that end and, in the Irish Republic, Irish has had its position as national language and first of two official languages (Irish and English) enshrined in the Constitution and in the Official Languages Act.[19] In Northern Ireland, Irish is in a different position due to the nature of its fractured community and the conflicting perceptions of identity which have manifested themselves in the contrasting political allegiances of its people (see Introduction). The language has been contentious, therefore, disowned for the most part by the unionist community while cherished as the national language by nationalists even if, as in the Irish Republic, this may be no more than a symbolic attachment for many. Developments in support of Irish, therefore, have traditionally been at grass-roots level, whether these take the form of the establishment of Irish-medium schools or of the first new Irish-speaking community, or Gaeltacht, in the Shaw's Road in West Belfast in the 1960s.

In more recent years, and in the context of the peace process, some of the traditional binaries have been breaking down with the result that increasing numbers of unionists have taken steps to learn Irish; the role of TURAS (which has been facilitated by the East Belfast Mission) has been particularly significant in that regard.[20] The other indigenous language, Ulster-Scots, which was introduced into Ireland in the seventeenth century in tandem with settlements of large numbers of people from Lowland Scotland, is spoken not only in what is now Northern Ireland but also in those parts of Ulster that are in the Irish Republic (particularly Donegal). This language too has been contentious but what is striking, in this case, is that scepticism in relation to its status as a language distinct from English has been expressed very forcefully by some within the unionist community, the very community which might be most expected to support it. On the other hand, the language has not been met with any hostility by Irish speakers; both language communities are aware of the precariousness of their position in some respects and of the need to be seen to co-exist and work together, wherever possible.

The need to support linguistic diversity was first articulated by the Good Friday/Belfast Agreement of 1998 in which all the participants (the British and Irish governments, and all the NI political parties) 'recognised the importance of respect, understanding and tolerance in relation to linguistic diversity', including Irish, Ulster-Scots and the 'languages of the various ethnic communities'.[21] The agreement led to the establishment of six North–South implementation bodies on the island of Ireland; the Language Body is comprised of the Irish Language Agency (Foras na Gaeilge) and the Ulster-Scots Agency, both with an all-Ireland remit and funded by the two governments through the Department for Communities in Northern Ireland, and the Department of Arts, Heritage and the Gaeltacht in the Irish Republic. More problematically, the support enshrined in the agreement was qualified by the stipulation that the new devolved Northern Ireland Assembly would sustain its commitments to the indigenous languages 'in a way which takes account of the desires and sensitivities of the community';[22] as Northern Ireland is a divided community, the desires and sensitivities of its people differ in the contested area of languages.

The question of support was revisited again in the context of the St Andrews Agreement of 2006. The British government undertook to introduce an Irish Language Act to enhance and protect the language as part of that agreement and also iterated its belief in the need to enhance and develop the 'Ulster-Scots language, heritage and culture'.[23] However, in giving legislative effect to the agreement, the St Andrews Act omitted any reference to an Irish Language Act and instead empowered the NI Executive to adopt strategies for both Irish and Ulster-Scots. The two separate strategies which eventually emerged, the 'Strategy to Enhance and Protect the Development of the Irish Language' and the 'Strategy to Enhance and Develop the Ulster-Scots Language, Heritage and Culture' cover the period 2015–35 and include among their aims the desire to facilitate language acquisition and learning, and build sustainable networks and communities. The extent to which these aims are supported, however, may vary in accordance with the political outlook of the minister of the day. In an earlier iteration of the Department for Communities (Arts, Culture and Leisure), the Sinn Féin minister supported the establishment of a Gaeltacht quarter in West Belfast and invested in infrastructural and other initiatives. She also initiated the Líofa project in 2011, the purpose of which was to encourage 20,000 people to become fluent in Irish by 2015; almost 19,000 to date have signed up.[24] On the other hand, the reassignment of this portfolio after the assembly election in 2016 to a minister from the Democratic Unionist Party resulted in a change of priorities and the cutting of Líofa grants to learners of Irish from disadvantaged socio-economic backgrounds. The subsequent furore was a factor in the deterioration of relations between the two parties of government which culminated in the fall of the Assembly at the beginning of 2017.[25] There does seem to be consensus between the government parties in terms of support for the Ulster-Scots Institute and an Irish Language Academy (the latter had been mooted by the previous minister and appeared in the most recent Programme for Government, despite the change of minister). This could be interpreted, however, as a bid to balance the scales between the two languages politically rather than signalling any broader change in attitude towards supporting the indigenous languages. Tensions remain, particularly in relation to renewed pressure from Sinn Féin for the introduction of an Irish Language Act. The new political landscape post-Brexit means that the North–South structures which have had the most positive impact on promoting linguistic diversity now find themselves having to transcend a new UK–EU boundary, adding further layers of complexity, potentially, to what is already a complicated picture. The issue of funding will be a key concern for community-based projects, in particular, as these have benefited from a variety of EU support mechanisms in the past.

Heritage Languages As mentioned above, heritage languages are not taught as such in the mainstream school system but several are taught in community schools, particularly where there is a substantial critical mass of speakers. Where this is the case (e.g. for Chinese, Arabic, Polish), the heritage languages in question are thriving in sections of the communities where they are spoken and many mainstream schools will normally facilitate entry for GCSEs in the languages concerned. Maintaining and developing fluency in heritage languages is extremely important for identity and cohesion within these communities. However, despite explicit mention in the Good Friday Agreement (see above), and the normal provision of interpreters for services such as health, there is no formal proactive support from public funds for learning or maintaining heritage languages.

Future Perspectives

Although the overall situation is extremely challenging for languages in Northern Ireland, there are, nonetheless, a number of significant positives. The Irish-medium primary sector is thriving, as is Irish language learning outside formal education, notably through classes in local communities, including a growing interest amongst the PUL community.[26] Irish in the post-primary sector is also fairly healthy. Moreover, the decline in raw numbers taking foreign languages at GCSE and A level masks the fact that the proportion of pupils has remained steady over several years.

As far as foreign language learning is concerned, many of the challenges in Northern Ireland are similar to those that are well documented for the rest of the UK and are much discussed elsewhere in this volume. The figures certainly indicate a clear fall in numbers at GCSE and A level and the range of languages available in the university sector has narrowed considerably in the last 20 years. Yet, as is the case elsewhere in the UK, the acute need for high-level language and intercultural skills is acknowledged by some important bodies: for example, the Chamber of Commerce in NI has recently published a report making clear how vital foreign languages are for our export market, which is key to the local economy.[27] The situation of Irish also has risks attached as we head towards Brexit: the bodies designed to protect and support Irish form part of the North–South dimension of the Good Friday Agreement and could be more vulnerable in the volatile political environment of Northern Ireland where a future EU border is likely to traverse the landscape.

Urgent steps need to be taken in the education sector if current uptake trends are to be stalled and turned around. There is certainly a need to address the primary-school context, as NI pupils are the only children in the UK not to study a second language. Just as importantly, in the post-primary sector, tangible support will be required to enable schools to make A-level classes in certain languages viable in the current financial climate. Similarly, schools will need to be supported in maximising the possibilities of Area Learning Communities, where this is the most sensible solution in terms of making a particular A-level language available to pupils.

But solving the problem goes well beyond the education sector. What is now needed is a radically different level of awareness in wider society in Northern Ireland and in local government, of the importance of languages for international business, international relations, peace, community cohesion, security, diplomacy and crucially, for intercultural understanding (at home and abroad).[28] If this challenge could begin to be addressed, the more buoyant elements in the languages landscape of Northern Ireland could be harnessed and capitalised upon in order to create a step change that would benefit everyone, both locally, and in terms of our global aspirations in a post-Brexit world.

Notes

1. The census is available on http://www.nisra.gov.uk/archive/census/2011/results/key-statistics/summary-report.pdf (accessed 2 February 2017). The percentages do not total 100% because other options were available.

2. There are only two schools where a compulsory fee of over £200 per year is charged. In the 'voluntary grammar' sector, there is a small compulsory fee ranging from £12 to around £150 per year.

3. Note that the census question asks about speakers' 'main language', so it is possible that the responses do not give the full range of languages spoken: many speakers of languages other than English may be responding 'English' due to the nature of the question.

4. https://www.education-ni.gov.uk/sites/default/files/publications/de/languages-for-the-future.pdf.

5. We are extremely grateful to Sarah Malcolmson and Dale Heaney from the Department of Education for supplying us with data and for sharing their expertise. We are also very grateful to Sharon Jones (Stranmillis University College) and Ian Collen (QUB) for sharing their expertise at primary and post-primary levels, respectively.

6. The 2017 review, led by Sharon Jones, was funded by the Northern Ireland Languages Council and is accessible at http://www.stran.ac.uk/media/media,748093,en.pdf. The quotation from the Chief Inspector can be found at: http://www.nisra.gov.uk/archive/census/2011/results/key-statistics/summary-report.pdf, p. 23.

7. See http://ec.europa.eu/eurostat/documents/2995521/7008563/3-2409 2015-AP-EN.pdf/bf8be07c-ff9d-406b-88f9-f98f5199fe5a.

8. See http://www.legislation.gov.uk/nisi/1998/1759/article/89/made.

9. See http://www.comhairle.org/gaeilge/ or http://www.comhairle.org/english/

10. We will refer to the languages of immigrant communities as 'community' or 'heritage' languages.

11. See https://www.barnardos.org.uk/feels_like_home_exploring_the_experiences_of_newcomer_pupils_in_northern_ireland.pdf.

12. An important report, funded by the Northern Ireland Languages Council and authored by Ian Collen, Eugene McKendry and Leanne Henderson, will be published imminently on *The Transition from Primary Languages Programmes to Post-Primary Language Provision*.

13. A very small number of schools offer Italian; and an even smaller number offer Russian.

14. These are collaborations between schools in the same area where pupils can take a subject which is not offered in their own school.

15. See https://www.education-ni.gov.uk/news/odowd-officially-opens-new-post-primary-irish-medium-school-dungiven.

16. See http://ccea.org.uk/sites/default/files/docs/news/2016/Oct/Annual%20Qualifications%20Insight%202016_(web).pdf.

17. All data are taken from the Annual Qualifications Insight for 2016, published by CCEA: http://ccea.org.uk/sites/default/files/docs/news/2016/Oct/Annual%20Qualifications%20Insight%202016_(web).pdf.

18. See http://www.cbi.org.uk/index.cfm/_api/render/file/?method=inline&fileID=DB1A9FE5-5459-4AA2-8B44798DD5B15E77.

19. Welsh Language Act (1993); Welsh Language (Wales) Measure (2011); Gaelic Language (Scotland) Act (2005); Official Languages Act (Republic of Ireland) (2003).

20. See http://www.ebm.org.uk/turas/ TURAS is an Irish language project designed to connect members of the Protestant community to their own history with the Irish language and it offers language classes, talks and other activities.

21. https://www.gov.uk/government/uploads/system/uploads/attachment_data/file/136652/agreement.pdf (p. 24).

22. https://www.gov.uk/government/uploads/system/uploads/attachment_data/file/136652/agreement.pdf (p. 20).

23. https://www.gov.uk/government/uploads/system/uploads/attachment_data/file/136651/st_andrews_agreement-2.pdf (p. 12).

24. See https://www.liofa.eu.

25. The minister eventually reversed his earlier decision and restored the Líofa grants.

26. Protestant-unionist-loyalist.

27. See http://northernirelandchamber.com/wp-content/uploads/2014/02/Exporting-the-Challenge-February-2014.pdf.

28. At least two responses relating to the importance of languages were submitted to the recent Programme for Government consultation.

15

Building Capacity in UK Higher Education

Jocelyn Wyburd

Such has been the alarm in the higher education sector in the UK about declining numbers of students taking languages degrees, that the Higher Education Funding Council for England (HEFCE) classified languages as strategically important and vulnerable subjects during the first decade of this century. This classification combines two vital notions—the fact that languages are strategically important, whether to the UK as a nation or to the well-being of the higher education sector, or both; and that the health of these disciplines is vulnerable. In this chapter I will explore the trends which gave rise to this classification and the role that higher education can play in rebuilding the UK's capacity to communicate with and understand the world.

Historical Context

It is often asserted that the decline in the study of languages at university was a direct consequence of languages being marginalised in our secondary-school curricula from 2004. However, the changes to the

J. Wyburd (✉)
University of Cambridge, Cambridge, UK

© The Author(s) 2018
M. Kelly (ed.), *Languages after Brexit*,
https://doi.org/10.1007/978-3-319-65169-9_15

National Curriculum which resulted in languages becoming optional from age 14 predominantly apply to England, not the UK as a whole, and in reality, the decline predated it. Indeed, even as early as the late 1990s, the Nuffield Languages Inquiry highlighted the closure of university language departments due to declining student numbers, alongside making a number of recommendations about the systemic, funding and policy initiatives required in respect to languages in higher education (Nuffield Languages Inquiry 2000: 54–57). The Higher Education context is, however, inevitably linked to issues in the supply chain from the statutory education sector, and to the status given to languages in government (mainly education) policies.

In spite of the adoption by the government of a National Languages Strategy for England from 2002 to 2011 (DfES 2002), in response to the Nuffield Report, the situation in higher education in the UK has become even more challenging. In the past decade, the numbers of universities offering degrees in the major traditionally taught languages (French, German and Spanish) has declined by over 50%, while HEFCE figures show total undergraduate enrolments in modern languages degrees in England has fallen by 52.7% between 2003–4 and 2014–15.[1]

In relation to higher education's supply chain, and in recognition of the importance of rebuilding capacity, recent positive initiatives have been taken in Scotland and Wales. The Scottish Assembly has adopted a 'mother tongue plus two' languages policy (Scottish Government 2012), mirroring the EU's own goals. Meanwhile, the publication of *Global Futures* (Welsh Government 2015) cemented a commitment to Wales's becoming a 'bilingual plus 1 nation'. In England, the inclusion of a language within the English Baccalaureate (EBacc) performance measure (subsequently turned into a goal) for schools was taken on academic grounds, rather than as part of a strategic drive to build capacity specifically in languages. The goal of 90% of pupils achieving GCSEs in the EBacc subjects by 2020 is a challenge for languages, whose take-up stood at 49% in 2016. It is too soon to assess how these initiatives will impact on progression through to higher education across the UK as a whole.

HEFCE's classification of modern languages as 'Strategically Important and Vulnerable Subjects' led to the establishment in 2006 of the national (England only) Routes into Languages programme of collaborative outreach activities by universities to schools. By the time funding ceased in 2016, hundreds of thousands of pupils had engaged in a wide variety of activities to motivate their language learning and progression to university, the programme had been adopted in Wales under separate funding arrangements and many of the activities developed by 'Routes' had been picked up within the mother tongue plus two implementation plans in Scotland. From data gathered by 'Routes' on the influence such activities had on students choosing to study languages at university, it appears that the declines in higher education enrolment would undoubtedly have been much greater, without this intervention.[2]

In the meantime, as was already the trend when Nuffield reported in 2000, the numbers of students in British universities taking up language learning alongside other subjects of study have been increasing dramatically. Indeed, numbers doubled in a decade (AULC 2013: #3.1 p. 3), in all likelihood partly due to the success of 'Routes'. This trend has also been driven by emerging university internationalisation strategies, recognising at institutional level the importance of developing an ever-more 'global' skillset in all graduates. It has also accompanied both national (UKHEIU 2014) and institutional strategies to increase international experience abroad, through engagement in outward mobility programmes of study and/or work.

Thus, when we consider the role of higher education in rebuilding capacity in languages, we have two contrasting scenarios at play. On the one hand, more students than ever before are acquiring language skills, and in an ever-wider variety of languages (AULC 2016). On the other hand, ever-fewer students are studying languages and related cultures in depth and to a high level of language proficiency. The former demonstrates an increasing awareness amongst university students of the instrumental skills associated with learning another language, even if only in one beginners' course during their university career. The latter, however, reflects a decline in the appeal of academic disciplines that involve studying other cultures (literature, film, society, cultural studies) through the medium of languages other than English.

Looking to the Future: Defining the Strategic Need

As a member of the EU, as well as of a broader global society, the UK already has an unfulfilled strategic need for language and intercultural skills. The need is likely to increase, not decrease, following UK withdrawal from the EU. One major dimension is, clearly, the economic one in relation to trade and exports. However, we should not ignore the dimensions of soft power (Hill and Beadle 2014), diplomacy and security (British Academy 2013) and social cohesion (Newby and Penz 2007) within the UK's own nations. These were helpfully summarised in the report of a national languages policy workshop held in 2015 (CPPSRI 2016). Employers have also repeatedly demonstrated an unfulfilled need for culturally agile 'global graduates', equipped with transcultural skills as well as language skills (most recently for example, CBI 2016; British Academy 2016a).

In theory, graduates in languages fulfil much of the profile of the culturally agile, transculturally competent and multilingual graduate called for in today's global society, and in tomorrow's more uncertain future outside of the EU. And yet, as we have seen, demand for degrees in languages has shrunk, posing a major challenge for university language departments to address. In the meantime, graduates with languages taken on the side may only partially be addressing the strategic needs identified above.

Degrees in languages are also vital in the supply chain of professional linguists, whether these are the academics, teachers, translators or interpreters required in education, business, government and public services. The secondary education sector is currently facing a major shortage of language teachers (the Department for Education estimates an additional 3500–4000 are needed), not least in order to deliver the EBacc goals mentioned above. This shortage may be further exacerbated by any restrictions on employment of EU nationals following Brexit. Rebuilding capacity in our universities to deliver languages degrees, and stimulating demand for them, should thus, in this respect alone, be regarded as a major national strategic priority.

Rebuilding Capacity: The Transnational Graduate

Languages departments in higher education have not simply relied on their outreach activities, such as 'Routes', to combat the declining take-up and to make the case for the study of their disciplines. On the contrary, there has been and continues to be considerable rethinking of curricula and the introduction of innovative degree programmes which combine languages with other disciplines, as well as new entry routes to take languages as specialist subjects *ab initio*. These moves have been driven in part by a necessity to attract students who might not wish to commit to a degree only in (one or more) language(s), or who might not have the confidence to do so, not having had the opportunity to take two languages post-16. There is, however, a risk involved in the range of routes and combinations available, which is that the skillset of graduates of these programmes is becoming ever-less transparent to employers. The Born Global research project, for example, demonstrated that employers have little understanding of the value of a languages degree and that graduates are failing to communicate it effectively during recruitment processes (British Academy 2016b: 11).

One challenge is recognition of the level of competence achieved in the relevant language(s) and the transferability of this competence to a work environment. The other challenge is the communication of the range of transversal academic and personal skills gained through the study of cultures, literatures and societies. It is also crucial that both graduates and employers recognise the skills and attributes developed during the period of residence abroad, which is inherent to the majority of languages degrees.

The interculturally competent, multilingual graduate is likely to be in increasing demand post-Brexit, should there be restrictions on the employment of EU nationals, who currently compete very successfully with their UK peers. Through the review in 2015 of the Quality Assurance Agency's Subject Benchmark Statement for degrees in and with languages (QAA 2015), the higher education sector has acquired some vital new definitions: both of language-based degrees, as *inherently intercultural* and *transnational* (§2.2, p. 8), and of their graduates, as equipped to *operate within different linguistic and cultural contexts* and to *compare and contrast diverse visions of the world, thereby promoting intercultural understanding* (§2.6, p. 9). University language departments are embracing these terms in order to reposition the unique strengths of their disciplines, both with respect to employers and for the purposes of marketing language degrees to prospective students.

In so doing, they have the opportunity to present language degrees as uniquely enabling the UK to gain an invaluable understanding of other cultures. By providing students with the opportunity to study cultural heritage and masterpieces, they are equally providing them with an invaluable insight into contemporary cultures and societies. Simultaneously, language degrees contribute enormously to the personal growth and development of the students who study them in depth and who experience living within other cultures and societies. The value of language degrees to the UK's knowledge base and citizenship cannot be underestimated.

University language departments can and should do more to package and market their degrees along these lines, and to continue to develop innovative pathways and interdisciplinary approaches. They continue to do so, however, in a national policy vacuum in respect of the value of languages and intercultural skills to all sectors of society and the economy. This vacuum was recognised in the *Manifesto for Languages* issued by the All-Party Parliamentary Group on Modern Languages in 2014 (APPGMFL 2014), which called on all politicians to support a Framework for National Recovery in Languages. In a higher education sector driven increasingly by market forces, and with reducing levels of government funding or intervention, there is a real risk for the provision of language degrees.

As noted above, the development of ever-broader Institution-Wide Language Programmes (IWLPs), available for credit and/or as extra-curricular courses, has successfully raised the profile of the importance of languages and intercultural skills for graduates of any discipline. One of the advantages of IWLPs is that they are not full degree programmes requiring constant revalidation and that the modular format is therefore able to respond flexibly to changing demands. In a post-Brexit UK,

IWLPs will thus be well placed to respond to shifts in geopolitical-economic trends. Annual surveys of the sector have demonstrated this level of responsiveness to date, for example the ability to cope with recent increasing demands for Japanese, or the widespread introduction of Swahili and Sign Language (e.g. AULC 2016). Furthermore, IWLPs typically offer a much wider range of languages than could be offered at full degree level.

It is, however, important to recognise that IWLPs are not a panacea when addressing the challenges of rebuilding capacity, not just in languages but in the accompanying transnational and intercultural competences and knowledge base required of today's and tomorrow's graduates. The majority of home students who take an IWLP course do so at beginners' or post-beginners' (e.g. post-GCSE) level. In many universities they may be limited to being allowed to take a language course in one or two of their years of study. Thus the majority do not reach a highly proficient level of language competence in what is for most only their second language. This especially contrasts with their European or international peers who are often taking courses in their third or fourth language and in many cases are building on more extensive prior language learning, coming from countries with more systematically embedded language education policies.

IWLPs are undoubtedly a symptom of the awareness of the importance of gaining skills in languages other than English. There is, however, a risk that a focus on gaining some language skills (however important) detracts from an understanding of the deeper cultural and intercultural understanding which is gained from the study of languages as a specialist degree subject, not to mention the much higher level of language competence gained in the process. Language departments are on occasion faced with having to defend their disciplines in the face of perceptions that IWLPs are the solution both to the challenge of building capacity and of developing 'global graduates'. Such perceptions may be held by prospective students, their teachers and parents, and senior management teams in universities alike. There is a real risk, therefore, that the very welcome success of IWLPs becomes a threat to languages departments, their degrees and their research.

One of the most valuable aspects of languages degrees is the period spent residing and studying or working abroad. As noted above, this experience has in recent years expanded considerably in respect of students of other disciplines also. There have been numerous studies of the benefits to students' intercultural as well as linguistic profile, not least in terms of their employability skills and life chances (e.g. Bøe and Hurley 2015). Student mobility has been one of the underlying principles of the EU, facilitated through the Erasmus+ programme, of relevance both to work and study placements. The future of the UK's participation in Erasmus+ is, at the time of writing, uncertain.[3] It comes with EU membership, but is also available to non-EU members who choose to subscribe to it. There is widespread anxiety, as noted also in the recent report of a small-scale study of students of German (Klaus and Mentchen 2016), that without Erasmus+ such experiences would be unattainable or unaffordable in the future for swathes of UK undergraduates. However, we should note that students already engage in mobility to Latin America, the Middle East, East Asia and Russia (for example) without the benefits of Erasmus+, and that other arrangements are in place to ensure access to these opportunities for students, regardless of background. While arrangements will vary locally, we must also recognise that these come at a cost to the host university. As has already been noted, universities are working in an increasingly monetarised and market-driven economy, and any loss of access to Erasmus+ will necessarily raise major questions about the affordability of outward mobility programmes for universities and their students, thus threatening the potential for higher education to rebuild capacity in languages and transcultural skills.

Conclusions

Universities are in a very strong position to build capacity in tomorrow's graduates to address national and international strategic needs—not least in light of Brexit. Degrees in languages are already developing a wide range of skills that have been identified as needed by employers across a range of sectors. Both universities and their students still need to communicate the profile of language graduates more consistently in terms which are understood by employers and which demonstrate the unique value of these degree subjects. There are, furthermore, increasing numbers of graduates in other disciplines entering the workforce equipped with at least some skills in an additional language as a result of IWLP provision. This trend should be celebrated and fostered, without positioning it as an alternative to the specialist degrees in languages and related studies.

UK universities are in many ways extremely well positioned to deliver in response to a wide range of strategic needs in relation to both language skills (in a very wide range of languages), cultural knowledge and intercultural understanding. Languages in UK higher education are more strategically important than ever. While departments conducting language-based research and delivering degrees remain vulnerable, they are in the strongest position they have been for many decades to make an evidence- and demand-based case for the importance of their disciplines, given the policy vacuum in which they are working.

At a national level, the All-Party Parliamentary Group on Modern Languages has repeatedly called on government to establish a cross-departmental policy initiative, supported ideally by a Minister for Languages. In light of forthcoming Brexit negotiations, it would be timely to revive this proposition and to invite higher education specialists in a range of languages, cultures and societies to contribute to the formation of national policy in this vital area of importance. It is also vital that government recognises the benefit of outward mobility for students of all disciplines and ensures that the UK can continue to participate in the Erasmus+ scheme.

Notes

1. Data obtained through the HEFCE interactive data set: http://www. hefce.ac.uk/analysis/supplydemand/ug/ November 2016.
2. Analysis of data from surveys of first-year undergraduates in successive years showed that 48–54% agreed that these interventions had influenced their decision to study languages at university (Gallagher-Brett 2016: 16).
3. For information on Erasmus+ see the website: https://www.erasmusplus. org.uk/.

References

APPGMFL. (2014). *Manifesto for Languages*. All-Party Parliamentary Group for Modern Languages/British Council. https://www.britishcouncil.org/sites/default/files/manifesto_for_languages.pdf.

AULC. (2013). *UCML-AULC Survey of Institution-Wide Language Provision in Universities in the UK 2012–13*. Higher Education Academy. http://www.ucml.ac.uk/sites/default/files/pages/160/UCML_AULC_2013-2014.docx

AULC. (2016). *UCML-AULC Survey of Institution-Wide Language Provision in Universities in the UK 2015–16*. UCML/AULC. http://www.ucml.ac.uk/sites/default/files/pages/160/UCML_AULC_2015-2016.pdf.

Bøe, L., & Hurley, D. (2015). *Gone International*. UK Higher Education International Unit. Retrieved from http://go.international.ac.uk/content/research-and-evidence/go-international-research/gone-international-mobile-students-and-the-0.

British Academy. (2013). *Lost for Words. The Need for Languages in UK Diplomacy and Security*. British Academy. https://www.britac.ac.uk/publications/lost-words-need-languages-uk-diplomacy-and-security

British Academy. (2016a). *Born Global: Reports and Data Sets from the Born Global Research Project*. British Academy. http://www.britac.ac.uk/born-global.

British Academy. (2016b). *Born Global: Implications for Higher Education*. British Academy. http://www.britac.ac.uk/sites/default/files/Born%20Global%20-%20Implications%20for%20Higher%20Education.pdf.

CBI. (2016). *The Right Combination*. CBI/Pearson Education and Skills Survey. CBI. http://www.cbi.org.uk/cbi-prod/assets/File/pdf/cbi-education-and-skills-survey2016.pdf.

CPPSRI. (2016). *The Value of Languages*. Cambridge Public Policy Strategic Research Initiative. University of Cambridge. http://www.publicpolicy.cam.ac.uk/pdf/value-of-languages.

DfES. (2002). *Languages for All: Languages for Life. A Strategy for England*. DfES Publications. http://webarchive.nationalarchives.gov.uk/20130404073225/. https://www.education.gov.uk/publications/standard/publicationDetail/Page1/DfES%200749%202002

Gallagher-Brett, A. (2016). *Routes into Languages 4th Annual First-Year Undergraduate Survey in England: Students' Prior Engagement with Languages Outreach and Enrichment Activities 2014–15*. Southampton: Centre for Languages Linguistics and Area Studies/Routes into Languages.

Hill, C., & Beadle, S. (2014). *The Art of Attraction: Soft Power and the UK's Role in the World.* British Academy. https://www.britac.ac.uk/events/art-attraction-soft-power-and-uks-role-world

Klaus, A., & Mentchen, S. (2016). *Why We Cannot Afford Losing Erasmus+.* (Report of a small-scale study disseminated) by UCML. http://www.ucml.ac.uk/news/340.

Newby, D., & Penz, H. (Eds.). (2007). *Languages for Social Cohesion. Language Education in a Multilingual and Multicultural Europe.* ECML, Graz, Austria.

Nuffield Language Inquiry. (2000). *Languages: The Next Generation. Final Report and Recommendations of the Nuffield Languages Inquiry.* The Nuffield Foundation. http://www.nuffieldfoundation.org/nuffield-languages-inquiry-and-nuffield-languages-programme

QAA. (2015). *Subject Benchmark Statement: Languages, Cultures and Societies.* Quality Assurance Agency. http://www.qaa.ac.uk/publications/information-and-guidance/publication?PubID=2982#.V0LZfuR-5fY.

Scottish Government. (2012). *Language Learning in Scotland. A 1+2 Approach.* © Crown Copyright. http://www.gov.scot/resource/0039/00393435.pdf.

UKHEIU. (2014). *UK Strategy for Outward Mobility.* UK Higher Education International Unit/BIS/HEFCE. http://www.universitiesuk.ac.uk/policy-and-analysis/reports/Documents/2014/UK-strategy-for-outward-mobility.pdf.

Welsh Government. (2015). *Global Futures. A Plan to Improve and Promote Modern Foreign Languages in Wales 2015–2020.* © Crown Copyright. http://gov.wales/docs/dcells/publications/151019-global-futures-en.pdf.

16

Support Unsung Heroes: Community-Based Language Learning and Teaching

Kate Borthwick

Introduction

There are young people and adults walking among us who carry within them a hidden and valuable ability to enrich our society: knowledge of a language other than English and of a culture other than British. The UK is home to an extraordinary number of languages and it is a tremendous advantage to be able to communicate in one of them, besides English. As other chapters show, it opens up job opportunities, enhances general literacy, improves cognitive abilities and broadens the mind. However, traditionally we have not been good at valuing community language skills or at working to enhance and develop them. This is short-sighted. The UK has the potential to jump-start its capacity for language skills if it begins to pride and support the language knowledge held by its community groups. Community-based language teaching and learning is widespread across the UK but relies heavily on volunteers and charitable work to survive. Yet the creativity, innovation and collaborative nature of

K. Borthwick (✉)
University of Southampton, Southampton, UK

M. Kelly (ed.), *Languages after Brexit*,
https://doi.org/10.1007/978-3-319-65169-9_16

community-based classes and supplementary schools offers us a vision of how language skills and cultural knowledge could be built up and embedded across society. Learning lessons from community-based language classes will help the UK to meet the challenges and realise the opportunities of an interconnected and globalised future.

UK Context

The UK is a wonderfully multilingual country. In London, it has been reported that over 300 languages are spoken (Von Ahn et al. 2010) and in the wider UK, 7.7% of the population report having a main language other than English. A selection of the 'other' main languages cited as spoken in England and Wales includes Polish, Punjabi, Urdu, Bengali, Gujarati, Arabic, Cornish, Manx Gaelic and Spanish (ONS 2011). Yet, the majority of these are not taught or learnt within the mainstream education system. Much of the learning and development in these languages goes on in supplementary schools based within community settings.

It has been estimated that there are between 3000 and 5000 supplementary schools in the UK, teaching subjects ranging from maths to Urdu (2017, from the website of the National Resource Centre for Supplementary Education). It is difficult to ascertain an exact number as many supplementary schools operate in informal settings outwith recognised reporting structures and therefore, are effectively invisible. Several recent studies commissioned by the Royal Society for the Encouragement of Arts, Manufactures and Commerce (RSA, Nwulu 2015) and Institute for Public Policy Research (IPPR, Ramalingam and Griffith 2015) have shown how important these schools are in raising the educational attainment of children in black and ethnic-minority (BME) communities.

A significant dimension of the work of supplementary schools is the offer of classes in mother-tongue languages (languages other than English), which may be spoken within the family or be part of an individual's cultural heritage. These languages are often described as minority languages spoken in majority-language contexts, or as less widely taught (or learnt) languages. Knowledge of these languages and community support for developing skills in these languages is an important element in the language landscape of the UK.

The UK has a rich history of support for community-based language learning through initiatives mostly driven by charitable organisations but often in partnership with local and national government. For example, the RSA and the British Council are active in funding research into the benefits community language learning and the promotion of cultural knowledge bring to communities. Both the Paul Hamlyn Foundation and John Lyon's Charity have been long-term supporters of research and practical projects aimed at understanding and assisting the work of community-based language teachers and learners. These charities are two of the many supporters of the National Resource Centre for Supplementary Education (NRCSE), an organisation that draws together partners from across the supplementary education sector and acts as a national champion for supplementary schools. This important centre works to enhance the quality of supplementary education and to promote excellence and innovation in the field, as well as providing resources for community-based teachers and learners.

Another important support network for community languages is the National Association of Teaching English and Community Languages to Adults (NATECLA). This charitable association brings together teachers of English as a Second Language with teachers of other languages and offers a forum for professional discussion, training events and other support for language teachers. In addition, there are many small-scale local projects which support language learning in the community in diverse ways. These projects are often flexible and dynamic collaborations between a range of partners including charities, local government, volunteer teachers, parents, pupils and educational institutions. This collaborative, cross-sector way of working is characteristic of the supplementary sector and, alongside support for languages in the mainstream education sector, offers a potential model for sustaining and enhancing language learning more broadly across the UK.

Why Is It Important to Support Community-Based Language Learning?

There is a body of research that demonstrates that the development of language skills—in any language—are beneficial to individuals and to society at large. For example, learning a language has cognitive benefits to individuals in delaying the effects of ageing and the onset of dementia (Leca 2016), and the development of language skills improves performance in educational tasks and enhances literacy (reported in McPake and Sachdev 2008). In this way, the teaching and learning of community languages has the potential to have an impact on general educational attainment and the cognitive ability of individuals. Children who have a head start in linguistic and cultural knowledge due to their ethnic background or family heritage need to be encouraged to develop and prize their skills. Their knowledge enriches the lives of all of our children through the sharing of cultural and linguistic perspectives and by exposing others to ideas outside of their own understanding.

Subsequent research, including the British Academy's Born Global project, which reported in 2016, have emphasised the UK's need for languages in business and society (see Chap. 6). Our community language speakers and learners constitute a considerable, valuable and ready resource to help us meet the challenges of the future. The challenge for our society is to find ways to ensure that young people and adults who are fortunate enough to know a second language are nurtured and supported. If this happens, then we will all realise the benefits that such language knowledge can bring.

The Current Challenging Climate

Despite the manifest benefits to learning a language and to investing in our community language learners, supplementary schools operate in increasingly challenging circumstances. Much of the government support and sources of funding for community-based language classes have been reduced or have disappeared entirely. This includes national initiatives which comprised the support of community-based language teaching in their work, such as Routes into Languages or CILT, the former National Centre for Languages. Local government support projects are also subject to drastic cuts. As we have seen, community-based language learning is already heavily reliant on charitable work and the input of enthusiastic volunteers. Every year, even more is asked of these supporters. The RSA's recent research highlights the danger to the existence of supplementary schools from shrinking funds and 'volunteer fatigue' (Nwulu 2015).

In addition to this climate of austerity, many qualifications in community languages have been withdrawn (e.g. A levels and GCSEs as well as qualifications in the Asset Languages programme). This removes an important incentive for pupils to continue with community languages to a high level, and downgrades the importance of knowing community languages. Alongside the loss of qualifications, which would add prestige and value to language knowledge, there are challenges around the implementation of exams in many community languages. The exams can be expensive to run unless there is a high number of students taking them; appropriately qualified examiners can be hard to find; and exam papers in foreign scripts are at a higher risk of containing errors (Steer 2015). Access to exam centres can also depend on the size of the local student cohort, with students having to travel to different towns or regions of the UK if they wish to sit an exam in their particular community language.

Sensible discussion of the challenges facing community-based language learning is often complicated by issues around identity, politics and race. Advocating support for the learning of heritage languages spoken in the wider community can be politically charged. In this context, languages spoken in the community might be perceived as a threat to the importance of the English language. This is a false perception: while some supplementary schools teach English, the majority of community-based language learners are children growing up speaking English fluently, educated through UK educational systems, with an intimate, lived experience of UK culture. Let us be clear: when we talk about supporting the learning of community languages, we are mostly talking about learning and developing a second language: a language in addition to English.

Governmental leadership on language learning and a strategic vision which incorporated community-based languages would help to address these challenges by encouraging society to value the language knowledge in the people around us, developing processes and qualifications to support language knowledge and creating mechanisms to develop the sustainability of community-based learning and teaching.

A Case Study of Community Language Learning: Southampton

The city of Southampton is in Hampshire, on the south coast of the UK. It is one of the UK's major commercial ports and it has a population of about 250,000 people. Its long history as a port city means that it has always attracted a diverse population. I have been closely involved with community language learning in the Southampton area for some years. The situation in Southampton is typical of the situation across much of the UK: there are a number of community–based language classes reflecting the ethnic mix of the region including classes for Polish, Hindi, Punjabi, Russian, Persian, German and Italian. There is no 'one size fits all' description for any of the classes, pupils or teachers: in some cases, language learning goes on in formalised school-like structures featuring a number of classes, trained teachers and well-resourced settings. In other cases, classes are given by an untrained, enthusiastic volunteer who rents space on a weekly basis in a local school or community centre. Language classes are also run by religious institutions, churches, mosques or temples, or by other local organisations or schools. Many of our classes in Southampton are hosted by local schools, who rent space and facilities to community classes.

Community language teachers work in a challenging environment with limited access to teaching resources and materials. They often have little teacher training and have full-time responsibilities alongside their volunteer work. They deliver their language classes at weekends and out of hours. They often create their own materials and frequently at their own cost. In addition, pupil needs, skills and abilities are dazzlingly diverse. Some pupils can neither speak, understand nor write their heritage language; others can speak but not write; others have knowledge of the written language but limited experience in speaking—and amongst this diversity, all levels are represented. It is entirely possible to have, in one class, pupils ranged in age from 6 to 16, and language skills (in speaking, writing, reading and listening) from beginner to advanced. Contrary to expectation perhaps, these challenges often combine to make community language classes inspiring places: pupils are typically motivated and keen to learn and achievement rates are high. Due to the diverse nature of the pupil cohort, teaching is often inherently personalised and rich, with a high use of authentic materials. Where skill levels are diverse, teachers also often involve pupils in peer teaching, which generates learning experiences valuable to all involved.

In common with the national picture, funding for community-based language classes in Southampton has shrunk over the last six years. For over 25 years, to 2012, the city council maintained a community languages service that was co-ordinated by a dedicated council employee; it offered premises for teaching, organised the training of teachers and provided teaching materials and a small honorarium for each teacher. This co-ordinated service included the county of Hampshire and the city of Portsmouth within its remit. At its height, it saw nearly 1300 pupils a year, awarded annual certificates for achievement, funded an exam programme and ran classes in nearly 20 languages. Cuts to local government funding have meant that the service—as a co-ordinated activity—has ended, but many of the classes remain. Within the city of Southampton, the classes that have survived have done so due to increased efforts from volunteers, and a shared-cost model which sees parents paying some costs while the city council pays for room rental. Sympathetic local schools assist by hosting classes on their premises at the weekends. Inevitably, where community groups are larger and have access to sources of funding, language classes continue. However, community groups, which are smaller in size and less well-established financially, often cannot sustain the costs of running language classes and so the classes die away. It is no coincidence that this latter trend is likely to affect the most disadvantaged groups and children in society.

The benefit of a locally co-ordinated service was that a collective approach meant that all languages and groups in the city could be supported regardless of their individual abilities to pay. Another benefit was the ability to collect data about the classes in order to measure their uptake, exam entry numbers, impact and success. In other words, it is not only more difficult to deliver good quality classes, but it is more difficult to manage and co-ordinate the classes that do exist to make a case for support to potential funders, local government and the general public. The excellent work of teachers and pupils is becoming less and less visible. The loss of leadership, co-ordination and funding has fragmented community language support, and rising costs mean that the classes are endangered again. Parents, teachers and pupils in the city are once more searching for solutions as to how community language classes can continue to exist.

Despite the gloomy economic situation and challenging diversity of the community language classes, there is one shining factor which unites teachers, parents, pupils and other supporters: a love and appreciation for education. An irresistible desire for our young people to develop their skills and abilities to the very best level possible—and to work through any obstacle to help them do this. I am continually impressed and humbled by the dedication of parents, teachers and community groups to the education of their children in the face of relentless challenges. The times may be tough, but the dynamism and energy of community language teachers, parents and pupils, will ensure that the classes find a way to go forward.

Conclusion

The pattern in Southampton of collaboration between schools, local councils, community groups and dynamic, enthusiastic volunteers is repeated in many cities and regions across the UK and it is a model that we can learn from. The IPPR report *Saturdays for Success* (Ramalingam and Griffith 2015) recommends greater coordination between mainstream and supplementary schools, with both sectors learning from the successes and excellent practice found in each other. If language learning is to survive and expand in the UK, we need to consider flexible and innovative models of working, and include all sectors delivering language education in the discussion. At a time when fewer pupils are choosing to learn languages in mainstream schools, we need to find a range of ways to provide opportunities for language education.

It would be useful to see the development of a national language policy that reflects the diversity and range of languages in the UK and unequivocally prizes language knowledge. Too often, I hear children and adults belittling their own language skills or those of others: 'Oh I speak Hindi but I don't write it', 'I can understand German but I can't really speak it' or 'My Dad speaks Thai, but I only know a few words.' The possession of linguistic and cultural knowledge is a source of pride. We need to harness and make use of that knowledge and there is a simple way to do it: create environments that support and enable language classes to flourish, and give financial and vocal assistance to community language classes that do exist. There is a powerful symbolic value in how public funds are allocated and even a small amount of funding would convey legitimacy to community-based schools and reflect how they are valued by society. My own experience has shown me that a small amount of resource can go a very long way. At a time when it is widely acknowledged that the UK needs more linguists, it is perverse to ignore the language skills and knowledge held by the diverse groups within our communities.

The volunteer teachers, the charitable foundations and supporters of community-based language classes are the unsung heroes of language teaching and learning in the UK. Their energy and excellent work in the service of our children's education goes largely unpraised and unrecognised, as does the impact of their work on children's literacy and educational attainment. If our education system aspires to encourage children to explore and develop their individual abilities and skills, then we need to find ways of supporting and sustaining heritage languages and cultural knowledge. Forcing a monolingual, monocultural straitjacket of English onto children hurts all of us. Language skills give access to cultural knowledge and educated, culturally adept people benefit all of society. They prepare the UK to meet the challenges of internationalisation for business, society and education, and to realise the opportunities of our digital, interconnected and globalised world. Community language learners and teachers contribute a great deal to our society and it is time that we recognised this and that we gave them the encouragement and support that they richly deserve.

References

British Academy. (2016). *Born Global.* http://www.britac.ac.uk/born-global.

John Lyon's Charity. http://www.johnlyonscharity.org.uk/initiatives/schools/. Accessed 26/08/2017.

Leca, I. (2016). Lifespan Multilingual Education, a Long-Term Investment. *European Journal of Language Policy, 8*(1). doi:https://doi.org/10.3828/ejlp.2016.3.

McPake, J., & Sachdev, I. (2008). *Community Languages in Higher Education: Towards Realising the Potential.* Southampton: Routes into Languages.

National Association of Teaching English and Community Languages to Adults (NATECLA). http://www.natecla.org.uk/content/478/Community-languages. Accessed 26/08/2017

National Resource Centre for Supplementary Education (NRCSE). http://www.supplementaryeducation.org.uk/. Accessed 10/02/2017

Nwulu, S. (2015). *Beyond the School Gates—Developing the Roles and Connections of Supplementary Schools.* A Report for The Royal Society for the Encouragement of Arts, Manufactures and Commerce (RSA) Investigate-Ed Series. https://www.thersa.org/discover/publications-and-articles/reports/beyond-the-school-gates.

Office of National Statistics: Languages in the UK. (2011). Data from the 2011 National Census, article released online March 2013. https://www.ons.gov.uk/peoplepopulationandcommunity/culturalidentity/language/articles/languageinenglandandwales/2013-03-04

Ramalingam, V., & Griffith, P. (2015). *Saturdays for Success: How Supplementary Education Can Support Pupils from All Backgrounds to Flourish.* Report for the Institute for Public Policy Research (IPPR). http://www.ippr.org/publications/saturdays-for-success.

Steer, P. (2015). Cambridge Assessment, Blogpost on Language Qualifications 'Why We Can't Go on Like: This Language Qualifications in the UK.' http://cambridgeassessment.org.uk/insights/why-we-cant-go-on-like-this-language-qualifications-in-the-uk/.

The Paul Hamlyn Foundation. http://www.phf.org.uk/. Accessed 26/08/2017

Von Ahn, M., Lupton, R., Greenwood, C., & Wiggins, D. (2010). *Languages, Ethnicity, and Education in London* (DoQSS Working Paper No. 10–12). Institute of Education University of London. http://repec.ioe.ac.uk/REPEc/pdf/qsswp1012.pdf.

17

Language Learning by Different Means: Formal and Informal Developments

Tim Connell

Informal Language Learning

The British have a bad reputation as linguists and regularly appear at the bottom of international lists of language learners.[1] That is just not sustainable in a post-Brexit world. And yet historically colonial officers were required to learn local languages, and until fairly recently a modern language and even Latin were requirements for university entry.

Many people now regret not having learnt a language properly (or at all) at school. Even Australian students sign up for Japanese classes while they are in London, as they did not pay attention to learning it while they were at school in the same way that the British tend to regret having overlooked French. However, on top of the decline in formal language learning there are also cuts in language classes in further education, arising from pressures on the sector and changes in funding.[2] Organisations such as the Royal Society of Arts or the London Chamber of Commerce have dropped their own specific foreign language examinations,[3] although

T. Connell (✉)
City, University of London, London, UK

© The Author(s) 2018
M. Kelly (ed.), *Languages after Brexit*,
https://doi.org/10.1007/978-3-319-65169-9_17

various alternatives have emerged for students at post-compulsory education level, adult learners and those who do not wish to take GCSE or A level as a formal qualification. It is also possible that in their particular circumstances they wish to focus on speaking and listening, perhaps reading, but with no particular interest in acquiring accurate writing skills. In such cases informal learning can be part of an ongoing process: someone may learn a particular language simply because it is on offer at school or college; then they find they have a need to come back to it for reasons of travel, family or work. Nor may they have an interest in acquiring formal qualifications as this would often mean enrolling in formal classes at regular times at the same time of year, something which may not be possible for personal, professional or family reasons.

Those involved in formal modes of delivery need to be aware of both the benefits and challenges of more informal styles of learning as resources may now be selected to meet individual interests or needs. And they can of course be mixed with the formal—especially as the number of teaching hours has been steadily reduced by many universities. In addition there is an increasing demand in universities for the so-called Institution-Wide Language Programmes (IWLPs) which allow students to register for language study either as an add-on to their degree or as a freestanding subject. University HEFCE data shows that enrolments for undergraduate language degrees declined by 36% between 2003 and 2014, with post-1992 institutions suffering a 55% decrease over the same period.[4] This decline has even caused entire language departments at some universities to close while many have reduced the variety of language programmes available. On the other hand the figures for students taking IWLPs have more than doubled in a decade and are currently estimated at over 60,000, appreciably more than the 39,000 enrolled on full-time language degrees.

Technology Today

Informal methods of learning have become an increasingly valuable tool as the technology has advanced—not only with the power of computing but also with provision such as e-books and online sources, which make the internet an indispensable part of both private and public life. Nor should the impact of social media be underestimated, with advances in the sharing of content between individuals and the level of interaction with other users worldwide.

Gone now are the dusty, bulky tomes of yesteryear. Publishers have taken their dictionaries and encyclopaedias online or made them available as CDs and there is a plethora of multilingual dictionaries out there. The instant-translate or -interpret market is becoming highly competitive, with an increasing number of apps available. Individual travellers may not have got into sharing earbuds or passing their iPhones backwards and forwards yet, but it is not unknown in Japan for a friendly member of staff to be carrying an iPad with a link to an interpreter to assist hapless Western visitors. More and more languages are becoming available on such apps (iTranslate handles 80 languages).[5]

The young in particular have become adept in the use of personal handheld equipment, which seems to be advancing in sophistication and power at a remarkable rate. Recent advances include small devices that will translate short phrases by using Bluetooth technology which then connects to Google Translate.[6] More recently Bluetooth earphones have appeared which are designed to link up conference calls and which are claimed to operate at conversational speed in 37 languages.[7] Japanese hi-tech firm NTT Docomo has created a pair of augmented reality spectacles that will translate menus, timetables or whatever documents are being viewed, to be launched in time for the Tokyo Olympics in 2020.[8] This is likely to be a pivotal time in the development of facilities for online language support as Japanese, Chinese and Korean offer particular challenges there will be a clear demand for such languages in future, and scope for further development in this area.

Modern technology gives us the chance to personalise learning in terms of level, pace and content plus an opportunity to establish contact with native speakers and to rehearse real-life situations, covering anything from choosing from menus through to making travel enquiries and learning about places to visit. Informal media may be used simply for reinforcing the classic elements of language learning, such as memorisation, repetition, listening and responding. That does, however, give rise to the danger of applying nineteenth-century pedagogy to twenty-first-century technology. It may therefore be necessary to develop new practical skills in order for people to make full use of that technology—especially in the case of older users (who can still remember technology of the sort that had a key in the side). It is important for them not only to become self-reliant in the use of such equipment as it becomes available but also to have the confidence to search online for suitable material and to know how to make the best use of it.[9]

Informal learning is a valuable means of support also at higher levels. Networking is not the only valuable resource offered online. For professionals, and freelance workers in particular, internet resources can not only keep them in touch with fellow workers in the same field and keep them up to date with developments in their particular field, but will also give them access to CPD information and even online courses. Maintaining standards and informal upskilling are other possibilities.[10] The Chartered Institute of Linguists, for example, offers webinars, videos and training courses as part of its eCPD programme, available for experienced linguists, newcomers and examination candidates.[11] The whole approach to translation at professional level has changed in recent years, with some debate as to whether online translation programs should be used either exclusively or in support of the human input. Software like TRADOS, MemoQ 2015 or cloud-based technologies are now essential translation tools.[12]

The Right Material

It is also incumbent on publishers and writers to take informal learning into account when producing new material, something which, fortunately, has begun to happen. The long-standing Teach Yourself series covers the mainstream languages of French, German, Italian and Spanish—plus 63 other languages, ranging from Afrikaans to Zulu. Participants can join study groups that will allow them to review fellow learners' work and receive feedback. Or there is the online language community called Open Road, which puts learners in touch with each other. It provides information about travel and culture as well as language.[13] The British Council Connecting Classrooms project goes even further and links schools across the world, providing all sorts of opportunities for teachers and learners to develop a wide range of skills.[14] Classic providers such as Berlitz are also up to date with an array of group courses, crash courses, one-to-one teaching and cultural consulting, whilst eBerlitz offers a virtual classroom, and blended learning with cyber-teachers.[15]

Learning and Testing

Flexible learning may also entail flexible testing. Many further education colleges will offer part-time courses leading to GCSE or A levels, but then the number of languages being offered by examination boards has declined, although the recently revised A levels will now include 12 non-traditional languages which are defined as 'smaller cohorts'.[16] However, there will be no spoken component for these because of the practical difficulties of arranging oral exams. Oral development will still be encouraged but not assessed, though there will be orals for French, German, Spanish, Chinese, Italian and Russian, some of which are languages frequently used by ethnic groups in the UK.[17]

There are opportunities in the mainstream languages for examinations which are outside the standard UK offering. The principal cultural institutes such as the Institut Français, the Instituto Cervantes, the Goethe Institute, the Japan Foundation and (more recently) the Confucius Institute with its HSK exam all offer examinations which are calibrated to the Common European Framework (CEFR) and have the advantage of being recognised internationally, and particularly in the target country.[18]

But how do informal learners know what their level of language is? There is a need here for a straightforward online test, supplemented by an oral interview via Skype in particular for people who have lived or worked abroad, have family connections or who own a property abroad. The European Language Portfolio and the Language Passport did set out to provide a recognised form of certification but the system was not taken up widely.[19] The BBC still has a handy page on its website, though it has not been updated since 2014.[20] (Given its venerable ancestry, language provision via the BBC should be revived!) The Open University gives assistance to potential students as to which intermediate level they should opt for in the languages that it offers.[21]

This illustrates a problem arising from the developments in adult language learning in particular, and the fact that it tends to be provided at beginners and intermediate levels only. The Foreign Office does, however, examine languages for diplomats going to serve abroad up to CEFR level C1 (Operational) and C2 (Extensive) within the CEFR.[22] Employers in particular see a need for language skills at the higher levels. They are also concerned that a proliferation of qualifications makes it difficult for them to understand quite what specific language skills a candidate might have and to what level, although most qualifications nowadays seem to be mapped on to the CEFR. It would help if there could be greater standardisation in the production of certificates, so that these state clearly the individual levels of attainment within particular skills in such a way that they can be understood by non-linguists. An authoritative website outlining the language qualifications available with a note on relative levels would also be useful in the same way that the NARIC website provides data on foreign qualifications and skills.[23]

The Potential of the Heritage Language

Herein lies a massive potential input of linguistic skills to national life, as demonstrated in the 2011 Census, which was the first to incorporate a question on languages.[24] Twenty main languages were identified, though it was acknowledged that over 100 are in use in some London boroughs.[25] This is no longer simply a matter of immigration, or languages being spoken by the second or third generation. The 2011 Census identified a growing trend in mixed marriages and a high proportion of children under the age of 16 with a mixed family background.[26] There are however some difficulties to be overcome before this linguistic diversity can be put to good use in a post-Brexit world. Children from a bilingual family background tend to have a high degree of oral fluency in a domestic register, but one which will not be adequate in a professional context, especially if a non-Roman alphabet is involved. Suitable materials and learning opportunities are needed to take Britain beyond the standard language sets of French, German or Spanish, plus other languages which generate a lower level of interest such as Italian, Russian, Japanese or even Korean.

(Chinese is in a separate category with increasing rates of growth, though of course many people in the UK will be speakers of Cantonese rather than Mandarin.)

Important work is being done in supplementary schools, of which there are now between 3000 and 5000 nationwide.[27] A process of formalisation has been taking place, coming from within communities and informal support organisations, which appears to be moving towards greater recognition of these schools from mainstream schools and local authorities as they are perceived to be filling a gap and providing a useful social, cultural and educational service which could only be filled with some difficulty by mainstream organisations. It is interesting to note that supplementary schools (which are being referred to increasingly as 'complementary' schools as their function changes) are beginning to cater for teenagers and adults, some of whom are returning to their heritage language, which they never learnt as children, or who wish to make contact with relatives in the country of origin.[28]

The numbers involved are quite striking and the languages covered tally with calculations as to which languages will be of commercial or strategic importance in future: these include Arabic, Persian/Dari, Hindi and Malay as well as Spanish and Portuguese for the Hispanic and Lusophone worlds.[29] There are some disadvantages, however, in the current rather informal approach to the languages concerned, namely standards and recognition. Work is going on to train teachers to meet national standards, but there is still a dearth of teaching material if these languages are to be used in a professional context, and testing needs to go beyond the 'smaller cohort' languages being offered at A level. The Chartered Institute of Linguists does offer bespoke examining (which can be arranged in over 50 languages), or the recently launched Certificate in Language Skills for Business could also be used.[30]

Conclusion

There is a growing awareness that with Brexit the UK will need to look to the wider world for new markets (unless we wish to export exclusively to the cricket-playing countries), so that skills in languages which have not hitherto been taught in schools and only rarely in universities will be a definite advantage. We will also have to defend ourselves more in Europe, though it is most unlikely that English will cease to be used in Brussels post-Brexit. The possibility has been mooted, as neither Ireland nor Malta have declared English as their national language and the rules do not currently allow for second official languages, even though minority languages are firmly encouraged.[31]

For those who believe that all foreigners should speak English, there are doubts as to whether English will maintain its current dominance worldwide, given the power of the internet and the growing practice of putting a row of flags on the home page of a website. In a report for the British Council, the author David Graddol also questions whether English will maintain its global dominance in future and argues that there are already indications that its influence is beginning to decline.[32] Instead he foresees a world in which trading blocs will form worldwide in which certain languages will be of particular value. This may be the case with the BRICs,[33] but the slowdown in some economies and political difficulties in some of the countries concerned suggest that the matter is by no means clear-cut, though other country groupings, such as the CIVETs, may well appear in future.[34]

Given the need for language skills in a far wider range of languages than hitherto, there is a need for informal language learning to be formalised to a far greater extent. The withdrawal of mainstream examining boards from a wide range of languages suggests that there should be a more directed approach at government level, giving more scope to those organisations which are willing and able to provide assessment both for the language and the areas of specialisation that might be required.

Arguably, with Brexit the world is our linguistic oyster. But this means that there is an urgent need to stem the decline in language capability in order to meet new challenges worldwide. The decision of the BBC to add 11 new languages to its World Service offering will hopefully reach out to new societies and economies, and provide a useful source of listening comprehension to people in this country who wish to listen in.[35] But to use the language appropriately and to maximise any advantage means knowing how to work with different cultures, an important topic which is not always as closely linked in to language learning as it should be. Simply watching Scandi Noir films on a Saturday night is just not enough!

Notes

1. http://ec.europa.eu/public_opinion/archives/ebs/ebs_386_en.pdf.
   See also http://ec.europa.eu/eurostat/statistics-explained/index.php/Foreign_language_learning_statistics.
2. In 2008 the government introduced ELQs (Equivalent or Lower Qualifications), whereby students in higher or further education would not receive a government fee subsidy if they were taking a subject at a lower level than their highest qualification. See http://www.hefce.ac.uk/lt/elqs/.
3. The RSA merged with Oxford and Cambridge in 1998 to form the OCR Examinations Board and the LCCI discontinued its respected FLIC programme—Foreign Languages for Industry and Commerce.
4. The number of students enrolling for languages as a first degree fell by 16% between 2007–8 and 2013–14, from 9550 to 8030. See *Born Global* (British Academy 2016) especially the Preamble and page 7: *http://www.britac.ac.uk/born-global*.
5. itranslateapp.com. Just put 'translation apps' into Google for many more examples.
6. Sigmo covers 25 languages—and was developed with crowdfunding.
   See https://www.indiegogo.com/projects/sigmo-talk-understand-in-more-than-25-languages#/.
7. For example: Mymanu Clik at https://mymanu.com/mymanu-clik/.
   Read more at http://www.stuff.tv/news/mymanus-clik-wireless-earbuds-are-real-life-babel-fish#tEIRFSzYZeBla2gl.99we.
8. See http://www.telegraph.co.uk/technology/news/10344580/Augmented-reality-glasses-translate-foreign-menus-as-you-read.html. Google Translate also has Word Lens, which will do much the same thing.
9. See Agnes Kukulska-Hulme, 'Re-Skilling Language Learners for a Mobile World', on the website of The International Research Foundation for English Language Education (Monterey, CA, 2013).
   See http://www.tirfonline.org/english-in-the-workforce/mobile-assisted-language-learning/.

10. See 'The Tablet Interpreter' by Alexander Drechsel in *The Linguist* 56.2 (2017), 16–17.

11. See ciol.org.uk/cpd/webinars.

12. See http://www.translationzone.com/ for Trados and also https://www.memoq.com/en/memoq-2015.

13. See https://www.teachyourselflanguagesonline.com/.

14. See https://schoolsonline.britishcouncil.org/about-programmes/connecting-classrooms.

15. See http://www.berlitz.co.uk/language_training/for_companies/.

16. Arabic, Bengali, Gujarati, Modern Greek, Modern Hebrew, Japanese, Panjabi, Persian, Portuguese, Polish, Turkish and Urdu.

17. See https://www.gov.uk/government/uploads/system/uploads/attachment_data/file/596783/MFL-smaller_cohort_A_level_subject_content_government_response.pdf.

18. A simple search on the appropriate website will bring up all the information required.

19. See http://www.coe.int/en/web/portfolio/the-language-passport.

20. See http://www.bbc.co.uk/languages/, covering French, German, Italian and Spanish. Although still accessible, it was archived in 2014.

21. See http://fels.open.ac.uk/language-diagnostics/ Again, the same four languages are covered as for the BBC.

22. In 2016 30 languages were tested by the CIOL at C1 and 12 at C2 for the FCO (figures supplied by the CIOL).
    The Common European Framework details are to be found at: https://www.coe.int/t/dg4/linguistic/Source/Framework_EN.pdf.

23. See http://naric.org.uk/naric/.

24. See https://www.ons.gov.uk/search?q=language.

25. See http://www.standard.co.uk/news/london/census-data-shows-100-different-languages-spoken-in-almost-every-london-borough-8472483.html.

26. See the Office for National Statistics: https://www.ons.gov.uk/peoplepopulationandcommunity/birthsdeathsandmarriages/marriagecohabitationandcivilpartnerships/articles/whatdoesthe2011censustellusaboutinterethnicrelationships/2014-07-03.
    And press reports such as:
    http://www.independent.co.uk/news/uk/home-news/one-in-10-relationships-now-cross-racial-boundaries-9582976.html.

27. See www.supplementaryeducation.org.uk.

28. See www.**natecla**.org.uk. NATECLA (National Association for Teaching English and other Community Languages to Adults) is the national forum and professional organisation for ESOL teachers.

29. David Graddol, *The Future of English?* (British Council, 1997), p. 29. See also the list in: Teresa Tinsley and Kathryn Board (2013) *Languages for the Future* (British Council, 2013), pp. 7–8. https://www.britishcouncil.org/sites/default/files/languages-for-the-future-report.pdf

    The list does not differ markedly from the languages suggested by the *Daily Telegraph*: http://www.telegraph.co.uk/education/9487434/Graduate-jobs-Best-languages-to-study.html?frame=2314809.

30. See http://www.ciol.org.uk/qualifications.

31. An interesting list of world leaders' views and a potted history of UK–EU relations is to be found here: http://www.telegraph.co.uk/news/2016/06/28/english-language-could-be-dropped-from-europe-an-union-after-brex/. There were even suggestions in 2016 that Michel Barnier, the EU's chief negotiator, wanted to conduct the Brexit talks in French: http://www.independent.co.uk/news/world/europe/brexit-negotiator-talks-french-michel-barnier-negotiation-insists-eu-article-50-conducted-a7373556.html.

32. See http://englishagenda.britishcouncil.org/sites/ec/files/books-english-next.pdf.

33. Brazil, Russia, India, China. The acronym BRICs was coined by Jim O'Neill at Goldman Sachs in 2001 (the s is just the plural).

    Scholarships to BRICs countries are to be found at: https://www.topuniversities.com/student-info/scholarship-advice/scholarships-study-brics-countries.

34. Colombia, Indonesia, Vietnam, Egypt, Turkey and South Africa. See http://www.investopedia.com/terms/c/civets.asp.

35. See Philip Harding-Esch in *The Linguist* 56.1 (2017), 25.

18

Translation and Interpreting in a Post-Brexit Britain

Myriam Salama-Carr, Svetlana Carsten,
and Helen J. L. Campbell

The efforts deployed, over the last few decades, by the translation and interpreting community to promote the profession, and the key role it plays in exchanges, have long gone beyond foregrounding the instrumental value of languages in business and global trade exchanges. The wider language community, including researchers, teachers and practitioners, seems to be constantly having to counter the 'widespread underestimation of the significance of language in the production, maintenance, and change of social relations of power' (Fairclough 2001: 1). This significance needs to be highlighted with particular vigour and clarity in the current climate of uncertainty and looming cultural insularity that has followed the UK referendum.

M. Salama-Carr (✉)
University of Manchester, Manchester, UK

S. Carsten
York, UK

H.J.L. Campbell
Brussels, Belgium

Translation, Interpreting and the European Project

The dominance of English as a global language is unlikely to wilt, considering the fact that it has become a lingua franca in many areas of human activity including IT and the sciences. However, employment opportunities for UK graduate linguists, including translators and interpreters, are likely to suffer within the European Union Institutions, which are among their largest employers.

Most translators and interpreters work for the private sector on a freelance basis, but it is their engagement with international and national institutions such as the European Commission and European Parliament, the UN and its agencies, FCO, GCHQ and MoD, which helps give the profession its 'lettres-de-noblesse'. Their affiliation with the professional bodies, such as CIOL, ITI and AIIC,[1] has helped to raise their status to almost the same level as that of other professions, such as engineers, nurses, doctors and architects. The support of EU institutions, both strategic and practical, has been huge over the last decade. The ambitious European Masters in Translation Project is a particularly striking example of collaboration between the EU and universities in the member states to ensure the sharing of good practice. Whilst accounting for the diversity of patterns of training across the EU, the Masters project has helped to develop a template of required components in a translator-training programme.

Following reports of the declining language learning trends in the UK after the removal of languages from the compulsory list of subjects at GCSE in 2004, the Directorates General of Translation and Interpreting at both the European Commission and the European Parliament began lobbying the UK government to improve language policies and invest in language provision. It was felt that the impact of downward trends on Translation and Interpreting courses and on workforce recruitment to language services would be disastrous, especially for the recruitment of linguists with English as their first language. The EU institutions' efforts greatly contributed to the rise of the Routes into Languages programme and the creation of its two associated networks—one for interpreting and the other one for translation. This helped to forge even closer links between EU employers and universities regarding language skills training. The employers were ready and willing to provide expert advice on curricula, hands-on training in relevant skills and work experience. The European Masters in Translation is one example. The Masters model had a precedent in the European Masters in Conference Interpreting Consortium, for which an agreement was signed on 9 May 2001, with the same goals, to set standards and maintain quality of interpreting training in university courses.[2] This blueprint has allowed universities to follow the EU 'approved model' when setting up and running such courses, and continues to do so.

What Future?

At this point in time, two viewpoints could be offered: one highlights the disastrous impact that Brexit is likely to have on the translation and interpreting professions, and the other one is a more optimistic view on job opportunities beyond the EU. With regard to the first point, it would be useful to mention the 'Brexit and Languages' Checklist of the APPG (see Chap. 1) put forward in October 2016 (All-Party Parliamentary Group on Modern Languages 2016). One of the objectives on the checklist calls for 'A commitment to legislate the rights enshrined in the 2010 European Directive on the Right to Interpretation and Translation in Criminal Proceedings', for instance, the right to use one's own language. This Directive has had considerable impact on rendering this type of interpreting more visible and more regulated, albeit with more recent setbacks brought out by cost-cutting measures in the public sector. The more optimistic view would be with regard to the new role that the UK is seeking on the global stage. This new role would make it even more crucial to engage with other linguistic constituencies, which would presumably lead to a greater development of translating and interpreting training in global languages used for new directions (for instance, Arabic, Chinese or Russian, to name only the three official non-European languages of the UN). Such a scenario would lead to an exponential growth of translation and interpreting work.

The main difficulty here when attempting to map possible future developments in the field of translation and interpreting is that the profession is by nature transnational. The use of new technologies, particularly for translators, but increasingly for interpreters too, means that UK businesses commission much of their work from translators based outside the UK, and particularly in the other EU member countries. The opposite is also true: UK-based translators work for clients based outside the UK. All this is facilitated by the principle of freedom of movement for goods and services. Translation and interpreting conferences, whether they focus on academic research or on the challenges and opportunities for the profession, are hardly ever only national. Interpreters cross borders to do their job regardless of their nationality.

So far the reaction from the translation and interpreting industry has been one of concern and disquiet, with a few brave voices urging for optimism in a future which might bring real opportunities in a global cross-continental communication. Professional associations have welcomed the objectives proposed in the APPG Checklist for Government negotiators and officials (Harding-Esch 2016). The objectives listed cover residency status for EU nationals living in the UK, participation in the Erasmus+ programme, rights to translation and interpreting in criminal proceedings and the place of languages in education. All are very relevant to the short- and medium-term future of translation and interpreting.

Translation and Interpreting and English as a Global Language

It is too soon to know what the impact of Brexit will be on translation and interpreting courses offered in the UK. Translation and interpreting are nowadays graduate professions. There is no reason to think that the predicted, and indeed registered, drop in applications from EU students outside the UK, is not going to impact on the financial viability of existing training programmes in the same way as it will impact on all other courses. At present, course leaders only report anecdotal evidence of students withdrawing their applications for interpreting and translating courses. The reasons include a reluctance to study in a post-Brexit Britain, or some concern that withdrawal from the European Union would definitely entail a reduction in the volume of translation and interpreting workflow available to graduates of these courses.

Concerns raised by higher education institutions in general, and translation and interpreting course providers in particular, go well beyond the drop in EU applicants. The visa restrictions imposed on non-EU international students over the last five years, as well as Brexit anti-immigration rhetoric, have caused much anxiety in higher education. To quote a student recruitment consultancy, Hobsons, '30 per cent [of international students] said they were not likely to come to the UK, while six per cent said they would definitely not choose Britain as a study destination as a result of the EU referendum' (Ali 2016). Even before the referendum, the media warned 'Brexit risks international students' recruitment' (Burns 2016).

Paradoxically, while foreign languages in the UK have lost their appeal over the last 15 years, this trend has been counterbalanced by a huge increase in interest in English abroad (see Chaps. 4 and 11, 12, 13, 14, 15). The increase in the number of international students in the UK over that period could partly be explained by the expansion of the EU to the east and by breathtaking developments in information technology which have given the English language an unprecedented world dominance. The 2004 EU expansion made English a 'pivot language' in the EU's interpreting and translation services as it had already become a lingua franca and the most popular language of study in Eastern Europe. This meant that translation and interpretation from less familiar languages, for example Lithuanian, Estonian or Hungarian, was performed into English and then interpreted or translated from English into all the other languages of the EU. An ever-growing number of international trainees flocked to the UK to improve their active English and enhance their job opportunities.

To put this into an economic context, the recent parliamentary briefing on 'International Students and Immigration' estimated that in 2011–12 non-EU students made a £7.3 billion contribution to UK GDP (£9.1 billion when EU students are included), reaching around £9 billion in 2014–15, 'and supported 137,000 FTE jobs across the UK (170,000 when EU students are included)' (Universities UK 2016). We can forecast that Brexit will have a large-scale impact on universities and colleges, in particular on already depleted UK modern languages departments and on translation and interpreting training provision. It is unclear how UK universities, modern language departments and interpreting and translation training courses could possibly gain. Of course, English will still be in use but what might well follow is that the highly specialised, high-register, sophisticated English language skills normally performed by native English speakers will be more frequently performed by non-native speakers who learn English in their own countries and enhance it through the means of social media and the internet. One only hopes that the command of English of such linguists will be much better than that of their ministers who choose to speak it instead of their mother tongue, just to save on the interpreting services which are available to them. For pragmatic reasons and as a lingua franca, English will continue to be used within the walls of the EU, in meetings and debates. However, our EU partners in interpreting services suspect that the regime of languages might be adjusted as the English constituency will be much reduced, comprising just the Irish and Maltese. Interestingly, a formal application to include English as an official EU language will have to be made, since only the UK had requested this, in 1973. Each member state may notify one official language, thus Ireland—several years after its accession to the EU—requested Irish and Malta, on accession, requested Maltese, making English, officially at any rate, redundant, or no longer accepted after the UK leaves. At any rate, changes to the EU language regime must be agreed upon unanimously by the Council of Ministers, making the removal of English from the official languages unlikely, albeit not impossible. In addition, English would remain a working language even if stripped of its 'official' status.

The real threat of job losses in the EU will be for English-speaking *fonctionnaires*, but job opportunities for freelance interpreters and translators will remain strong since English is unlikely to disappear. And yet, if UK courses are not producing sufficient number of skilled linguists, other nationals will be recruited to perform services which in the past would have been done by native English speakers. Course providers continue receiving messages, from the European Parliament in particular, about the EU's need for strong English-speaking linguists with two or three passive languages from which they can work. However, such jobs will be available on a freelance basis only. Of course there will be a need for work outside the EU but would there be enough course providers in the UK to train in the needed skills? That remains to be seen. But that does not mean the world will stop speaking English. To quote Simon Keper of the *Financial Times,* who was referring to the recent hacking scandal concerning the US election: 'The English language used to be an asset of the US and UK. Now it has become a weakness …' 'The US has just been outsmarted by foreigners it didn't understand. Britain may be next' (Kuper 2017).

Kuper further refers to the asymmetry of knowledge between English-speaking countries and their rivals, and the consequent ease with which such rivals can hack into US and UK systems—because they understand the language. As he puts it, 'being an English-speaking country is like living in a glass house; it makes you transparent'. It is not difficult to see how important it has become for Chinese and Russian elites to send their children to British and American universities: the numbers have increased each year, despite the high cost for international students. According to Project Atlas, in 2006 14.5% of the overseas students enrolled in UK universities were from China, and in 2015 that number had increased to 19.1%.[3] On the positive side, *The Independent* reported that there has been an increase in the number of UK students choosing to study Chinese (Pells 2016). This at least suggests an interest in other countries and by definition, their languages, so while the intake of British students applying to study European (and generally perceived as easier) languages has been dropping over the last 15 years, insofar as we can guess, the number of those interested in global languages, particularly Chinese, look set to increase. It is possible that a system of visas will be introduced for EU nationals once the UK leaves, and the threat of visa restrictions is a major concern, both for EU nationals wanting to come to Britain and for British students hoping to spend all or part of their studies in an EU country. The higher education community has appealed for the adoption of a pragmatic approach to dampen down the impact of Brexit.

Catherine Barnard, professor of EU law at the University of Cambridge, who appeared before the House of Commons Education Committee recently, proposed: 'If you accept the argument that higher education is one of the jewels in the crown of the British system, then what might the government do to protect higher education? One way would be to have a sector-specific deal which continues with free movement [for students and academics] much on the terms that we've got at present.'[4]

Alas, all such propositions are based on guesswork until the negotiations are completed. Questions and theories abound, but the simple answer to them all is 'no one knows' as Jonathan Faull, European Commission Director-General and former head of the Task Force for Strategic Issues related to the UK Referendum, stated publicly in Brussels recently. It would be fanciful to predict the outcome of these complicated and difficult negotiations. One cannot help but regret that the general public voted on something that most had little idea of, and were swayed mainly by the tabloids in making their decisions. For, as Mr Kuper also underlines: 'the twin centres of political power, Westminster and the tabloid newspapers are almost entirely monolingual and British voters were entirely unaware of how other EU countries would respond to the vote to leave.'

Looking for a moment to possible future developments and the likely repercussions of Brexit for linguists, starting with the European Union institutions, we see a continuing trend in translation towards post-editing and revision as opposed to 'pure' translation. This is nothing new: it has been in evidence since the 2004 enlargement in particular and will increase further, as English is used for most communication purposes in the EU, informally among staff and in written texts, both official and informal. Reports are written by staff of all EU nationalities chiefly in English, which needs correcting or 'revising' to a greater or lesser extent depending on the linguistic abilities of the author. The language is no doubt acceptable for the purposes of comprehension but it is a draft, a guideline, not a polished, English version that is fit for purpose, whether that be for a Draft Regulation, or Directive, a Recommendation or even for a text to be circulated through one or more institutions.

What this means is a lot more work for future English-language staff, but doing a rather different job from that of the pure 'translator'. It is simply a change, not necessarily negative. For those ready to face up to these new challenges, there will be employment as an in-house official, or, more probably, as a freelance. At present in the European Commission's Directorate-General for Translation there is a cohort of 115 English-language translators and revisers and 15 English-language editors, which will not diminish, and is more likely to increase.

For conference interpreters, there are also many new challenges; indeed, the issue of 'new technologies' for translation and interpreting would deserve a chapter in itself, although both have adapted quickly to the new challenges and skills involved and do not seem to have found technologies a problem. Interpreters, in their relatively more limited area in international organisations or as freelances in the private sector, have adapted quickly to the new landscape. Online conferences, telephone interpreting, video-interpreting and the like are part and parcel of the interpreter's daily life. In addition, as for the translator, the use of English by non-native speakers in meetings has been a challenge for some time. Since English is now the main lingua franca in multilingual meetings, be they in international organisations, the EU, UN and so on, or in the private sector, the job of the interpreter is now to decipher 'global English'. The constant complaint of non-English speaking interpreters is that they are faced with non-native speakers who simply do not speak English well enough to be clear, but who still continue to speak it. It is a problem in both professions and one that needs to be addressed during training.

As Simon Kuper also points out, English is the main language in cyberwarfare, but so far the hacking has tended to be one-sided: i.e. they understand us, we do not understand them, to put it in simple terms. This imbalance is being taken seriously by government agencies, like GCHQ, MI5 and MI6. In particular, as the role of GCHQ becomes more crucial, more staff with languages need to be recruited and trained to fight cyber-attacks. According to the *Sunday Times*, a major attack planned by Russia against the BBC and government websites during the 2015 election was detected in time by GCHQ and thus prevented. These tasks, performed by British linguists, will become increasingly vital as cyberwarfare increases, as it inevitably will.

Finally, a word on the Directive on the right to interpretation and translation in criminal proceedings (2010/64/EU of 20 October 2010), and the Directive on the right to information in criminal proceedings (2012/13/EU of 22 May 2012). These were milestones in terms of human rights and in particular the rights of all citizens, suspected or accused, to interpretation and translation services. It reads:

Translation and interpretation services should be of a quality sufficient to ensure that suspected or accused persons understand the case against them and are able to exercise their right of defense.

To ensure access to qualified legal interpreters and translators, EU countries are asked to set up a register of independent and qualified translators and interpreters which should be available to legal counsels and relevant authorities. Judges, prosecutors and judicial staff involved in criminal proceedings should be trained to communicate efficiently with interpreters.[5]

Such a register, the National Register of Public Service Interpreters, exists in the UK; it is the envy of many.

It is of course to be hoped that this important piece of legislation will continue to apply in the UK after Brexit, and the signs are that it will. In all countries, courts of law are increasingly dealing with cases involving immigrants and asylum seekers. Their rights are therefore to be protected, as are every citizen's, hence the need for more interpreters and translators qualified to work in a legal setting, court of law, police station or immigration centre. The same applies to those working in the health sector. The Chartered Institute of Linguists (CIOL) examinations, awarding (uniquely) the Diploma in Public Service Interpretation and the Diploma in Translation, continue to be the chief qualifications for successful linguists in this area. There have been recent setbacks, notably the decision by the Ministry of Justice to outsource its recruitment, and the widely publicised problems that sprang from it. It is clear to all that *qualified* linguists are not only wanted in such crucial sectors, but are needed, for the sectors to function successfully. The development of public service interpreting, together with the vibrant growth of volunteer translators and interpreters' platforms at a global level, are significant changes that will help with this.

Conclusion

There is a clear rationale for ensuring that the need for translation and interpreting provision is met and for supporting the development of training towards realistic and fulfilling career options. However, as aptly suggested by Adrian Armstrong, Head of the School of Languages,

Linguistics and Film at Queen Mary University of London, it may be that in the current climate an emotional case too needs to be made in defence of languages as a matter of social justice.[6] The centrality of language mediation, and hence of translation and interpreting, can perhaps help reinforce this argument in a world which appears to be increasingly talking in confrontational terms.

Notes

1. These professional bodies are the Chartered Institute of Linguists (CIOL), the Institute of Translation and Interpreting (ITI) and the International Association of Conference Interpreters (AIIC).
2. See the website of the European Masters in Conference Interpreting: http://www.emcinterpreting.org.
3. See the website of Project Atlas: https://www.iie.org/Research-and-Insights/Project-Atlas.
4. See the website of Public Law for Everyone: https://publiclawforeveryone.com/2016/11/04/cambridge-university-brexit-week-talk-the-process-of-leaving-the-eu/.
5. See the text of the 2012 Directive on the right to information in criminal proceedings: http://eur-lex.europa.eu/legal-content/EN/TXT/?uri=celex:32012L0013.
6. See Professor Armstrong's report on the website of UCML January Plenary 2017: Post-Brexit implications for HE languages: http://www.ucml.ac.uk/events/06-01-17.html.

References

Ali, A. (2016, July 29). Brexit: Almost a Third of International Students Less Likely to Come to the UK to Study, Survey Finds. *The Independent*. http://www.independent.co.uk/student/news/brexit-international-students-in-the-uk-after-eu-referendum-hobsons-survey-a7161661.html.

All-Party Parliamentary Group on Modern Languages. (2016). Brexit and Languages: A Checklist for Government Negotiators and Officials. https://www.britishcouncil.org/sites/default/files/appgmfl-mflbrexit_oct16.pdf.

Burns, J. (2016, May 17). Brexit 'Risks International Student Recruitment'. *BBC News*. http://www.bbc.co.uk/news/education-36286057.

Fairclough, N. (2001). *Language and Power* (2nd ed.). Harlow: Longman.

Harding-Esch, P. (2016). Brexit Plea to the Lords. *The Linguist, 56*(6), 6.

Kuper, S. (2017, January 12). The Problem with English. Foreign Countries Are Opaque to Mostly Monolingual Britons and Americans. Foreigners Know Us Much Better Than We Know Them. *Financial Times*. https://www.ft.com/content/223af71a-d853-11e6-944b-e7eb37a6aa8e.

Pells, R. (2016, September 14). Number of British Students Choosing to Study in China Soars. *The Independent*. http://www.independent.co.uk/student/study-abroad/number-of-british-students-choosing-to-study-in-china-soars-a7307261.html.

Universities UK. (2016, November 15). International Students and Immigration. Parliamentary Briefing. http://www.universitiesuk.ac.uk/policy-and-analysis/reports/Documents/2016/international-students-and-immigration.pdf.

19

Language Teacher Supply: The Vicious Cycle, the Effects of the EU Referendum and Attempts to Solve Supply Shortage

René Koglbauer

Introduction

Alea iacta est; the die is cast. With this phrase, I opened a blog post on my initial thoughts on Brexit and its effects on education (Koglbauer 2016) a couple of days after the EU referendum in June 2016. I argued that EU citizens have been part of a solution to the teacher supply crisis. At the time, it became clear quite quickly that the outcome of the EU referendum was to be accepted by the government, despite the later (unsuccessful) attempt by the House of Lords to introduce a number of amendments to the Article 50 bill. Alongside all the political discussions, soon after the referendum, some made the claim that the status of languages in the school curriculum will be reduced in light of the EU referendum. Some language teachers reported that pupils had made comments such as 'Now we are leaving the EU, we won't need to learn French any longer.' Others reported that some pupils challenged them by asking native language teachers, 'Miss, when do you leave the

R. Koglbauer (✉)
Newcastle University, Newcastle, UK

© The Author(s) 2018
M. Kelly (ed.), *Languages after Brexit*,
https://doi.org/10.1007/978-3-319-65169-9_19

country?'; some were even more challenging, 'Sir, I don't have to listen to you. You won't be allowed to stay.' Abuse of foreign-born teachers in general has since been a growing concern for the profession, teaching unions and society in general (NASUWT 2017). In spite of these initial reactions and the experienced or witnessed abuse, those secondary native language teachers who have decided to quit their job and move back to their home countries are few and far between—at least to date. In this chapter, I will argue that EU citizens make a vital contribution to language teaching and learning but they are not the only contributing factor to this multifaceted issue.

The Status of Languages and Language Teacher Recruitment: A Vicious Cycle

Firstly, let's look at the context. Since June 2016, many conferences, symposia, blog posts and press releases have stressed the importance—or even the greater importance—of languages, and therefore also the need for adequate provision for language learning, in light of the EU referendum. Yes, English is widely accepted as a lingua franca: however, if the UK wants to stay competitive on the global stage, it will find that language, communication and intercultural awareness will be essential skills during the two years of negotiation, and then, obviously in the post-EU era. As several chapters in this book have argued, let's assume that we agree that language learning is going to be essential for future generations.

The Department for Education (2013) sets out what could be seen as a clear strategy for language learning in its preamble to the *Languages Programmes of Study* for Key Stages 2 and 3:

> Learning a foreign language is a liberation from insularity and provides an opening to other cultures. A high-quality languages education should foster pupils' curiosity and deepen their understanding of the world. The teaching should enable pupils to express their ideas and thoughts in another language and to understand and respond to its speakers, both in speech and in writing. It should also provide opportunities for them to communicate for practical purposes, learn new ways of thinking and read great

literature in the original language. Language teaching should provide the foundation for learning further languages, equipping pupils to study and work in other countries.

Many of us will be able to relate to and even endorse this strategy or 'wish'. Many of us welcome this commitment to language learning. With all such strategies, though, the proof of the pudding is in the eating, i.e. their implementation.

In England, studying a foreign or ancient language is now compulsory at primary level (from Year 3 onwards). Language learning and teaching feature as a small aspect of most primary initial teacher training courses but the majority of primary trained teachers are generalists rather than specialists, many without foreign or ancient language skills. A good number of generalists have either upskilled their language skills over the years and/or worked closely with primary language consultants, language specialists from local secondary schools or native speakers (often pupils' parents or other relatives). Some schools are able to employ a language specialist as a peripatetic language teacher: others engage with the British Council scheme of Primary Language Assistants,[1] where European primary trainee teachers work in primary schools as language assistants. One of the aims of this scheme is that the classroom teacher(s) will be able to develop their own language skills while working alongside the assistant. The overall picture of language provision at primary level in England is therefore patchy. Although primary trainee places have been oversubscribed in the last couple of years, according to the latest initial teacher training census (Department for Education 2015), without a greater number of generalists specialising in language learning, in my view this patchy provision will unavoidably continue. In addition, while some pupils make immense progress due to their skilled teachers, others might not go beyond word level or might experience an incorrect model of language or even no language progression over the four years at primary school. One way forward would be a required language qualification for primary (trainee) teachers, as suggested in the report into primary language teaching by the Scottish Parliament, European and External Relation Committee (2013). In addition, it might be worth considering a common practice from the

Continent, where language upskilling has become an integral part of primary initial teacher training courses.

The language experience in primary schools will without doubt influence the pupils' opinions of, and motivation for, language learning and their openness towards language learning in the future. Therefore, if we are really dedicated to our overarching strategy of developing our future generation's language skills, we will have to invest in (initial) language teacher education at all levels. In the last couple of years, the shortage of language teachers for secondary schools has definitely been a focus for the government, language associations, school leaders and initial teacher training providers. Despite generous bursary offers for language trainee teachers, the census report (Department for Education 2015) shows that in 2015/16, 13% of training places allocated for secondary language trainees were not filled. For the academic year 2017/18, initial teacher training providers are allowed to over-recruit and additional incentives are being offered to draw language graduates towards the teaching profession, such as 100 language trainee teacher scholarships of £27,500 each, administered by the British Council.

A crisis in language teacher supply is not a new phenomenon in the education landscape. For instance, Convey and Merritt (2000) reported a lack of language teachers in the late 1990s; this contributed to the then government's decision to make languages optional beyond Key Stage 3 in 2004. The current situation is somewhat different. The government's aim has been to strengthen languages through the implementation of the English Baccalaureate, for which a 'good' GCSE in a language is required, along with a GCSE in English, maths, science and either geography or history. The government would have liked to see that 90% of each GCSE cohort would take a language and has put this out for consultation. Should this be implemented within the next few years, we would need thousands of additional teachers. In other words, even if 100% of our language graduates of 2017 went into secondary language teaching, we would not be able to fill the vacancies. Anyway, this is somewhat utopic, as around 6% of language graduates end up in education.

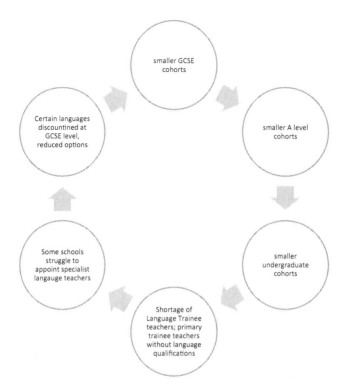

Fig. 19.1 The vicious cycle of language teacher supply

Making languages optional for GCSE in 2004 has led to what I call a vicious cycle of language teaching and language teacher supply (see Fig. 19.1).

The diagram shows that smaller GCSE cohorts trigger a causal effect on language provision in general and on language teacher supply specifically. Although the introduction of the English Baccalaureate bucked the trend of GCSE language entry decline initially, last summer a decline was reported and when we look at the GCSE language entries for summer 2017 a further decrease is expected.

Should the government insist on the English Baccalaureate for 90% of the GCSE cohort, it will be essential that this cycle is broken. This is also important in light of the increased demand for language skills the country is likely to experience in the post-EU era.

Immediate Steps and Mid-Term Solutions

A good number of language departments at UK universities have changed their degree programmes and nowadays offer greater flexibility, with combined honours degrees with languages on offer, as well as *ab initio* language courses. Alongside these developments, some other universities have taken a more radical step, and closed their language departments or parts of them. Through national initiatives such as Routes into Languages, universities have started to work much more closely with schools; collaboration between schools, universities and other stakeholders plays a vital role in tackling the vicious cycle and consequently the language teacher supply issue.

For decades, secondary school language departments have relied not only on home-grown talent but also on those who have come from the Continent or other native-speaking communities. Many stay after one or two successful years as language assistants. It is therefore a common feature in language departments in schools (and universities for that matter) that a good proportion of their teaching staff are EU citizens. In the past the government welcomed EU citizens with open arms, particularly from France and Spain, to reduce the shortage of language teachers. CILT (the now-defunct National Centre for Languages) and later CfBT (now known as the Educational Development Trust) offered bespoke language teacher training programmes for EU nationals. Learning from the past, the Department for Education together with its National College for Teaching and Leadership has identified that a continuous focus and advertising campaign in French-, German- and Spanish-speaking countries is one of many approaches with which to deal with the language teacher supply issue.[2] For instance, the Department for Education is currently planning to pilot an advertising campaign in Spain to recruit Spanish graduates to fill the allocated secondary language trainee places.

On the one hand this demonstrates a commitment to language learning: on the other hand the question emerges of what status these newly recruited trainee teachers will have in a post-EU era, as even the future of EU national language teachers already in the UK is yet to be negotiated. In addition, we will have to ensure that the perceived anti-Europeanism is not leading towards an anti-languages movement as, according to Convey and Merritt (2000), a tendency towards anti-Europeanism in British society, media and parts of the government had contributed to the decline of language learning they noted two decades ago. During the looming negotiations, it will be of importance to ensure that all language teachers employed in UK schools will have a fair and equal deal and that it does not come to an 'us' and 'them' situation. Home-grown teachers and EU nationals, whether trained in the UK and/or in the EU will have to have equal rights, career and professional development opportunities in order to successfully implement the language strategy in their schools and consequently across the country.

Without doubt, it will not be easy. Therefore, speaking from personal experience, I would like to see an induction programme for language teachers trained outside of the UK, whose qualifications are currently accepted for 'Qualified Teacher Status', to provide them with an insight into the ins and outs of the UK school system; to enable them to be fully prepared for the daily challenges and opportunities of language teaching and learning; and to help them to understand the complex and somewhat different daily routines of a teacher in the UK system, including the pastoral responsibilities and the different levels of teachers' accountability. This will, on the one hand, support new arrivals in their first year of teaching in a new and often very different context to that which they are familiar with; on the other hand, it will also reduce the burden on language departments and schools, as their newly appointed language teachers will have a sound understanding of what it means to teach in a British school.

However, these immediate and mid-term attempts at reducing the language teacher supply issue will, in my view, not solve the problem at its roots. The long-term solution is to tackle the vicious cycle, including the language teacher training and professional development for primary level. Next to teacher supply, funding and motivation are aspects that need addressing. Most importantly, and I have been arguing this for years, is the disentangling of pupils' GCSE/A-level results from school performance tables. This has led over the last two decades to the encouragement of 'opt-out' for less able language pupils by senior leaders, career advisors, (language) teachers and parents. If we see languages as a vital skill for the future of our country outside the European Union, it must not become an elite subject. This must be coupled with a greater effort to raise the status of the teaching profession in society, whilst supporting language teachers in their desire to bring language learning alive through trips, foreign exchanges and e-twinning partnerships, and supporting the involvement of foreign nationals, including language assistants, in the enrichment of language learning in UK schools.

Notes

1. For further information, see British Council: *Information to Language Assistants for Primary Schools*: https://www.britishcouncil.org/language-assistants/employ/primary-schools.
2. For further information on Initial Teacher Training see Department for Education website: *Get into Teaching*: https://getintoteaching.education.gov.uk/explore-my-options/training-to-teach-secondary-subjects/training-to-teach-languages.

References

Convey, A., & Merritt, A. (2000). The United Kingdom. In C. Brock & W. Tulasiewicz (Eds.), *Education in Single Europe* (2nd ed., pp. 377–403). London/New York: Routledge.

Department for Education. (2013). *National Curriculum in England: Languages Programmes of Study.* https://www.gov.uk/government/publications/national-curriculum-in-england-languages-progammes-of-study/national-curriculum-in-england-languages-progammes-of-study.

Department for Education. (2015). *Initial Teacher Training Census for the Academic Year 2015 to 2016, England.* https://www.gov.uk/government/uploads/system/uploads/attachment_data/file/478098/ITT_CENSUS_SFR_46_2015_to_2016.pdf.

Koglbauer, R. (2016, June 27). BREXIT—Initial Thoughts on Effects on Our Schools. *BERA* blog. https://www.bera.ac.uk/blog/brexit-initial-thoughts-on-effects-on-our-schools.

NASUWT. (2017, April 14). Teachers Concerned About Impact of BREXIT on Education. NASUWT article. https://www.nasuwt.org.uk/article-listing/teachers-concerned-impact-of-brexit-on-education.html.

The Scottish Parliament, European and External Relation Committee. (2013). *3rd Report, 2013 (Session 4): Foreign Language Learning in Primary Schools.* http://www.parliament.scot/S4_EuropeanandExternalRelationsCommittee/Reports/Foreign_language_learning_in_primary_schools_-_Inquiry_report.pdf.

Part IV

What Can Be Done to Make the UK Language-Ready?

20

Collaboration, Connectedness, Champions: Approaches Within Government

Wendy Ayres-Bennett

In this chapter, I will argue for the need for concerted cross-government action to promote languages in the UK and propose a number of measures to this end. The lack of a coherent government-wide policy for languages was discussed and lamented at a national languages policy seminar held at the University of Cambridge in October 2015, which produced the report, *The Value of Languages*.[1] Fifteen years earlier the final report of the Nuffield Languages Inquiry, *Languages: The Next Generation*, had already included as one of its major findings the fact that 'Government has no coherent approach to languages'.[2] The result of the referendum in June 2016 has given fresh urgency and importance to the issue.

As a specialist in the French language, the absence in the UK of what the French call a *politique linguistique* has always struck me as surprising. Interestingly, the French have felt the need for such a policy for two main

This chapter has been written as part of the AHRC-funded project, 'Multilingualism: Empowering Individuals, Transforming Societies' (www.meits.org) of which I am the Principal Investigator. I am grateful to Philip Harding-Esch of the APPG for Modern Languages for his help in its preparation.

W. Ayres-Bennett (✉)
Murray Edwards College, Cambridge, UK

© The Author(s) 2018
M. Kelly (ed.), *Languages after Brexit*,
https://doi.org/10.1007/978-3-319-65169-9_20

reasons: the need to continue to promote French as a major world language, and the perceived need to defend French against the influence (often described as 'contamination') of English. The *Délégation générale à la langue française et aux langues de France* (General Delegation for the French language and the languages of France or DGLFLF) is:

> a government department whose role is to guide national language policy at inter-ministerial level. Attached to the Ministry of Culture and Communication, the department's role is to examine, pilot and co-ordinate issues, and to track the application of legislative and statutory mechanisms. (Cited from the Presentation of the DGLFLF on the website of the Ministry of Culture and Communication)[3]

As speakers of a global language, the British have been complacent about the value of languages, and languages have not featured highly enough on the political agenda. Whilst there is an effective All-Party Parliamentary Group on Modern Languages (APPG), chaired by Nia Griffith, MP and co-chaired by Baroness Jean Coussins, which has lobbied strongly for modern languages in parliament and beyond,[4] compared to France—where there are high-level government committees looking at language issues and terminological commissions within different ministries—the lack of attention to language issues as part of UK government policymaking is notable.

In its 2014 'Manifesto for Languages', circulated before the 2015 general election, the APPG called for a National Languages Recovery Programme to address the decline of languages and language learning in the UK and its cost to the UK economy and society.[5] It proposed an audit of language skills across the UK civil service and a step change in policy to make commitments towards improving school language learning: a wider recognition of linguists and language skills; wider participation of schoolchildren in language learning; encouragement of the involvement of business and employers including tax breaks and other incentives to train and recruit home-grown linguists; and a commitment to maintaining and developing expertise in modern languages and cultures in the UK university sector. These recommendations for the promotion of foreign languages are still highly pertinent. Indeed, in its 2016 document on

Brexit and languages,[6] the APPG underlined the need for a post-Brexit plan for languages in education, business and the civil service, without which, it argued, the UK will be unable to meet its security, defence and diplomacy requirements.

In this chapter I will focus particularly on cross-government collaboration and the need to adopt a more holistic view of languages and language policy. Here are six recommendations which could help promote a more coherent and integrated approach to language policy in the UK:

1) Languages and language policy should not just be a matter of education policy

In the UK, the question of languages is often conceived as relating predominantly, or even exclusively, to the teaching and assessment of languages, and therefore as a matter for the Department for Education, and possibly Ofsted and the Higher Education Funding Council for England, and their counterparts in the devolved administrations. Whilst education is, of course, essential to the promotion of languages, a narrow focus on languages underplays the vital importance of languages across a wide range of ministries, and this demands a coherent cross-government language policy.

2) A more holistic approach to languages in the UK should be developed

One of the reasons for the association of languages with education is that the focus of policy has often been the teaching of (a small number of) modern foreign languages in schools. In other words, there is often a disjuncture between thinking about foreign language learning and about the language skills of speakers of the indigenous languages of the UK (such as Welsh, Irish, Scottish Gaelic) and of community languages (such as Polish, Punjabi, Urdu, Bengali, or indeed French or Italian). An exception to this is the Army, which, as we will see, is beginning to value language skills whatever their origin. Knowing another language—being multilingual—gives access to culture and cross-cultural understanding; it allows us to view the world through other people's eyes and this cultural agility can be acquired by a monolingual British citizen learning a first or second foreign language, by a citizen who is brought up bilingually, say in English and Welsh, or by someone who acquires English as an additional language. In policy terms, language learning is divided across different departments, each with a different set of priorities and language policies. For example, foreign language learning in England is the responsibility of the Department for Education, whilst languages including Welsh, Scottish Gaelic and Irish are the responsibility of the devolved administrations of Wales, Scotland and Northern Ireland.[7] As for the provision of English language teaching, notably for immigrants, this is partly the concern of the Department for Communities and Local Government (DCLG), with its responsibility for community-based language English language provision; partly a matter for the Department for Education, responsible for ESOL provision (English for Speakers of Other Languages); and partly a question for the Home Office, particularly in terms of visas and immigration. Promotion of the Cornish language has come under the DCLG, although funding for the previous programme stopped in April 2016.

3) **Senior civil servants acting as language officers or language co-ordinators are needed within different Whitehall government ministries and departments and in the devolved administrations of Scotland, Wales and Northern Ireland**

When we started preparing for the National Languages Workshop held in Cambridge in 2015, it was surprising how enquiries to various Whitehall departments about speaking to someone responsible for languages or language policy within that ministry were met either with incomprehension, hesitation or a simple denial that languages were of any interest to that area. Yet the contribution of languages to the UK's economy and society is both rich and varied. It stretches from enabling economic growth and prosperity, through the language and communication skills required to allow UK business to participate in the global marketplace; to the 'soft power' and diplomatic skills through which the UK's role and authority in foreign policy is manifested; to national security, defence and conflict resolution; and to enhancing the cultural capital, educational attainment and social cohesion within England and the devolved communities of the UK. To say nothing of the translation and interpreting services required in legal and health services or in international organisations such as the United Nations. Acknowledging the importance of languages through identifying within each ministry or department a senior civil servant responsible for language policy would have both practical and symbolic value.

4) More collaboration across Whitehall and the devolved governments is required

There is currently a cross-Whitehall language focus group, but not all departments where languages are important to their policy work are represented. In October 2015 it had representatives from the Ministry of Defence, the Foreign and Commonwealth Office, the National Crime Agency, the Metropolitan Police, HM Revenue and Customs, the Department for International Development, the British Council, the Home Office and the Ministry of Justice. It is an operational group reporting to the International Next Generation HR Group, which seeks to find efficiency savings through joint procurement and the pooling of resources. As such, it is a valuable forum for exchanging ideas and sharing best practice and information on training opportunities. On 16 November 2016 Baroness Coussins tabled a written question in the House of Lords 'To ask Her Majesty's Government whether they intend to extend participation in the cross-Whitehall language focus group to more government departments' (HL3284). The reply by Baroness Anelay of St Johns, given on 2 December 2016, was very encouraging: 'The cross-Whitehall Language group was re-launched on 10 November and we are keen to include other government departments who have an interest in, or need for, foreign language skills'.

Collaboration could, however, extend further to the devolved administrations in Scotland, Wales and Northern Ireland, all of which are facing different, but related, challenges. Scotland has launched a 'Mother Tongue plus two' or '1+2' languages policy (*Language Learning in Scotland: A 1+2 Approach*[8]), whilst Wales is promoting a 'Bilingualism (in Welsh and English) + 1' policy (*Global Futures: A Plan to Improve and*

Promote Modern Foreign Languages in Wales 2015–2020[9]): both administrations are grappling with how these can be implemented by the target
date of 2020. In Northern Ireland, the politically charged situation has
hindered the development of policy (see Chap. 14). The lack of a coherent UK policy has been exacerbated in the post-devolutionary context
which, to cite Andrew Hancock (2015: 189) in his study of language
education in Scotland, has given rise to 'language silos' with responsibility delegated to the devolved administrations; the result is 'policy formation and provision [which] has been fashioned separately for different
categories of languages, through a variety of mechanisms, such as legislation, policy statements and individual school or community initiatives
but independent of any comprehensive and integrated national policy for
languages'.

5) To facilitate collaboration across government and raise the profile of languages, champions for languages are required

More champions for languages are required within (and indeed outside) government. It is significant, for example, that there is a Chief
Government Scientist but not a Chief Government Linguist, despite the
very obvious benefits of languages for the economy, security and
well-being of the nation. However, previous experience of when there
was a so-called 'languages tsar' suggests that initiatives of this kind will
only be successful if such an appointment is given well-defined targets,
resources and the authority to be able to make policy decisions. As
National Director for Languages from 2003 on, Lid King was indeed
given a clear set of tasks—including the primary languages programme,
the development and rollout of the Languages Ladder as a national recognition scheme for languages, teacher training and curriculum development around the Key Stage 2 and Key Stage 3 frameworks, and a
promotional campaign aimed at encouraging young people to take up
languages. It is notable, however, that the focus remained in the sphere of
education and the compartmentalisation of government meant that it
was difficult to develop cross-government co-ordination across different
departments, which often had differing language-related priorities.
Funding for these projects was cut in April 2011 as other subjects and

areas of government were prioritised. At the time of writing (June 2017), there are some positive signs: a Senior Champion for Languages has been appointed from the Foreign and Commonwealth Office (FCO) to help co-ordinate language policy across Whitehall. It would be helpful to have a government minister with similar responsibility.

6) Examples of good practice, such as recent initiatives in the armed forces, should be disseminated and used to inform more widespread cultural change

Following the experiences of the conflicts in Afghanistan and Iraq, the Army has come to realise the importance of having personnel with language skills. In a recent House of Lords debate on languages in the armed forces (27 October 2016), arising from a question from Lord Harrison as to 'whether the United Kingdom has sufficient speakers of foreign languages serving the Armed Forces and defence services', the Minister, Earl Howe, spoke of the importance now attributed to languages: 'The Army now insists that officers must have a survival level of speaking and listening to a foreign language prior to the appointment of command at the rank of major'.

In response to a question from Baroness Coussins as to whether the measures adopted by the Army would be extended across the services, the reply was equally encouraging: 'the answer is yes. All measures that I have highlighted are common across all defence personnel, both regular and reserve, and the language competency award schemes are in play here. We are [...] conducting a 100% audit of all personnel with a latent language skill'.

I will focus here on three possible lessons that could be learnt and applied more generally. First, as well as offering MOD training in languages as required through the Defence Centre for Languages and Culture (DCLC), the Army is conducting an audit of language skills through the Defence Requirements Authority for Culture and Languages (DRACL). Language examination results are recorded as a competence for three years, which can be utilised, at short notice, for operations or urgent tasks. Such an audit across the whole civil service would be invaluable, but in response to a written question tabled by Baroness Coussins on 15 November 2016: 'To ask Her Majesty's Government whether they are planning to conduct a language skills audit across the whole civil service; and if so, whether they will publish the results' (HL3198), the reply from Baroness Chisholm of Owlpen was that there were no plans for this.

Second, there is a 'Whole Force' approach to the issue. Army personnel are encouraged to come forward to have their language skills assessed, whether these have been acquired through foreign language learning or as a home or community language. Whilst the learning of English is vital for the social integration of immigrants, as a recent report from the APPG on Social Integration has highlighted,[10] it is equally important for the first language of immigrants to be respected and valued as an integral part of their identity and culture.

Third, there is financial reward for demonstrating language competence on a sliding scale depending on level of achievement and the importance of the language to the armed forces. Again, there is nothing similar in the civil service. Yet, language skills would be an advantage, for example, to those civil servants concerned with international trade, the promotion of export growth and international development or, in the light of the Brexit vote, more generally, in the new Department for Exiting the European Union.

In short, as we noted in the *Value of Languages* report, a national strategy for languages must cut across departmental interests and thereby support the Department for Education in delivering an education policy grounded in national priorities and promoting a cultural shift in the attitude to languages. Whilst some of the above recommendations require investment of time and money, others—such as the strengthening and consolidation of the existing cross-Whitehall language focus group—could be relatively quick fixes and would represent an important first step towards greater cross-government collaboration and cohesion.

Notes

1. See http://www.publicpolicy.cam.ac.uk/pdf/value-of-languages.
2. See http://www.nuffieldfoundation.org/sites/default/files/Languages_the_next_generation_execsummary(2).pdf.

3. See http://traduction.culturecommunication.gouv.fr/url/Result.aspx?to= en&url=http://www.culturecommunication.gouv.fr/Politiques-ministerielles/Langue-francaise-et-langues-de-France/La-DGLFLF/ Qui-sommes-nous/Presentation-de-la-DGLFLF-en-d-autres-langues.

4. See https://www.britishcouncil.org/education/schools/support-for-languages/thought-leadership/appg/about.

5. See https://www.britishcouncil.org/sites/default/files/manifesto_for_languages.pdf.

6. See http://brexitlanguagesappgmfl.weebly.com/downloads.html.

7. See http://gov.wales/topics/welshlanguage/?lang=en and http://www.gov.scot/Publications/2010/07/06161418/5.

8. See http://www.gov.scot/resource/0039/00393435.pdf.

9. See http://gov.wales/docs/dcells/publications/151019-global-futures-en.pdf.

10. See the All-Party Parliamentary Group on Social Integration, *Interim Report into Integration of Immigrants*, January 2017: http://d3n8a8pro7vhmx.cloudfront.net/themes/570513f1b504f500db000001/attachments/original/1483958173/TC0012_AAPG_Interim_Report_Screen.pdf?1483958173.

References and Further Reading

British Academy (2013). *Languages: The State of the Nation*. http://www.britac.ac.uk/publications/languages-state-nation.

Hancock, A. (2015). Scotland: Issues in Language Education. In C. Brock (Ed.), *Education in the United Kingdom* (pp. 177–194). London: Bloomsbury.

University of Cambridge (2015). *The Value of Languages*. http://www.publicpolicy.cam.ac.uk/pdf/value-of-languages

21

Speaking to the World About Speaking to the World

David Crystal

So how *do* we 'speak to the world'? I don't mean in the sense of 'learning and using foreign languages', which is what earlier chapters in this book have been about. I mean: how do we speak to the world about the importance of languages? We have a critical message to communicate. How do we set about conveying it to the general public?

We can of course lecture to them, and write books like this one—but let us not fool ourselves. Even if one of our academic books sold out, we would be talking only about a few thousand copies and a relatively small number of readers. Academic textbooks have an important role in forming intellectual opinion, but they don't usually get into a Xmas must-buy bestselling list. We have to find other ways of getting people to pay attention to languages. What initiatives would make a permanent impact on the consciousness of the general public, so that people would never forget the important role languages play in their well-being and begin to be active in their support?

Getting people to pay attention is by no means easy. We are part of an intensely competitive world. Human beings are able to take in only so

D. Crystal (✉)
University of Bangor, Bangor, UK

© The Author(s) 2018
M. Kelly (ed.), *Languages after Brexit*,
https://doi.org/10.1007/978-3-319-65169-9_21

much information, and are willing to devote attention, time and money to only a tiny number of the laudable projects that are placed before them. We need to find ways of making languages stand out, appealing to hearts as well as heads. Every now and then an initiative does reach a wide audience. The UNESCO International Year of Languages in 2008 was a case in point, received with great acclaim around the linguistic world—but the British general public had little awareness of it. There was very limited promotion of it in the media. Apart from anything else, it was in competition with other 'years': 2008 was also the International Year of Sanitation, the Reef, Planet Earth and the Potato. Even if the notion had grabbed public attention, it would have been a temporary victory only. Once over, these years are largely forgotten. How many remember the IYL and its achievements now? The same point applies to Language Days. We have two: 26 September is European Languages Day and 21 February is World Mother-Tongue Day. But most people do not know about them, and in any case they are only two days out of 365. What do we do the rest of the year?

People need constant reminders to keep an issue in front of their minds. With a topic as wide-ranging and multifaceted as language learning, the reminders need to be many and various. I am a great believer in copying the successes of others. How have other enterprises behaved when faced with the problem of how to gain and maintain the attention of the public? How do the conservationists do it? The scientists? The artists? What happens to make their enterprises front-page news? Or front-screen news? There are three main ways that others have used to achieve a noticeable public presence.

Awards

Literature, medicine, economics, cinema … these domains become front-page news by being associated with awards—most famously, the Nobel prizes and the Oscars. The UK has its Turner Prize for contemporary art. In the USA, there are 21 categories of Pulitzer Prize. In relation to language, there is very little. I know of the annual International Linguapax Award, rewarding work in the field of linguistic diversity and multilingual education. In Ireland, to celebrate the European Day of Languages, Léargas—the Irish organisation that supports international collaboration and exchange—each year holds a competition to encourage learners and teachers to engage with languages in different ways (in 2016, the competition connected languages with geography to explore climate change). The prize is an environmental field trip in a European country. It generates a remarkable range of innovative projects, with the best initiatives awarded the European Language Label and individuals receiving the Language Learner of the Year award.

In the UK, the Chartered Institute of Linguists in the UK has over a dozen awards, including the Threlford Memorial Cup (named after Sir Lacon Threlford, Founder of the Institute of Linguists), awarded annually to a person or organisation, or for a project that has inspired others with an original language initiative. For many years the awards have been presented at an annual ceremony by Prince Michael of Kent, himself an accomplished linguist—a noteworthy indication of the high social profile that languages can achieve. Another of their trophies was in 2016 given a wider remit, now awarded to an individual who has made 'an outstanding personal contribution and commitment to promoting the understanding of languages, multilingualism, and the values and benefits of language learning'.

Prestigious within the language professions as they are, these awards do not make the headlines. I wonder if anyone outside of those professions is aware of them. Why aren't there more, and why aren't there any really well-known ones? The value of an award is not its monetary value, which can be quite low, or even non-existent. Rather, it provides professional recognition to an individual or institution, motivation for action to that person's or institution's peers and an opportunity for publicity for the subject that the prizewinner professes. Annual prizes keep a topic in front of the public's attention. And not just once a year, when they are announced, but often when the recipients are mentioned. Write-ups tend not to say 'director Anthony Minghella' but 'Oscar-winning director Anthony Minghella'. The attribution is significant: it transforms a name from someone we might not know about (if one is not a specialist) into someone that we *should* know about. And it identifies subjects—areas of knowledge—that we feel we ought to know about. We need to get languages into that position.

Modern society is obsessed with prizes—Oscars, Grammys, Emmys, Golden Globes, Bookers, Pulitzers, Goncourts—and they gain a level of publicity that far exceeds their monetary (if any) value. Anticipation of Oscar nominations lasts for months. The Turner Prize, in its often controversial decisions, has generated a remarkable amount of discussion about the nature of art. So why could there not be an annual national prize for an incarnation of multilingualism—a school, a course, a publication, an individual, an artistic achievement—to be announced perhaps on European Languages Day? A dimension of this kind would complement our professional linguistic activities, and ultimately aid them, for public awareness and sympathy is prerequisite if we are to alter the intellectual, emotional and financial climate within which linguists have to work.

Artworks

An artistic achievement … How do we remember someone or some event? We build a monument or statue: *Nelson, Churchill*. We write a play or make a film: *Henry V, Amadeus*. We compose a piece of music: *1812, War Requiem*. We sing a song: *The Ballade of Casey Jones, Woodstock*. We paint a picture: *Mona Lisa, Guernica*. Commemorative artworks keep a topic in the forefront of our eyes and ears. But where are the artworks devoted to languages or linguists? I have seen major public exhibitions devoted to plant and animal conservation, or the history of books, or motor cars, but never seen one that deals solely with foreign language teaching and learning.

I am not talking about the individual works that have been created to celebrate a particular language. I can think of several poems and folk songs which celebrate Welsh, for example, and there are similar compositions about many other languages. I am talking about artworks specifically created to celebrate languages in general, the benefits of multilingualism and the principles and practices of language teaching and learning. Some organisations do promote artistic competitions, such as the BBC's International Radio Playwriting Competition, the BP Portrait Award or the Sunday Times Watercolour Competition. Somebody ought to establish an annual commission or competition to provide an artwork on the theme of languages, perhaps with a different art form every year—literature, film, photography, painting, music, dance ... The topic deserves at least a symphony, a fantasia, an opera, a ballet, or—to change the genres—a jazz piece, or a guitar extravaganza. Even the folk singers have failed to lament the dangers caused by the loss of language proficiency.

We might hope the language arts would be in the forefront of such activities, but we would be disappointed. There are still far too few poems, plays, novels and works in other literary genres in which notions of language aesthetics, expressiveness, and identity provide the dominant theme. Yet verbal art is a major way of boosting linguistic self-esteem, through the promotion of storytelling sessions, drama groups, poetry readings, public-speaking competitions, singing galas and cultural gatherings. The Welsh National Eisteddfod is a shining example of what can be done. There needs to be an English equivalent.

Within a country, people do not change their minds, or develop positive attitudes about languages, just by being given information; the arguments need to capture their emotions, and art forms are the main way in which this can happen. I am not talking just about artworks of the most expensive kind, produced by professional artists. Amateur art, of the kind frequently devised by teachers in classrooms, can be extremely effective in raising local public awareness. There have been several such initiatives that have produced ingenious products, such as multilingual calendars, postcards, birthday cards and festival posters. I recall a very successful schools competition in 2009 to make cards to celebrate World Language Day, sponsored by the Association for Language Learning, and each year some schools do similar things. At a professional level, a few artists have specialised in providing multilingual items, such as Canadian artist Ilona Staples, who produced a set of greetings cards in several languages, or American sculptor Tim Brookes, who makes wooden carvings containing messages in endangered alphabets.

However, despite all this effort, relatively few artworks retain a permanent presence in a public space. Most artistic creations, of the kind that are produced in schools, arts centres, studios, community centres and other exhibition or performance spaces, disappear from public awareness once the presentation moment has passed. They need to be archived in an easily accessible way. The best might gain an afterlife through a publication, an audio or video recording, or via the internet—and it is in relation to the increasingly multilingual internet (and especially through mobile phones) where future ingenuity in our field needs to be primarily focused, for the internet is the ultimate archive. A Google day-animation devoted to languages would have a real impact. But what happens offline, in the physical world? Some arts organisations do archive their creations: Shakespeare's Globe, for example, has an archive of all its productions, but it is not publicly available. Accessibility is a critical factor, so how is that to be achieved?

Arenas

If you are interested in accessing the world of science, you can visit a science museum. Plants and animals, a natural history museum. Painting, an art gallery. In London there are over 300 major exhibition centres which keep their subject matter in front of the public—textiles, transport, maritime, musical instruments, dolls, lawnmowers ... All the major UK cities have an array of spaces devoted to the accessible presentation of some domain of human knowledge, inventiveness or creativity. But for the 6000 or so languages in the world there is nothing, in country after country, other than the occasional local institute devoted to a single language.

Languages ought to be given the same kind of public presence that other domains of knowledge receive. Every city should have a language museum, or gallery, hall, house ... The terminology is debatable, but the reality is not. There is no arena where people can go to see how languages work, how they are used and how they evolve; no space where they can see presented the world's linguistic variety; no public place where they can meet linguists—private as well as professional—and reflect on ways of promoting multilingualism and language diversity.

It has not been for want of trying. The World of Language was one such concept, promoted during the late 1990s in the UK by the British Council and others. This would have been a multistorey building, the first of its kind, with floors devoted to the world of speech, the world of writing, the world of meaning, the world of languages and the world of language study. A building had even been identified, in Southwark, opposite the new Shakespeare's Globe. The plans had reached an advanced stage, and all that was required was a small tranche (£25 million) of government funding to get the project off the ground. Things were looking promising, but then the government had a better idea, called the Millennium Dome, and all funding stopped.

The money that was wasted on the Dome project would have supported over 20 'worlds of language'. We still have none in the UK. A second attempt in 2006 to develop such a presence also failed, because all available funding was being directed towards the Olympics. Proposals to capitalise on the Games, through the notion of a 'languages legacy', also came to nothing, despite vigorous efforts by supporters. Perhaps, if there had been more multilinguists in Parliament, things might have turned out differently—but here too there is a conspicuous absence, both in the Commons and in the Lords. Despite the avowedly fundamental role of languages in relation to human society and thought, there is an inexplicable reluctance to give them the public presence they demand.

Other countries have come up with similar ideas, under a variety of names, such as 'the language city' and 'the town as a linguistic landscape', but all projects have suffered from a lack of finance, and every major initiative that was being developed in the early 2000s has foundered, either because of a downturn in the economy (which caused the demise of the Casa de les Llengues, 'House of Languages', in Barcelona in 2012, after eight years of development) or changes in political policy (such as the withdrawal of support for the Welt der Sprachen, 'World of Languages', in the Humboldt-Box, Berlin in 2015). The Casa also had a touring exhibition, which I saw in Lleida some time before the project closed, containing an array of innovative presentations and activities. The privately funded Mundolingua in Paris is a rare success story, a fine example of what can be done by filling a small building with linguistic artefacts and interactive opportunities.

The most promising major development is in Iceland, where the former president of Iceland, Vigdís Finnbogadóttir, has given her name to the Vigdís International Centre of Multilingualism and Intercultural

Understanding, located on the campus of the University in Reykjavik, and inaugurated in April 2017. Another is in the USA, where a proposed Planet Word is at an early stage of development in Washington DC. On a smaller scale, the USA also has the National Museum of Language in College Park, Maryland, originally established within a building, but now a virtual presence. In the UK, an exemplary initiative is the multilingual lending library set up by the Kittiwake Trust in Newcastle-upon-Tyne—a space that contains artefacts as well as books. Local developments of this kind are hugely important, but we still await the creation of a purpose-built national house of languages in the UK.

The world needs houses of languages for the same reason that it needs expositions of all kinds, from the arts to natural history—to satisfy our curiosity about who we are, as members of the human race, where we have come from and where we are going, and to demonstrate that we, as individuals and as communities, can make a difference to life on this planet. We expect, in a major city, that there will be a museum or gallery or other centre which will inform us about the main fields of human knowledge and creativity—to show us what others have done before us and to suggest directions where we can stand on shoulders and see new ways forward. Most of these fields, indeed, now have their expositions. But languages have been seriously neglected.

Houses of language are so important. There is a fascination about language and languages deep within everyone. We are all intrigued by the names of people and places. We think long and hard of what names to give our children. We worry endlessly about changes taking place in the language we hear and see around us. We watch in awe as children learn to speak, often more than one language at a time. We are diverted by the different accents and dialects of a region, and, as tourists, by the languages of the countries we visit. We are curious about the history of words. Everyone has these interests because everyone speaks, writes or signs. And people want to share their interests.

Not so long ago, I received a letter from an old man in the north of England who had been collecting local dialect words for years. He had a collection of several hundred, many of which, he said, were not recorded in the local dialect dictionaries. What could he do with them? Where could he archive them, so that other people could enjoy them too? If there were a house of languages in Britain, I could have told him. That is what a house of languages does. It provides a focus, a locus, a means of directing the linguistic energy that lies within all of us. It is a place to which we can turn when we want a question answered or believe we can provide an answer ourselves. It is a place, moreover, where we meet like-minded people, and encounter their enthusiasm. We value the atmosphere that comes from the shared experience of seeing a film in a cinema, rather than on a DVD at home, and the same kind of synergy would come from a visit to a house of languages. In an increasingly multilingual and multicultural UK, the case for such a development is stronger than ever.

Based on the experience of visitor footfall in the few cases where language-related exhibitions have taken place, it is clear that a sound business case could be made to justify the establishment of such spaces. When the British Library launched its Evolving English exhibition on 2010, which I helped to curate, there was concern in that institution about the level of public interest. They need not have worried. I was told after it finished that it was the best-attended winter exhibition the Library had ever had. School groups travelled from far afield, just as they still do for Shakespeare's Globe, the Natural History Museum and other such places. One of the most appreciated features was the way visitors could leave their linguistic footprint, in the form of an audio recording of their own accent and dialect. I can easily imagine such a facility forming one of the most appealing elements of a multilingual enterprise.

The three as—awards, artworks, arenas—could provide the basis of a PR policy that would complement the initiatives being taken to rebuild the UK's capacity for languages. The support might come from government, language-related businesses, organisations such as the Arts Council or philanthropic institutions and individuals. Despite a widespread belief to the contrary, the UK has always been a multilingual territory, thanks to the indigenous Celtic languages, and it is now a major multilingual nation, as a result of waves of immigration. There is a much stronger awareness of linguistic diversity today than there was a generation ago, and the revitalising focus on foreign language teaching and learning that this book represents could lead to any or all of the three As becoming a reality in the lifetime of its contributors. This would be the best way of showing that the UK is serious when we talk about 'speaking to the world'.

22

Conclusion: Steps Towards a Strategy for the UK

Michael Kelly

Why Do We Need a Strategy?

This book begins with a call to action on behalf of parliamentarians who are concerned that languages are being neglected because they 'belong everywhere a bit, but nowhere holistically or strategically'.[1] They call for a comprehensive strategic plan to ensure that the UK produces sufficient linguists to meet its future requirements. They also identify concrete steps that can be taken immediately to improve our language capacity.

The need for a strategy arises from the 'transversal' nature of languages. Languages run through every part of our life, but very rarely appear as a major issue or a high priority, except to the specialists who work behind the scenes to keep the show on the road (including translators, interpreters, teachers and researchers). For most people, languages are taken for granted and only pop up occasionally as an issue when something goes wrong. Brexit increases the chances of things going wrong because our language infrastructure is not up to the job. And so it is the right time to call for a national language strategy for the UK.

M. Kelly (✉)
University of Southampton, Southampton, UK

© The Author(s) 2018
M. Kelly (ed.), *Languages after Brexit*,
https://doi.org/10.1007/978-3-319-65169-9_22

251

The need for a holistic strategy is echoed in many of our chapters. It is an ambitious aim, and we try to lay down the groundwork for developing a strategy. We identify some of the main areas in which languages are needed, show how far we are from meeting those needs and make recommendations for what can be done to meet them more effectively.

Most of the issues we discuss were already known about, and our contributors refer to many previous attempts to draw attention to the UK's language deficit in different areas. One thing that we think has changed since June 2016 is the dawning realisation that complacency about languages is now a greater obstacle to our country thriving. Languages are more important than ever for our political partnerships, our economic relationships and our personal and cultural growth.

We live in a world of languages, and three chapters show some of the broader challenges for us in a multilingual world.[2] We suggest reasons why so many people seem resistant to other languages, and why the success of English as an international lingua franca holds threats as well as opportunities for native English speakers. And we suggest that learning other languages is how we can build trust and friendly understanding with international partners.

The second group of chapters looks in detail at some important areas where the UK needs strong language capabilities. An awareness of 'linguanomics' reveals the close relationship between languages and economics, which is confirmed by research on the increasing value of language and culture to British business. Despite the prevalence of English, multilingualism is important in an understanding of global scientific research. Languages are vital to public services, such as policing and justice, or supporting refugees. And as individuals, we need a healthy diet of languages to keep our brains in good shape.

We then offer an assessment of what capacity the UK has to respond to language needs. An important part is the role of schools, but we also look at other ways of building capacity. There are some very positive signs in different parts of the education system, but overall it is not an encouraging picture. Languages are fragile in English secondary schools despite some government efforts to offer incentives. There are high aspirations for languages in Scottish education, but a lack of resources means they may not be achieved in practice. Similarly in Wales, there is an ambitious strategy but it may not have caught people's hearts and minds. In Northern Ireland languages are at a low ebb, and though there is some goodwill, there are also political complexities that take priority.

Universities are well placed to build capacity in languages among graduates, but there is a worrying decline in specialist languages programmes. Community-based schemes build valuable language skills and cultural knowledge in less-taught languages, but are increasingly dependent on volunteers and charities as public funding dwindles. Many of the informal routes to learning languages are very popular, but there are fewer facilities for recognising achievement in formal qualifications. The demand for translation and interpreting services is continuing to grow rapidly and so far supply has kept up with demand, but there are risks to future supply and to maintaining the quality of services. Underlying the UK's capacity are language teachers, whose services are more needed than ever, but who are in short supply and increasingly difficult to recruit from abroad.

What Can Be Done?

Concerned parliamentarians are calling for a comprehensive strategic plan to ensure that the UK produces sufficient linguists to meet its future requirements. They also identify concrete steps that can be taken immediately to improve our language capacity. Many contributors echo this view, pointing to specific actions that can be taken to improve the situation. Two concluding chapters lay out recommendations for action at government level and more widely in public life.

The first argues that there is need for concerted cross-government action to promote languages in the UK, taking a more holistic approach. It is important that languages and language policy should not just be a matter of education policy. Senior civil servants and perhaps even a government minister could be given responsibility for championing languages and fostering co-operation between government ministries and departments and in the devolved administrations.

The second chapter in the final section broadens the scope to ask how the message about languages can be conveyed to the general public. Learning from how other important public benefits are promoted, we should consider developing a stronger range of national awards for activities in languages, along the lines of the Booker or Turner prizes. We should find ways of presenting languages in works of art, including visual and performing arts and online platforms. And we should find ways of showcasing languages in exhibitions and galleries, perhaps including a House of Languages that would generate excitement and cater for public curiosity about languages. All of these recommendations are captured in the Appendix, which provides an aide-memoire for steps that might be taken.

Developing a strategy does not impede the implementation of specific recommendations. However, it does recognise that many of the potential actions are interdependent. Some actions form long cycles, where, for example, the take-up of languages at school affects the number of languages graduates, which in turn affects the supply of teachers to teach languages in schools. Some actions form short cycles, where, for example, an audit of language skills enables a government department to allocate the most suitable staff to a particular task. Many actions that have been suggested have the potential to act as pilot schemes, providing a positive example of benefits, for example where the armed forces have devised incentive schemes to encourage personnel to develop their proficiency in other languages and cultures.

A more wide-ranging strategy could find the synergies between actions and have a dynamic effect in making the UK more language-capable. It will need to be inclusive: recognising the distinct situation of the four home nations and the different priorities and responsibilities of government, of the public services, of the private and voluntary sectors and of public opinion. It will need to be based on co-operation: involving policymakers, languages professionals and those organisations who are in most need of better language capability. It will need to learn lessons from the experience of other countries, especially the English-speaking world and Europe.

A strategy should also learn from previous experience in the UK. There have been many briefing reports and policy initiatives on languages over the past 40 years, since an HMI Report of 1977 articulated a 'rapidly growing concern about the future of language learning in our schools'.[3] Many of the most recent reports are referenced in the different chapters of this book, particularly those commissioned by the British Academy and the British Council. The most wide-ranging initiative over that period, and probably the most influential in British policymaking, was the report produced by the Nuffield Languages Inquiry (1998–2000).[4] It operated in a different political and economic environment, that of 20 years ago, and much has changed, but the Inquiry offers a valuable model of co-operation. It was chaired by prominent national figures, sponsored by a major charitable trust and steered by a high-level committee in which language professionals were a minority. It carried out detailed research and undertook widespread consultation, including with government. An initiative of comparable scope and ambition could be the catalyst for a strategy that fits the UK for the 2020s.

We hope that this book may trigger a strategic initiative, and lead to productive discussions on the importance of languages for the future of our country. And we hope that it will prompt actions to address the short- and long-term issues that it raises. Wittgenstein famously said that 'Die Grenzen meiner Sprache bedeuten die Grenzen meiner Welt', which might be translated as: 'The borders of my language mean the borders of my world'.[5] If the UK is not to be locked within the borders of the English-speaking world, we need the language capability to talk with our neighbours, scan the far horizons and speak to the wider world.

Notes

1. See Chap. 1.
2. The names of contributors have not been repeated in the Conclusion, in order to highlight the arguments of the chapters in this short summary of the book. Contributors' names are shown at the head of their chapter, and short biographies are included in the Notes on Contributors.

3. See: Department of Education and Science, 'Modern Languages in Comprehensive Schools' (1977): http://www.educationengland.org.uk/documents/hmi-discussion/modlang-comp.html.

4. See: Nuffield Foundation, 'The Nuffield Languages Inquiry and Nuffield Languages Programme'. The main documents of the Inquiry are stored on the project website: http://www.nuffieldfoundation.org/nuffield-languages-inquiry-and-nuffield-languages-programme.

5. Ludwig Wittgenstein, *Tractatus Logico-Philosophicus* (1922), 5.6.

Appendix: Summary of Proposals

Throughout this book, contributors make suggestions for actions that should be taken to enable the UK to develop the knowledge and skills in languages that will be needed for the future. In many cases, several contributors develop similar ideas, and many refer to the recommendations of the All-Party Parliamentary Group for Modern Languages, which are developed in Chap. 1. This Appendix attempts to capture the proposals, whether couched as suggestions or as recommendations and for each proposal, at least one chapter is indicated where the point is developed. The proposals are grouped thematically in nine lines of action:

1. Develop a comprehensive strategic plan
2. Manage the impact of Brexit
3. Improve collaboration across government
4. Raise the public profile of languages
5. Improve language education
6. Improve intercultural and other skills
7. Support teachers
8. Recognise community languages
9. Recognise languages outside the education system

© The Author(s) 2018
M. Kelly (ed.), *Languages after Brexit*,
https://doi.org/10.1007/978-3-319-65169-9

1. Develop a comprehensive strategic plan

(a) Develop a comprehensive strategic plan to ensure that the UK produces sufficient linguists to meet its future requirements post-Brexit (Chaps. 1, 20, 22 and elsewhere).

(b) Plan and fund research to support the implementation of strategy (Chap. 12)

2. Manage the impact of Brexit

(a) Guarantee the residency status for non-UK EU nationals already living in the UK and agree favourable terms for the future recruitment of EU citizens who are needed (Chaps. 1, 18 and elsewhere).

(b) Ensure that the UK retains access to and participation in the EU's Erasmus+ programme, which funds study and work experience abroad (Chaps. 1, 15 and elsewhere).

(c) Negotiate free movement for students and academics (Chap. 18).

(d) Introduce no new impediments to mobility for education, such as visa requirements or loss of funding streams (Chap. 11)

(e) Legislate to replicate the rights enshrined in the 2010 European Directive on the Right to Interpretation and Translation in Criminal Proceedings (Chaps. 1, 8, 18)

(f) Measure and monitor the ongoing impact of Brexit on language learning (Chap. 11).

3. Improve collaboration across government

(a) Establish a cross-departmental policy initiative, supported by a Minister for Languages, with the participation of specialists in a range of languages, cultures and societies, from higher education and elsewhere (Chaps. 1, 15, 20)

(b) Appoint senior civil servants acting as language officers or language co-ordinators within government ministries and in the devolved administrations of Scotland, Wales and Northern Ireland (Chap. 20)

(c) Ensure that languages and language policy are not just a matter of education policy (Chap. 20).

(d) Maintain momentum in the strategic discussions around languages in Scotland, Wales and Northern Ireland (Chaps. 12, 13, 14, 20)

(e) Carry out an audit of the civil service to find out what language resources we may already have (Chaps. 1, 20)

(f) Implement more widely across the civil service the existing good practices in some departments (Chaps. 1, 20)

(g) Introduce tax breaks and other incentives for language training and language expertise (Chaps. 1, 5, 20)

4. Raise the public profile of languages

(a) Establish an annual national prize for an incarnation of multilingualism—a school, a course, a publication, an individual, an artistic achievement (Chap. 21)

(b) Establish an annual commission or competition to provide an artwork on the theme of languages (Chap. 21)

(c) Develop arenas where people can go to see how languages work, how they are used, and how they evolve: a place in every city, and a national House of Languages (Chap. 21)

(d) Promote storytelling sessions, drama groups, poetry readings, public-speaking competitions, singing galas and cultural gatherings, to increase linguistic self-esteem (Chap. 21)

(e) Design language-themed products, such as multilingual calendars, postcards, birthday cards and festival posters (Chap. 21)

(f) Propose a Google day-animation devoted to languages (Chap. 21)

(g) Find ways of getting languages to be given the same priority as STEM (sciences, technology, engineering and maths) subjects (Chap. 12)

5. Improve language education

(a) Act at national level to ensure that more young people leave formal education with the ability to speak at least one other language and be conversant with other cultures (Chap. 6).

(b) Invest in improving school language learning (Chaps. 3, 11 and elsewhere)

(c) Allocate more time to language learning in the curriculum and in the school week (Chaps. 3, 6, 11)

(d) Give teachers time and space to develop exchanges and extra-curricular activities (Chaps. 11, 17)

(e) Provide sufficient access to native speakers (Chap. 6).

(f) Promote wider participation of schoolchildren in language learning, not just for the elite (Chaps. 3, 11 and elsewhere)

(g) Invest in a range of foreign languages in order to flexibly match the changing language needs generated by the market (Chap. 6)

(h) Invest long term in affordable and high-quality vocational education, including language and cultural training (Chap. 5)

(i) Extend the use of bilingual education, content and language integrated learning (Chap. 3)

(j) Maintain and develop expertise in modern languages and cultures in the UK university sector (Chap. 15)

(k) Explore incentives for undergraduates to continue language learning and to use languages in interdisciplinary and applied contexts (Chap. 15)

(l) Encourage co-operation between employers and education in designing appropriate curricula for the future (Chap. 16)

(m) Provide a broad suite of qualifications in languages (Chap. 13)

(n) Work with pupils to challenge monolingual mindset (Chap. 13)

(o) Disentangle pupils' GCSE/A-level results from school performance tables, so as to reduce pressure to encourage less able language pupils to opt out (Chap. 17)

6. Improve intercultural and other skills

(a) Promote intercultural skills and awareness of how cultural differences can affect social relationships and outcomes (Chaps. 4, 5).

(b) Encourage monolingual speakers to improve their transcultural communication skills so as to understand and make themselves understood by the majority of the world's English users (Chap. 3)

(c) Develop young people with relevant skills, aptitudes and attitudes to operate in a global labour market (Chap. 6)

7. Support teachers

(a) Safeguard the status of existing language teachers from other EU countries, and maintain the stream of new recruits (Chap. 11)

(b) Invest in (initial) language teacher education at all levels (Chap. 17)

(c) Provide professional development for teachers (Chap. 6)

(d) Introduce a required language qualification for primary (trainee) teachers, and introduce language upskilling as part of primary trainee courses (Chap. 17)

(e) Introduce an induction programme for language teachers trained outside of the UK, in order for them to get an insight into the UK school system (Chap. 17).

(f) Improve strategic planning of numbers of graduates with high-level language skills in a diversity of languages and who are suitably qualified for entering teacher training, including primary teaching Chap. 12).

8. Recognise community languages

(a) Recognise linguistic skills of bilingual pupils and students, providing support and accreditation (Chaps. 1, 16 and elsewhere).

(b) Promote greater co-ordination between mainstream and supplementary schools (Chap. 16)

(c) Use language diversity in the workforce (Chap. 5)

(d) Support the development of home languages to levels of operational literacy using a formal register appropriate to professional use (Chap. 6).

9. Recognise languages outside the education system

(a) Acknowledge the need for scientists to conduct and publish research across a range of languages (Chap. 7).

(b) Promote the value of a Healthy Linguistic Diet, for the development and protection of the brain and its cognitive functions (Chap. 10).

(c) Launch a campaign to promote the idea of lifelong learning, normalising the idea of language learning throughout life (Chap. 12).

(d) Revive BBC language learning programmes (Chap. 11).

(e) Provide learning and training opportunities in the workplace (Chap. 6).

Index

Note: Page numbers followed by "n" refer to notes.

27801131R00164

Printed in Great Britain
by Amazon